Living Be

ASA Monographs

ISSN 0066–9679

The Relevance of Models for Social Anthropology, ed M. Banton
Political Systems and the Distribution of Power, ed M. Banton
Anthropological Approaches to the Study of Religion, ed M. Banton
The Social Anthropology of Complex Societies, ed M. Banton
The Structural Study of Myth and Totemism, ed E.R. Leach
Themes in Economic Anthropology, ed R. Firth
History and Social Anthropology, ed I.M. Lewis
Socialization: The Approach from Social Anthropology, ed P. Mayer
Witchcraft Confessions and Accusations, ed M. Douglas
Social Anthropology and Language, ed E. Ardener
Rethinking Kinship and Marriage, ed R. Needham
Urban Ethnicity, ed A. Cohen
Social Anthropology and Medicine, ed J.B. Loudon
Social Anthropology and Law, ed I. Hamnett
The Anthropology of the Body, ed J. Blacking
Regional Cults, ed R.P. Werbner
Sex and Age as Principles of Social Differentiation, ed J. La Fontaine
Social and Ecological Systems, ed P.C. Burnham and R.F. Ellen
Social Anthropology of Work, ed S. Wallman
The Structure of Folk Models, ed L. Holy and L. Stuchlik
Religious Organization and Religious Experience, ed J. Davis
Semantic Anthropology, ed D. Parkin
Social Anthropology and Development Policy, ed R. Grillo and A. Rew
Reason and Morality, ed J. Overing
Anthropology at Home, ed A. Jackson
Migrants, Workers, and the Social Order, ed J.S. Eades
History and Ethnicity, ed E. Tonkin, M. McDonald and M. Chapman
*Anthropology and the Riddle of the Sphinx: Paradox and Change
   in the Life Course*, ed P. Spencer
Anthropology and Autobiography, ed J. Okely and H. Callaway
Contemporary Futures: Perspectives from Social Anthropology, ed S. Wallman
Socialism: Ideals, Ideologies and Local Practice, ed C.M. Hann
Environmentalism: The View from Anthropology, ed K. Milton
Questions of Consciousness, ed A.P. Cohen and N. Rapport
After Writing Culture: Epistemology and Praxis in Contemporary Anthropology, ed
   A. James, A. Dawson and J. Hockey
Ritual, Performance, Media, ed F. Hughes-Freeland
The Anthropology of Power, ed A. Cheater
An Anthropology of Indirect Communication, ed J. Hendry and C.W. Watson
Elite Cultures, ed C. Shore and S. Nugent
Participating in Development, ed P. Sillitoe, A. Bicker and J. Pottier
Human Rights in Global Perspective, ed R.A. Wilson and J.P. Mitchell
The Qualities of Time, ed W. James and D. Mills
Locating the Field: Space, Place and Context in Anthropology, ed S. Coleman and P. Collins
Anthropology and Science: Epistemologies in Practice, ed J. Edwards, P. Harvey and P. Wade
Creativity and Cultural Improvisation, ed E. Hallam and T. Ingold
*Anthropology and the New Cosmopolitanism: Rooted, Feminist and Vernacular
   Perspectives*, ed P. Werbner
Thinking Through Tourism, ed J. Scott and T. Selwyn
Ownership and Appropriation, ed V. Strang and M. Busse
Archaeology and Anthropology, ed D. Shankland
The Interview: An Ethnographic Approach, ed J. Skinner

Living Beings
Perspectives on Interspecies Engagements

Edited by
Penelope Dransart

B L O O M S B U R Y

LONDON • NEW DELHI • NEW YORK • SYDNEY

Bloomsbury Academic

An imprint of Bloomsbury Publishing Plc

50 Bedford Square	1385 Broadway
London	New York
WC1B 3DP	NY 10018
UK	USA

www.bloomsbury.com

Bloomsbury is a registered trade mark of Bloomsbury Publishing Plc

First published 2013

British Library Cataloguing-in-Publication Data
A catalogue record for this book is available from the British Library.

ISBN:	HB:	978-0-85785-841-2
	PB:	978-0-85785-842-9
	ePDF:	978-0-85785-844-3
	ePub:	978-1-47251-907-8

Library of Congress Cataloging-in-Publication Data

Living beings : perspectives on interspecies engagements / edited by Penelope Dransart.
pages cm. – (ASA monographs)
ISBN 978-0-85785-842-9 (pbk.) – ISBN 978-0-85785-841-2 (hardback) –
ISBN 978-0-85785-844-3 (epdf) – ISBN 978-1-4725-1907-8 (epub) 1. Human-animal
relationships–Case studies.   2. Human-plant relationships–Case studies.
I. Dransart, Penny.
QL85.L55   2014
590–dc23
2013035918

Typeset by Apex CoVantage
Printed and bound in Great Britain

Contents

List of Illustrations

Contributors

Carole Baker is an educator, writer and photographer who has taught in higher education since 2001 after gaining her doctorate on the 'Representation of the Animal in Photography'. Recent critical and practice-based work has explored phenomenological approaches to nature, place and vision. Carole is currently senior lecturer in photography at the University of Plymouth.

Rachel Ben-David earned a master's degree from Ben Gurion University of the Negev, Be'er Sheva, in 2012 and a bachelor's degree in biology from Hebrew University, Jerusalem, in 2001. She is an animal-assisted therapy lecturer at Sapir College, Israel. Her anthropological area of research is in human-animal relations in East Africa, informed by her work as a safari guide.

Sarah Jane Boss is the director of the Centre for Marian Studies at the University of Roehampton and has published monographs and chapters on the cult of the Virgin Mary, including *Empress and Handmaid: On Nature and Gender in the Cult of the Virgin Mary* (Cassell 2000), *Mary* (Continuum 2004) and, as editor and contributor, *Mary: The Complete Resource* (Continuum 2007). Her main interest is in the way in which Marian theology and devotion expresses Christians' relationship with nonhuman nature. She has taught a master's programme on religion and ecology and has taught for the Centre for Alternative Technology, Machynlleth.

Juliette Brown is cofounder of terra incognita arts organization. Following undergraduate work in English literature and Roman civilization, she completed a master's degree in gender, society and culture, and began doctoral work in social and political anthropology before electing to study medicine. She has published on art, psychoanalysis and gender and medicine. In medical practice, she specializes in psychiatry and is a member of the Royal College of Psychiatrists.

David Cockburn is emeritus professor of philosophy at University of Wales Trinity Saint David. His publications include *Other Human Beings* (Macmillan 1990), *Other Times: Philosophical Perspectives on Past, Present and Future* (Cambridge University Press 1997), *An Introduction to the Philosophy of Mind* (Palgrave 2001) and a wide range of papers on themes in philosophy of mind, ethics, Wittgenstein, philosophy of religion and philosophy of time.

Veena Das is Krieger-Eishenhow professor of anthropology and professor of humanities at Johns Hopkins University. She is the author, among other books, of

Life and Words: Violence and the Descent into the Ordinary (2007) and *Affliction* (forthcoming).

Penelope Dransart is reader in anthropology and archaeology at the University of Wales Trinity Saint David. Her research focuses on human-herd animal interactions from 5,000 years ago up to the present. Stemming from her interests in fleece-bearing animals is her interest in substances such as fibre, hair, colour, blood and water, and she has explored the thematic and symbolic meanings of these elements as indicators of life. She is author of *Earth, Water, Fleece and Fabric: An Ethnography and Archaeology of Andean Camelid Herding* (Routledge 2002) and *Textiles from the Andes* (British Museum Press 2011), and edits and contributes to *Kay Pacha: Cultivating Earth and Water in the Andes* (Archaeopress 2006).

D. S. Farrer is associate professor of anthropology, anthropology programme coordinator and interdisciplinary arts and sciences coordinator at the University of Guam. He was awarded a PhD in social anthropology by the National University of Singapore in 2007. Dr Farrer has taught anthropology, sociology, social psychology and martial arts since 1992. Before relocating to Guam, he lectured in universities and colleges in England, Zambia and Singapore. He conducted ethnographic fieldwork for almost a decade in Malaysia and Singapore and has also conducted fieldwork in Thailand, London and Hong Kong. His research specialties include visual anthropology, the anthropology of performance, art, religion, spiritual healing and Chinese and Malay martial arts. Dr Farrer has published an ethnographic book entitled *Shadows of the Prophet: Martial Arts and Sufi Mysticism* (Springer 2009) and has recently published a volume (coedited with John Whalen-Bridge) entitled *Martial Arts as Embodied Knowledge: Asian Traditions in a Transnational World* (SUNY 2011). In 2011, he won the University of Guam College of Liberal Arts and Social Sciences Research Excellence Award. On Guam, he is interested in mixed martial arts and indigenous cultural revival.

Ronit Grossman-Horesh is a PhD student (stage B) in the Department of Sociology and Anthropology at the University of Tel Aviv and a course coordinator in the Department of Sociology, Political Science and Communication at the Open University of Israel. Her fields of research are community studies, anthropology of religion, anthropology of tourism and the Kibbutz society. Her publications include 'Blogs of Israeli and Danish Backpackers to India' (with Yael Enoch) in *Annals of Tourism Research* (2010) and 'Tourism and Change in a Galilee Kibbutz: An Ethnography' in Yoram S. Carmeli and Kalman Applbaum (eds), *Consumption and Market Society in Israel* (Berg 2004).

Safet HadžiMuhamedović is a doctoral researcher in anthropology at Goldsmiths, University of London. He holds an MPhil degree in social anthropology from the University of Cambridge and BA degrees in history of art and sociology from the University of Sarajevo, and studies at Kenyon College. Currently, his research focuses on Bosnian sacral geography as the source of alternative histories. More broadly, his work engages with syncretic religiosities through ethnographic explorations of space, place and landscape, oral histories and endangered materiality.

Alana Jelinek is Arts and Humanities Research Council Creative Fellow at the Museum of Archaeology and Anthropology, University of Cambridge. She is an artist and writer whose publications include *This Is Not Art* (IB Tauris 2012), *Ohm's Law* (terra incognita 2007) and *terra incognita* (an art installation inaugurated in 1997). Exhibitions include Tall Stories: Cannibal Forks (Museum of Archaeology & Anthropology 2010), The Field (2009–ongoing) and Inter-weaving Cultures (Jim Thompson House & Gallery, Bangkok, Thailand, 2006).

Preface

The chapters in this book are based on a selection of papers presented at the 2011 annual conference of the Association of Social Anthropologists of the United Kingdom and Commonwealth (ASA), which met in Lampeter, Wales, under the title 'Vital Powers and Politics: Human Interactions with Living Things'. When the ASA accepted the proposal of what was then the University of Wales Lampeter to host the conference, the University was in a merger situation, and by the time that delegates gathered in Lampeter to attend the event, we had become the University of Wales Trinity Saint David. The disciplinary landscape for the teaching of anthropology at university level in Wales was rapidly changing. The disinvestment of the respected Department of Sociology and Anthropology at Swansea University meant that the Lampeter campus became the only remaining location in Wales where the teaching of undergraduate and postgraduate degrees is offered, and it has few anthropology lecturers. As a conference convener, I am grateful to the ASA committee for having the confidence in my institution to put on the conference.

The conference theme was related to research undertaken in the School of Archaeology, History and Anthropology, which is widely acknowledged as having longstanding interests in the study of environments, landscapes and human-animal interactions. This was the first occasion that the ASA conference visited Lampeter, where anthropology as a discipline was established in 1996.

With a population of less than 3,000 people, Lampeter is the United Kingdom's smallest town with a university, but the University's student body gives it a cosmopolitan character. Lampeter is a transition town in that it is endeavouring to achieve an environmentally sustainable future. Hence Lampeter's rural situation was appropriate to a conference whose theme concerned living beings.

As convener, I wish to thank NomadIT staff for their courteous support in their efficient organization of the conference (Rohan Jackson, Megan Caine, Darren Hatherley, Eli Bugler and Triinu Mets). Piers Locke and David Cockburn provided much help on academic matters. As editor, I am very grateful for the unstinting assistance provided by Betty Dransart, Jonathan Dransart, Felicia Hughes-Freeland, Colin Miller, Jonathan R. Trigg and Lynne Sharpe. James Staples, Publications Officer of the ASA, ensured the smooth progression of the book proposal through the ASA Publications Committee. Sophie Hodgson and Louise Butler at Bloomsbury guided me through the editorial process. I owe a debt of gratitude to the anonymous peer reviewers, many of whom reviewed chapter manuscripts at short notice yet provided insightful comments. Finally, I wish to thank the contributors for tolerating my many questions and cheerfully reworking their chapters in the light of the intriguing questions that the review process highlighted.

Penelope Dransart

Living Beings and Vital Powers:
An Introduction

Penelope Dransart

And for all this, nature is never spent;
There lives the dearest freshness deep down things.

(Gerard Manley Hopkins 1877)

But I don't want to end up with some smug trade-off between money and nature. I want to alienate money's alienation. Make its strangeness strange. I want to make going to a store and buying your daily food, for instance, seem like a miracle.

(Taussig 2004: 111)

The living beings inhabiting the pages of this book include mammal species (human and other), insects and trees. As a category, 'living beings' commands the interest of authors and readers, especially in relation to discussions concerning productive activities, as well as in debates concerning such themes as the body and personhood. In Louis Dumont's (1986: 587) definition, 'living beings' have a 'unity of their own, they tend to persevere in their being, and their relationship to their environment is vital'.

For much of the twentieth century, Western anthropologists explored cultural diversity while confidently relying on an anthropocentric notion that the human condition was a condition apart from that of all other animals. Yet the relationship between 'cultural' and 'natural' beings remains a perennial topic of investigation. A. R. Radcliffe-Brown's (1958: 96) programmatic declaration for social anthropology provided an epistemological basis for the discipline when he explained that social anthropologists apply 'the inductive method of the natural sciences to the study of human society, its institutions and its evolution'. Human interests are biological, and there can be no position of disinterest from which a researcher may investigate them objectively.[1]

John Beattie (1966: 11), however, took issue with anthropologists who treated the body politic as a discrete organism that might be vivisected. Tracing a lineage from Auguste Comte, who saw societies as systems beyond a mere aggregation of cells, Beattie objected to the teleological aspects of functionalism by making an analogy with the circulation and reoxygenation of blood in a breathing organism. He expanded on the analogy when he stated that functional explanations resemble

> what biologists do when they explain one part of an organism by reference to the contribution which its functioning makes to the life of the whole. But we must not ... suppose that societies are something like organisms; they are not ... An organism is a physical entity; you can put it on a table and dissect it. But a society, or a social institution, is not a thing at all. It is a concept. (Beattie 1966: 55)

Rather than engage directly with the grand functionalist, structural-functionalist and structuralist debates of the twentieth century, the contributors to this volume (who are social anthropologists, philosophers and artists) take a critical approach to views based on hierarchical oppositions concerning relationships between human and other living beings. They engage with debates that have emerged especially from late twentieth- and early twenty-first-century discussions concerning agency, Actor-Network Theory, phenomenology and relational ontologies. Early in what has been called the new 'biological century' (Brenner 2000), this volume's contributors consider frameworks for examining vital processes and recursive relationships between living organisms in their social and cultural contexts.

The different chapters examine interactions between living beings as organisms possessing a life cycle, from birth to maturation and from decline to death. They enquire into the vital powers emerging from human contact (and, at times, communication) with other animals, insects and trees. Although human practices may sometimes appear to exist in a realm beyond nature, those practices are nevertheless subject to the pull of natural forces, forces that may be brought into prominence through a consideration of the interactions between human beings and other inhabitants of natural worlds. Therefore the contributors are interested in more than just the social order of human interaction with other species. Hierarchies, moral universes and ethical engagements between living beings constitute their subject matter. Chapters in this book consider how activities of building and growing sustain people 'in their environments' (Ingold and Hallam 2007: 5) and notions of human indebtedness to other species. The fundamental contrast between nature(s) and culture(s)—or, following Descola and Pálsson (1996: 2), the dichotomy between the wild and the social—is still present in this volume, however, and the authors consider the changing and complex relationships between these phenomena in the ethnographic and historical materials that enrich their chapters.

Notions of relatedness between humans and animals are undoubtedly complex. Tim Ingold (1994: 15) pointed out that 'humanity', as a category, consists of individual members of the species *Homo sapiens,* while, at the same time, it represents a condition or status—one that is opposed to 'animality'. He noted that a turn from the inclusive to the exclusive has occurred in Western thought because the question 'What makes humans animals of a particular kind?' became 'What makes humans different in kind from animals?' In this argument, the notion that human beings comprise a province within a kingdom (that is, one animal species among many) has yielded to a view that the status of being human is opposed to that of being animal (Ingold 1994: 20).

The term 'animal', however, is a superordinate category not present in all languages. Laura Rival, for instance, was unable to find such a general term in her fieldwork among the Huaorani of Amazonia. Edible species that might be hunted are *oingairi* ('game'), but people would only speak with reluctance of 'monkeys', 'fish' and 'birds' in a collective sense, such as *gata* ('woolly monkey') to include all monkeys (Rival 1996: 162n1). In the Andes, the Aymara and Quechua languages do not have an all-inclusive term for 'animal' either, despite the attempts of seventeenth-century European linguists to introduce Aristotelian-inspired neologisms for quadrupeds (Dransart 2010: 89–90). To speakers of such languages, to refer to a human-animal divide would have little or no resonance. Veena Das demonstrates a nonunified province of 'animality' in the Vedic texts she discusses in Chapter 2. These texts differentiate between domestic and wild animals, but human beings are included in the former group of domestic creatures (*pashu*).

For readers who associate Western thought with a particularly ubiquitous and hierarchical attitude to dualism, however, the chapters by Sarah Boss (Chapter 3) and Safet HadžiMuhamedović (Chapter 4) demonstrate the dangers of making broad generalizations across time and space. Boss observes that if there has been a dominant intellectual strand of thought in Europe towards such a form of dualism, it has become much more marked since the modern period than it was in medieval times. For his part, HadžiMuhamedović considers the Basque Oak Tree of Gernika, whose 'eventful longevity' contributes to its singular importance as a 'nonhuman yet anthropomorphic being'. Trees, like humans, possess limbs, yet they have sap rather than blood coursing through their veins. They are long lived, yet, as with humans and other animals, they are vulnerable to diseases to which they have no resistance. Trees are therefore particularly apt in plant-based metaphors for relatedness, whether in the form of family or phylogenetic trees. HadžiMuhamedović argues that the Tree of Gernika belies orthodox understandings of Western worldviews, according to which trees cannot listen.

Changing directions or emphases in debates concerning continuity or discontinuity between species are often referred to as 'turns' when particular themes capture the imagination of readers and writers. The popularity of human-animal relations in the literature in the 'species turn' merits a consideration of what is involved in 'turning' one's attention to such topics.

'Turning' as a Concept

Dictionary definitions of 'turn' include 'to rotate, spin or move round an axis or point', as well as 'to hinge' and 'to reverse direction or tendency' (Simpson and Weiner 1989: 695–708). That the Old English and Old French terms, respectively *tyrnan* and *tourner,* seem to derive from the Latin *tornare,* which in turn came from the Greek *tornos* ('lathe' or 'compasses'), suits a theme which takes into account human and other animal species as productive workers.[2] The activities represented in this volume (sacrifice, the quest for food and clothing, participation in language, singing, wildlife safaris, martial arts, the making of artwork and so on) are productive acts. Contributors examine such activities in contexts that juxtapose human and other living beings in the light of themes including violence, difference, simulation and spiritual renewal. The notion of turning occurs at several critical junctions in this volume.

At the outset, Veena Das turns her attention to a classic theme of anthropological interest—that of sacrifice within the Vedic tradition of Hinduism. Her analysis leads to an examination of the 'ontological turn' in anthropology, through which a growing number of authors have contributed to the discussion of belief systems that offer different perspectives on the natural world. She warns the reader, however, that this ontological turn runs the risk of reinstating an unhelpful version of a human-centric understanding of the world. I will say more about this ontological turn later in this chapter.

In Safet HadžiMuhamedović's chapter (Chapter 4), trees turn; however, according to Yaghan accounts discussed in my contribution, there was a time when trees were formerly people. The geographers Paul Cloke and Owain Jones (2001, 2004) have discussed how trees might be considered to have relational agency. Cloke and Jones (2004: 314) considered how the trees 'turned' a formally designed Victorian cemetery into 'a more unkempt, wild and disorganized space' as human management became less vigilant. The concept of 'turning' in this context suggests that trees have the capacity to engage human attention. Both HadžiMuhamedović and Carole Baker draw upon Cloke and Jones's work in their respective contributions.

In Baker's chapter (Chapter 6), the world turns and fills with light; it is paralleled by a turn to the human body as a matter of enquiry for expressing relationships with other living things. This part of her discussion is inspired by the work of Michel de Certeau (1983: 26), according to whom vision is captivating because 'it is a journey toward external things.' Baker sees this journey as a turning of attention to objects in the world because, as de Certeau explained, travelling is a form of seeing.

Ronit Grossman-Horesh refers in Chapter 5 to secular Israeli citizens who seek refreshment in a turn towards spiritual renewal, while D. S. Farrer's Chow Gar martial arts adepts (Chapter 9) face each other in turning into other animal species or 'becoming' female in a symbolic awakening 'on the journey to becoming'. Finally, in the list of 'turns' I have observed in my reading of these chapters, David Cockburn (Chapter 10) discusses what happens in ape language research when a bonobo turns to make eye contact with a team of human researchers.

The 'Species Turn'

This volume's contributors attend to conceptual turns in the light of changing interests in a wider multidisciplinary literature concerning human relations with other species and the associated task of understanding animate nature. S. Eben Kirksey and Stefan Helmreich (2010: 549–56) examined a broad field of research, including contributions from biologists and philosophers, to demonstrate that social anthropologists from at least Lewis Henry Morgan (1868) have crossed disciplinary boundaries to maintain an engagement between the social and natural sciences. Restrictions on word allowance do not permit me to do justice to this literature. I merely draw attention to work by the biologist Donna Haraway, whose many publications have contributed to the 'species turn' in anthropology and philosophy. One of her areas of interest concerns the notion that different sorts of living beings coexist in 'contact zones', a phrase borrowed from Mary Pratt's *Imperial Eyes* (1992), although Haraway (2008: 216) did not wish to push the colonial parallels too far in her examination of human relationships with companion species. There are chapters in this volume by Grossman-Horesh (Chapter 5), Ben-David (Chapter 8) and myself (Chapter 11), however, where a consideration of what happens in interspecies contact zones under colonial or postcolonial conditions is relevant.

Haraway's main argument is that when species live together in contact zones, the boundaries can become blurred, or species can become habituated to each other's presence.[3] The term 'species', Haraway (2008: 17) observed, derives from the Latin *specere* ('to look' or 'behold'), and it therefore derives from a visual recording. Since the term is applied to the particular (the 'specific') as well as to classes of organisms sharing similar characteristics, it has caused biologists to address whether or not species are entities with an observable existence or merely conveniences established through some sort of taxonomic imperative (Haraway 2008: 17).

Arguing that revolutions in molecular and digital technologies have 'informationalized life' in contemporary biopolitics, Michael Dillon and Luis Lobo-Guerrero (2009: 1–2) point to three dictionary definitions for the term 'species'. In their list, the word has, first, the meaning of class membership (as opposed to an individual status); second, in a zoological or botanical usage, it is a term for the subdivision of a genus; and their third meaning relates to coinage, in designating a particular category of money. They comment that these meanings 'illustrate the deep complicity that obtains between classification, animation and monetary valuation' (Dillon and Lobo-Guerrero 2009: 4). Their argument is that, in the popular imagination since Charles Darwin, species-thinking has restricted the concept of species to animate rather than inanimate beings; however, developments in molecular and digital technologies are now problematizing distinctions between life and death. This argument is not entirely supported by the contributors to this volume, even in Western social contexts, as is evident from Jelinek and Brown's approach to multispecies engagements. Here, however, I wish to draw attention to Dillon and Lobo-Guerrero's discussion of the work of Western philosophers, such as Emmanuel Levinas and Jacques Derrida, whose writings disrupt classificatory attempts to reduce experience on the basis of species membership. Species-thinking, Dillon and Lobo-Guerrero (2009: 5) argue, is hegemonic because a living being has 'to be classifiable as informational code to be admitted to the category of contemporary biological species'. Distributive economies assign value, but they are also responsible for a parallel process in which devaluation occurs. In their insistence on the singular and the unclassifiable, philosophers pose a challenge to 'the inequitable distributive outcome of speciation' and the violent processes involved in excluding the invaluable/unclassifiable from the membership of positively viewed species (Dillon and Lobo-Guerrero 2009: 6). One might note my second epigraph, in which Michael Taussig (2004: 111) converted the more usual culture-nature dichotomy to a money-nature dichotomy.

The Levinasian ethics raised by Dillon and Lobo-Guerrero also feature in Jelinek and Brown's account of the difficulties in problematizing the notion of who 'we' might be in an art experiment that seeks to 'imagine difference in a nonhierarchical way'. This, too, is a strand of thought to which I will return.

'Perspectival' and 'Ontological' Turns

Eduardo Viveiros de Castro (2004) attempted to unsettle the nature-culture dichotomy in a discussion of 'perspectival multinaturalism', which drew attention to the plurality of natures in South American ontologies. He acknowledged that the contrast drawn by Native Americans between 'animals' and 'humans' might superficially be seen to be analogous to the distinctions Westerners make between nature and culture. In contrast, however, to Western 'scientific' evolutionist trajectories, which were intended to explain the distinctiveness of species, he pointed out that Amazonian peoples speak in their myths of a diversification of an original earthly condition populated by human beings. In the myths 'animals lost the qualities inherited or retained by humans'; therefore, human beings are not seen as ex-animals, but, rather, other species are seen to be ex-humans (Viveiros de Castro 2004: 465). He referred to a view held by Campa people in which humanity constitutes the 'primal substance out of which many if not all of the categories of beings and things in the universe arose' (Weiss 1972: 169–70). Furthermore, Yaghan people of Tierra del Fuego spoke of a time before a great flood when animals and birds were humans; they also believed that trees were formerly human beings (see Chapter 11).

Since the 1990s, anthropologists have intensively reconfigured their responses to nineteenth-century notions of animism, which had been so intimately associated with evolutionism that it has taken a century to realize its potential for approaching different worldviews on human relationships with other species. E. B. Tylor (1871: 260, 384) considered that the 'deep-lying doctrine of Spiritual Beings', which he saw as the basis for personification, gave 'consistent individual life to phenomena that our utmost stretch of fancy only avails to personify in conscious metaphor'. Animists, therefore, assign a spiritual essence to living beings and also to apparently nonliving entities such as stars and planets. Philippe Descola (2009: 147) found that Achuar people of the Upper Amazon endow animals and plants 'with a soul identical to the one they possess, thus opening the possibility of establishing social relations with them'. On the basis of a review of the literature with comparable evidence from other parts of the world, he argued that it 'becomes scientifically risky to go on using, even as a methodological prop, a distinction between nature and culture which is so uncommon elsewhere' (Descola 2009: 147).

Not all anthropologists would make such a bold claim. Reminding readers that the ontologies of Amazonian societies lack homogeneity, Terence Turner's (2009) interpretation of the situation among another Amazonian people is more complex. He found that Kayapo possess what might broadly be termed an 'animist' perspective, but they regard their 'own bodies as hybrid combinations of natural animal qualities of form and content, supplemented by acquired formal attributes of social identity' (Turner 2009: 33). To treat the 'spirit' or the 'soul' in essentially human terms would be to cast Amazonian views in an anthropocentric mould and, if people believe that animals or plants have 'a spirit or subjectivity', it does not necessarily follow that such beings consider themselves to possess human spirits (Turner 2009: 33). Veena Das (Chapter 2) recognizes that Viveiros de Castro's and Descola's positions allow for 'exciting possibilities for an expansion of thought on the being of animals'. She, like Turner, however, has reservations, and she observes that human views on the 'logical possibilities' concerning the position of animals cannot map onto a complete internalization of animal ways of being.[4]

Das also makes a very important point that other people's worldviews may incorporate the simultaneous presence of different ontologies, which invite further analysis: is it possible to trace the histories of such copresent ontologies in non-Western societies, and to determine which might be seen to be 'well' and which 'badly' made? Complex attitudes concerning human relationships with nature also emerge in Chapter 6, in Carole Baker's exploration of her own photographic practices in relation to work by the Japanese photographers Rinko Kawauchi and Masao Yamamoto, given that 'nature' is an incommensurable term belonging to different axiomatic systems in the English and Japanese languages (see Kawasaki 1999: 4–6).

Turning to Be Face-to-Face

A turn might be involved in the act of turning to face another being. Derrida (2008: 41) was uncomfortable with the singular and plural forms of the term 'animal' when applied to 'an irreducible living multiplicity of mortals'. He had been discomfited by the gaze of his cat, who saw him when naked. Unlike some other languages, which are not predicated on an opposition between animality and humanity (as I noted above), the French language does have a single term for a diversity of beings. Derrida (2008: 47) therefore felt the need to devise a neologism: *animot*. He instructed his readers to replace *l'animal* or *les animaux* with this 'chimera' term—which, of course, sounds like the latter when pronounced. This argument is, in part, intended to draw attention to how animal multiplicity disrupts human-animal divisions. This term was included in a book entitled *The Animal That Therefore I Am,* most of the content of which was published posthumously. The book's title is that of the first chapter (which Derrida had originally published before his death) followed by the phrase 'more to follow', a play on *je suis* ('I am' and 'I follow').

The metaphysical tracking that Derrida explored included a discussion of Levinasian ethics, but Matthew Calarco (2009) found his discussion of Emmanuel Levinas dutiful rather than insightful—he suggested that, were Derrida to have prepared the second chapter of the book for publication before he died, he would have felt the need to revise the section on Levinas. 'Tracking' indicates following from behind, whereas Levinas used the metaphor of turning to 'face' someone else.

Anthropologists have not responded to the work of Levinas to the extent that they have with other philosophers (see, for example, Chapter 9 by D. S. Farrer).[5] The responsibilities involved in face-to-face encounters between a fieldworker and his or her research participants, or between human and other beings, led Jelinek and Brown to explore the Levinasian notion that the face expresses vulnerability towards the 'Other' (Levinas 1989: 82–3). Transcendence for Levinas was an affair among human beings, and his ethics 'concerned intersubjective relation at its precognitive core' rather than having to do with 'rationalist self-legislation … the calculation of happiness … or the cultivation of virtues' (Bergo 2011). Jelinek and Brown discuss difficulties Europeans encounter in perceiving the face of the Other due to their Graeco-European inheritance of appreciation for notions of sameness.

Because her discussion is based on the notion of an interspecies blurring, Haraway (2008: 311n28) found Levinas's account of Bobby the dog, who greeted Jewish prisoners in a German labour camp, to be unsatisfactory because she argued that the encounter was grounded in face-to-face relationships. Levinas's analysis left Bobby on the 'wrong' side of 'a Great Divide' between humans and nonhuman species. Other attempts have been made to reread Levinasian ethics, exploring what 'the face' might mean. If Levinas used the phrase 'face-to-face' as a metaphor, Barbara Davy (2007: 49) argued that the 'Other need not be able to speak as a human for ethics to come to pass'. She admitted, however, that her 'reconstructive reading' of Levinas resulted in an 'extraneous' ethic that runs 'outside' his exclusion of 'nonhuman others in ethics' (Davy 2007: 39).

A discussion based on the notion in which a gaze is interrupted seems to privilege beings with certain facial features. In a radio discussion, the philosopher of science Peter Godfrey-Smith (2011) pointed out the relative ease with which it might be possible for humans to imagine thought processes of dogs and apes, as opposed to imagining those of an octopus. He noted that octopuses looked at him while he swam; he observed that for a human being to return an octopus's gaze is the closest one might get to an encounter with an intelligent alien. Whereas vertebrates have a centralized nervous system, Godfrey-Smith's description of the decentralized 'knots of neurons that are spread through the body and that are linked to each other in a ladder-like structure' in an octopus suggest a radically different form of brain activity. Yet the interspecies reaction still takes place. As I mentioned above, Yaghan people believed in the ability of trees to witness human actions, and the Basque Tree of Gernika listens and responds. It should be noted, however, that other disruptions of the senses might also be envisaged, such as the wordless screaming of cooked rice and barley mentioned by Das in Chapter 2.

Cycles of Life and Death

The concept of investigating the interactivities of living entities from an anthropological perspective provides scope for studying processes of growth, life cycles, entropy and death. The clinical precision of death in D. S. Farrer's discussion of martial arts contrasts with the multiplicity of many inefficient attacks on whales in Fuegian waters by orcas and humans in Chapter 11. A whale cannot easily be killed in a surgical strike.

Yet some people have maintained that death is meted out swiftly among animals. Until the nineteenth century, many European theologians and philosophers sought to prove the existence of God by arguing that the world was a morally ordained universe in which death amongst animals was expertly delivered; prey animals did not suffer the agonies of a slow death or a painful senescence. Quoting a letter written by Darwin to Asa Gray, Stephen Jay Gould (1994 [1982], cited by Lackey 2001: 85) argued that a wasp, rather than a lion, undid the long-prevailing argument that God designed nature. The ichneumon wasp paralyzes another living being, such as a caterpillar, by laying its eggs in the still living body. These eggs hatch and the larvae devour their host but instinctively avoid its vital organs because the death of the caterpillar would result in the loss of their food supply. For theologians, who saw God's design in a benevolent universe, knowledge of the behaviour of the ichneumon wasp was a great impediment to the coherence of their arguments.

Michael Lackey (2001) analysed the poem 'God's Grandeur' by Gerald Manley Hopkins as an exhortation addressed to authors such as Marx who had turned towards speculative atheism. Advances in entomological knowledge meant that Hopkins had to develop a different argument than one based on design to encourage such atheists to believe in the existence of God. According to Lackey (2001: 85), Hopkins used the poem to present a view of fallen humanity living in a world 'seared with trade; bleared, smeared with toil'. The Holy Spirit reanimates the vitality of nature in a regular resurrection. Admitting that the power of Hopkins's argument to convince is not a concern in his essay, Lackey (2001: 86, 89n18) noted the poet's concern was with 'the resurrection impulse within nature, a nature that is bleared and smeared with toil and wears man's smudge, but that also experiences a God-like resurrection on a regular basis'. The principle of resilience underscoring the poem ('There lives the dearest freshness deep down things') bears witness to the existence of God, without which this principle could not exist.

'Dearest freshness' lends itself to different interpretations. The poet might have been alluding to the cost or value of the things in nature, but the adjective 'dearest' is also a term of endearment for persons. I perceive an unsuspected conjunction between the poem by Hopkins and the work of Michael Taussig (2004: xviii). In the latter, a search for immanence and transcendence takes place in an irreducible and vengeful world of nature, in which human labour becomes 'the life-and-death play of nature with second nature'. Detailing the working lives of Afro-Colombian gold miners and panners, he comments that one goes

> beyond imitation to become one with what you are imitating, like the diver mingling with the elements as a fish and then as a mud crab burrowing in the dark. Here imitation undergoes a radical development. It passes from being outside to being inside, in fact to becoming Other. Imitation becomes immanence. Then there is the moment of the trick whereby in imitating and becoming Other, you stay right there, like water in water for the sheer hell of it, for the pleasure at the loss of self and the transformation of Being—or else you use that moment to dominate nature and seek profit from it. The fork in the road. (Taussig 2004: 80)

The conjunction between Hopkins and Taussig occurs in the periodic revitalizations and personifications of nature. They are at play in Hopkins's poem (in Lackey's [2001: 87] analysis of the '"charged" moments of resurrection' when God's presence is made manifest) and in Taussig's 'moment of the trick'. Taussig's approach to the vitalization of living beings and notions of relatedness between species is predicated on a different understanding of animation than in the approaches considered previously under the 'ontological turn'. In his hands, the human labour of placer mining equates the human being with a mud crab in a dignified life that combines the humdrum and the lethal.

The Chapters in This Book

In Chapter 2, Veena Das explores what she calls an 'enigmatic analogy between death and animality'. Her investigation of Vedic traditions concerning sacrifice enables her to peer into matters that are (and here she cites the work of Stephen Mulhall) 'resistant to human accessibility'. She develops the analogy between human imaginings of other animals' existence and human imaginings of death to argue that there are limits to the human understanding of the being of other animals. Although human and other animals can and do live with each other, unbridgeable cross-cultural differences remain—even though humans might be able to internalize 'animal modes of being ... they cannot assimilate these forms completely'.

In contrast to ancient Vedic texts, Sarah Boss turns attention to the work of the thirteenth-century Mallorcan philosopher Ramon Llull. His writings convey a sense of his wonder for the different beings of the world as well as his understanding of the purpose of those beings in the world. In order to share with his readers his knowledge of God, he developed a graphic device, a 'ladder of nature', to present his understanding of relationships between different orders of being through a graded sequence of faculties. At first sight, it might seem that this ladder enables a flow of vitality through the hierarchically ordered relationships, but Boss demonstrates that the hierarchical orders coexist in complex relationships, representing a mix of different physical and spiritual elements that make up heavenly bodies as well as those of men, women and other beings in the world. The gradualism implied by the steps of the ladder turns out to be fluid, yet at the same time, it is unified in the being of one God. In analysing Llull's writings, Boss approaches Veena Das's 'enigmatic analogy' from a different angle. Llull addressed a disconsolate Pagan who, confronted by a sense of nullity conveyed by the prospect of death, sought consolation among the living beings of the world. He offered the suffering Pagan a view of Christianity that was intended to grant people a meaningful place in a single universe of being in which the believer can find the presence of God in the world.

From ancient Vedic and Christian texts, attention turns in Chapter 4, by Safet HadžiMuhamedović, to the historical events of Gernika and the legitimating powers of an Oak Tree and its procreative genealogy. His subject matter concerns notions of rootedness and belonging associated with descendants of a Tree that survived the military destruction inflicted on Basque people on a market day in April 1937 by the German Condor Legion.

The treatment of historically recorded materials turns to the presentation of fieldwork findings by Ronit Grossman-Horesh. Her ethnographic description of the simulation of a conceptual forest in urban contexts by Israeli song circle members casts light on their spatial imaginaries within a naturalist paradigm. Their activities, designed to foster spiritual renewal, are intended to sing the vision of a green forest into existence in the minds of the participants, who are encouraged to make inner (introspective) and outer (communal) connections. This gathering of songs as a form of experiencing life in forests achieves its fullest expression in Costa Rica, but many circle members who are urban dwellers actualize their vision not through being physically present in a real forest, but through an ideal existing in the imagination. The infinite space of the imagined forest is located in Grossman's analysis on 'the margins of political discourse'. Circle members do not recognize themselves as having political interests and are secular in their beliefs, yet they engage in aPolitical political activism and they make aReligious religious observances.

Carole Baker demonstrates her engagement with living things (more specifically an orchard) through the use of analogue photography. She argues that such a photographic practice incorporates representational and phenomenological characteristics. Resisting the urge to contemplate how her viewers might engage with her photographs, she analyses her practice in juxtaposition to her responses to Kawauchi's and Yamamoto's photographs. She demonstrates that the nature of these photographs of living things is that of 'a ready-made analogon', adopting Sartre's term 'analogon' as the description of a thing that resembles the object it represents.

The 'art experiment' considered by Alana Jelinek and Juliette Brown explores principles and sentiments that are profoundly different to those expressed by the song circle members studied by Grossman-Horesh. This conceptual artwork is a physical 12.9-acre extent of land in Essex, England, known as *The Field,* and a series of multispecies encounters taking place on and in relation to the site. Juliette Brown's observation that 'nature can never not be political' makes an alternative stance to the mostly apolitical declarations of the Israeli song circle members. Jelinek and Brown are committed to *The Field* as a project with certain 'rules' or boundaries derived from the Conceptual Art practised in the 1960s and 1970s and in relationship to the philosophy of Levinas.

Rachel Ben-David examines an Israeli phenomenon in her chapter. Her study of 'family safaris' or 'Bar Mitzvah safaris' to Kenya and Tanzania demonstrates that middle-upper-class secular ecotourists regard wildlife as a means of assuaging modern feelings of alienation. In order to understand what motivates Israelis to go on safari in family groups, Ben-David enquires into the tourists' experiences and their attitudes towards the materialism and pace of urban life. For these tourists, it turns out that wild animals can become models for human behaviour related to 'forgotten' practices, including courtship and parental nurturing of children. She demonstrates how ecotourists access a magical 'sensual vitality' without necessarily feeling the need to communicate with other human beings in their paradoxical search for spiritual experience in nature. In her analysis, it turns out that 'watching wild animals from safe jeeps provides a break from modernity as well as being an enactment of modernity.'

D. S. Farrer explores the extent to which practitioners of Chow Gar martial arts can become replicas of other animal species in addressing what he calls 'somatic modes of attention'. He examines how the disciplining of physical and mental powers is 'assisted by reflex, but is not subject to reflex'. His discussion of the notion of becoming-animal focuses on the 'awakening' of vital powers associated with certain nonhuman species.

David Cockburn's chapter looks into the aims of ape language research and questions of 'anthropomorphism' or 'anthropocentrism' that such research has evinced. His discussion of these terms indicates that there is scope for general concerns in relation to all human studies of nonhuman worlds. Eye contact constitutes an important aspect of Kanzi's language skills. According to Cockburn, the bonobo's 'attempts to seek eye contact, far from clouding our judgment, are a legitimate, perhaps inescapable, part of the basis for a consideration of whether he has language.' Par Segerdahl and his team of fellow researchers who worked with Kanzi as a research participant found themselves in an interhuman-bonobo situation that was no longer just a human community. Cockburn argues that the standards embodied in this research into language use are no longer those of human beings alone.

My own chapter considers Yaghan attitudes towards clothing in Tierra del Fuego and how dressing oneself enmeshed people in a series of multispecies engagements. Using historical materials, it explores the recorded memories of Yaghan and ethnographic representations by outsiders, one of the most famous of whom was Darwin. While some anthropologists have accepted Darwin's comments that Fuegians had acquired a special physiological adaptation to the cold climate and did not need to clothe themselves to the extent that was necessary for outsiders, a close examination of the ethnographic evidence indicates that they felt the cold and dressed themselves accordingly. Being properly dressed by Yaghan standards involved wearing loose garments made of the fur of marine mammals and anointing their skin with seal, whale or fish oil. This dress served as a social skin expressing the wearer's subjective perspective concerning the fishing-gathering-hunting subsistence economy and, to use a phrase from Turner (2009: 36), it presented an 'objectified bodily form'. Because the Yaghan way of life came under threat from the sealing and whaling activities conducted on an industrial scale by people from the Northern Hemisphere, they were no longer able maintain their own dress standards. This examination of what at first may seem to be yet another case of locals and outsiders competing for the same animal resources, were it not for the annihilation of a way of life, reveals incommensurable approaches towards the objectification of bodily form.

In this introduction, I have attended to some of the strands threading their way through this volume. The study of living beings is one in which the researcher is deeply implicated with the subjects of the research. As Kay Milton (1993: 1) argued in her introduction to a book on anthropological approaches to environmentalism, the theme has 'to be explored rather than defined because it is still evolving'. My comments here should not be understood to imply that my fellow contributors share them. Finally, in a volume containing a discussion of anthropocentrism, I cannot resist drawing attention to a delightful (or unconscious?) animal pun in Comaroff and Comaroff's (1992: 10) comment that anthropocentrism 'dogs our desire to know' other species.

Notes

1. See Chapter 10 by David Cockburn in this volume. I am also grateful to Lynne Sharpe for discussing this point with me.
2. Both humans and animals featured in Karl Marx's analysis of the alienation or estrangement of production in capitalist society. Thomas E. Wartenberg (1982: 83) explained that his critique hinged on a concept of species-being, adapted from Feuerbach, but, unlike that author, he did not the restrict the concept to an ahistorical and asocial sphere of human essence. Instead, he developed a theory based on productive activity to account for the distinctiveness of human essence compared to that of nonhuman animals. Wartenberg (1982: 94) considered that

Marx recognized 'that many aspects of a so-called human nature are in reality nothing but hyposatized [*sic*] features of human social relations under capitalism'. Marx's critique was that human nature was not fixed: 'These conditions of existence are, of course only the productive forces and forms of intercourse at any particular time' (Marx 1970 [1932]: 85–6, cited by Wartenberg 1982: 94). The productive activities considered in the chapters of this volume have historical and spatial coordinates.

3. A Western view that there has been a gulf between humans and animals is countered by the proponents of other views arguing for a continuity of species—a chain of individual species each with their own special status. See Chapter 11 for a further discussion.

4. This area is another with a large literature that I cannot review fully here. Halbmayer (2012) and Hornborg (2006) have provided recent historical characterizations and bibliographies of the development of such anthropological thinking.

5. But see the article by Peter Benson and Kevin Lewis O'Neill (2007).

References

Beattie, J.H.M. 1966. *Other Cultures: Aims, Methods and Achievements in Social Anthropology.* London: Routledge and Kegan Paul.

Benson, P., and K. L. O'Neill. 2007. 'Facing Risk: Levinas, Ethnography, and Ethics'. *Anthropology of Consciousness* 18(2): 29–55.

Bergo, B. 2011. 'Emmanuel Levinas'. In E. N. Zalta, ed., *The Stanford Encyclopedia of Philosophy* (Fall 2011 Edition). Available at: http://plato.stanford.edu/archives/fall2011/entries/levinas/. Accessed 14 April 2013.

Brenner, S. 2000. 'Genomics—the End of the Beginning'. *Science* 287(5461): 2173–4.

Calarco, M. 2009. 'Tracking the Animal in Derrida'. *Humanimalia* 1(1). Available at: http://www.depauw.edu/humanimalia/issue01/pdfs/Calarco-Derrida.pdf. Accessed 14 April 2013.

Cloke, P., and O. Jones. 2001. 'Dwelling, Place, and Landscape: An Orchard in Somerset'. *Environment and Planning A* 33(4): 649–66.

Cloke, P., and O. Jones. 2004. 'Turning in the Graveyard: Trees and the Hybrid Geographies of Dwelling, Monitoring and Resistance in a Bristol Cemetery'. *Cultural Geographies* 11: 313–41.

Comaroff, J., and J. Comaroff. 1992. *Ethnography and the Historical Imagination.* Boulder, CO: Westview Press.

Davy, B. J. 2007. 'An Other Face of Ethics in Levinas'. *Ethics and the Environment* 12(1): 39–65.

de Certeau, M. 1983. 'The Madness of Vision'. *Enclitic* 7(1): 24–31.

Derrida, J. 2008. *The Animal That Therefore I Am,* ed. L. M. Mallet. New York: Fordham University Press.

Descola, P. 2009. 'Human Natures'. *Social Anthropology/Anthropologie Sociale* 17(2): 145–57.

Descola, P., and G. Pálsson. 1996. 'Introduction'. In P. Descola and G. Pálsson, eds, *Nature and Society: Anthropological Perspectives.* London: Routledge, 1–21.

Dillon, M., and L. Lobo-Guerrero. 2009. 'The Biopolitical Imaginary of Species-being'. *Theory, Culture & Society* 26(1): 1–23.

Dransart, P. 2010. 'Animals and Their Possessions: Properties of Herd Animals in the Andes and Europe'. In M. Bolton and C. Degnen, eds, *Animals and Science: Anthropological Approaches.* Newcastle: Cambridge Scholars, 84–104.

Dumont, L. 1986. 'Are Cultures Living Beings? German Identity in Interaction'. *Man* 21: 587–604.

Godfrey-Smith, P. 2011. 'How Do Octopuses Think?' Radio National: The Philosopher's Zone. Available at: http://www.abc.net.au/radionational/programs/philosopherszone/how-do-octopuses-think/3692530. Accessed 15 April 2013.

Gould, S. J. 1994 [1982]. 'Nonmoral Nature'. In S. J. Gould, *Hen's Teeth and Horse's Toes: Further Reflections in Natural History.* New York: W. W. Norton, 32–44.

Halbmayer, E. 2012. 'Debating Animism, Perspectivism and the Construction of Ontologies'. *Indiana* 29: 9–23.

Haraway, D. 2008. *When Species Meet.* Minneapolis: University of Minnesota Press.

Hornborg, A. 2006. 'Animism, Fetishism, and Objectivism as Strategies for Knowing (or Not Knowing) the World'. *Ethnos* 7(1): 21–32.

Ingold, T. 1994. 'Humanity and Animality'. In T. Ingold, ed., *Companion Encyclopedia of Anthropology: Humanity, Culture and Social Life.* London: Routledge, 14–32.

Ingold, T., and E. Hallam. 2007. 'Creativity and Cultural Improvisation: An Introduction'. In E. Hallam and T. Ingold, eds, *Creativity and Cultural Improvisation.* Oxford: Berg, ASA Monographs No. 44, 1–24.

Kawasaki, K. 1999. 'A Deductive Description of Cultural Diversity of "Observation" in Science Education'. *Journal of Science Education in Japan* 23(4): 258–70.

Kirksey, S. E., and S. Helmreich. 2010. 'The Emergence of Multispecies Ethnography'. *Cultural Anthropology* 25(4): 545–76.

Lackey, M. 2001. '"God's Grandeur": Gerard Manley Hopkins' Reply to the Speculative Atheist'. *Victorian Poetry* 39(1): 83–90.

Levinas, E. 1989. 'Ethics as First Philosophy'. In S. Hand, ed., *The Levinas Reader.* Oxford: Blackwell, 75–87.

Marx, K. 1970 [1932]. *The German Ideology,* ed. C. J. Arthur. New York: International.

Milton, K. 1993. 'Environmentalism and Anthropology'. In K. Milton, ed., *Environmentalism: The View from Anthropology.* London: Routledge, 1–17.

Morgan, L. H. 1868. *The American Beaver and His Works.* Philadelphia: J. B. Lippincott.

Pratt, M. L. 1992. *Imperial Eyes: Travel Writing and Transculturation.* New York: Routledge.

Radcliffe-Brown, A. R. 1958. *Selected Essays by A. R. Radcliffe-Brown,* ed. M. N. Srinivas. Chicago: University of Chicago Press.

Rival, L. 1996. 'Blowpipes and Spears: The Social Significance of Huaorani Technological Choices'. In P. Descola and G. Pálsson, eds, *Nature and Society: Anthropological Perspectives.* London: Routledge, 145–64.

Simpson, J. A., and E.S.C. Weiner. 1989. *The Oxford English Dictionary.* 2nd ed. Vol. 18. Oxford: Clarendon Press.

Taussig, M. 2004. *My Cocaine Museum.* Chicago: University of Chicago Press.

Turner, T. S. 2009. 'The Crisis of Late Structuralism. Perspectivism and Animism: Rethinking Culture, Nature, Spirit, and Bodiliness'. *Tipití: Journal of the Society for the Anthropology of Lowland South America* 7(1): 1–40.

Tylor, E. B. 1871. *Primitive Culture: Researches into the Development of Mythology, Philosophy, Religion, Art, and Custom.* London: J. Murray.

Viveiros de Castro, E. 2004. 'Exchanging Perspectives: The Transformation of Objects into Subjects in Amerindian Ontologies'. *Common Knowledge* 10(3): 463–84.

Wartenberg, T. E. 1982. '"Species-being" and "Human Nature" in Marx'. *Human Studies* 5(2): 77–95.

Weiss, G. 1972. 'Campa Cosmology'. *Ethnology* 11(2): 157–72.

Being Together with Animals: Death, Violence and Noncruelty in Hindu Imagination

Veena Das

How might we take animals as constitutive of our ways of world making?[1] In a deeply thoughtful discussion on the subject, Stephen Mulhall (2007) unfolds the underlying structure of Martin Heidegger's (1995) thought in his book, *The Fundamental Concepts of Metaphysics: World, Finitude, Solitude,* with regard to Dasein's kinship with the animal realm.[2] The three interlinked propositions that are taken to be fundamental for Heidegger, as Mulhall points out, are as follows: 'The stone is *worldless*; the animal is *poor in the world*; man is *world-forming.*' While many scholars have interpreted this sentence as Heidegger's denial or repression of a connection between human and animal modes of being, Mulhall invites us to take a different route to the understanding of what worldliness or its lack might mean for Heidegger. As against Alasdair MacIntyre's (1999) reading of Heidegger that says that he (Heidegger) leaves us with a very traditional picture of Dasein's being as distinguished from animal being by its possession of *logos*, Mulhall draws our attention to those sections of *The Fundamental Concepts of Metaphysics* in which Heidegger stumbles over words, asking us to read the expression 'world poverty' under erasure—so the animal elicits from the human, says Mulhall, a bewilderment, a difficulty in simply 'going along with'. It is worth citing Mulhall at length here:

> In other words, animals neither simply lack access to objects in their own right (as do stones) nor do they simply possess a humanly accessible mode of access to objects (as do other Dasein); their singularity in our experience lies in their having a mode of access to and dealing with the world from which we are excluded. Animal dealings with objects are accessible to humans, but only as resistant to human accessibility; hence to grasp animality is to grasp it as a mode of being from which human beings are fenced out, that they can grasp only as beyond them. The analogy with Heidegger's treatment of death is striking. (Mulhall 2007: 76)

What I find compelling here is Mulhall's recognition of the import of Heidegger's understanding that the human is not simply animal plus something else; rather, the weirdness of the animal world is experienced as somewhat similar to our strange

relation to death. Just as we must experience death not as an actuality but as a possibility that hovers over life (since my death can never be an event *in* my own life),
so there is an experience of being left out in relation to the animal life—we can never
quite grasp what the world of the animal is. As Mulhall puts it, death distinguishes
itself as our own most, nonrelational, not-to-be-outstripped possibility. What I admire in Mulhall's reasoning is the mirroring of a certain difficulty of reality (there
are aspects of our existence from which we are fenced out) and a certain difficulty of
philosophy. This way of looking at the problem of what it is to inhabit the world with
animals is very different from the stance of many scholars who have argued, for instance, that many Amerindian cosmologies allow us to decipher the being of animals
in an embodied sense—a point to which I shall return. But to return to Mulhall—he
ends up arguing that the Christian myth of the Fall is far better able to encapsulate the
'essentially enigmatic, uncanny, intimate distance' between humanity and animality
compared to the secular alternatives. He is, however, not interested in asking if other
traditions might have taken the enigmatic analogy between death and animality in
different directions.[3] This is a fair enough stance from where Mulhall stands, but
I am still puzzled by the lack of curiosity about other traditions, as if Christianity and
secularism were the only two viable options available for thought. I will return to the
difficulty of reality and the difficulty of philosophy with regard to animals and death
through the eyes of another philosopher (Cora Diamond) later. But first I want to
turn to a classic site of anthropology—that of sacrifice within the Vedic tradition of
Hinduism—to ask if the enigmatic relation between imagining animal existence and
imagining death within human life might provide a different route for conceptualizing the issues that Mulhall so masterfully opens up for us. I would like to think of
the Vedic–Hindu formulation as standing in a relation of dialogue with Heidegger's
thought in which our being fenced out from the experience of death might mirror the
experience of sustaining an intimate otherness with animals.

Animality, Humanity, Death

Why are animals killed in sacrifice? There is considerable anxiety in the Vedic texts
regarding the violence inflicted on animals. While neither the killing of animals in
sacrifice nor the anxiety surrounding the act is unique to Hinduism, the structure of
thought that is expressed in the justifications offered for the killing dramatizes the
way our relation to death and our relation to animals is encompassed within a notion
of the nature of life itself. In my earlier work, I have argued that instead of thinking
of sacrifice as primarily an act of communication between humans and gods (with
the animal offering as the object that mediates between the two), as dominant theories of sacrifice in anthropology are inclined to do (see Hubert and Mauss 1964), we
might apply a different cultural logic. In this logic, the eating and killing of animals
in sacrifice are integrally linked with the violent preconditions of our life, such that

far from death and life being opposite poles of existence, they become the conditions of possibility for each other (see especially Das 1983, 2012 [1977]). From this perspective, sacrifice provides a dramatic expression of the ambivalence that surrounds the idea that life feeds upon life—in order to live, we must inflict some violence on the world. One might regard ritual violence, then, as enacting puzzles about the costs we pay in order to live.

The first thing that we notice about how animals figure into the Vedic sacrifice is that there is no single realm of 'animality'—instead, the Vedic texts distinguish between domestic animals (*pashu*) and wild animals (*mriga*)—and notably, man himself is included in the category of *pashu*. What is the nature of this continuity being posited between certain kinds of animals and humans on the basis of their domesticity?

Heidegger's discussion on animals is sensitive to the varieties of animals (rather than a singular animality) that form a part of human experience. The way that we might be fenced off from the life of a giant lizard is not quite the same way that we feel left out from the world of dogs. The latter are in some communication with their human counterparts—they might, for instance, carry individual names as pets in our lives and learn to respond to our simple commands or to elicit a response from their human companions by deploying different kinds of vocalizations and gestures. The tracks that particular animals leave in philosophical texts are quite telling—lions, cows, dogs, beetles, flies and spiders in Ludwig Wittgenstein; and dogs, squirrels, moths and bees, among others, in Heidegger. Other philosophers too have made compelling points about the difference between animals such as moths or mosquitoes—which might lack the as-if structure to enable them to change perspective—and animals such as such as dogs, dolphins, chimpanzees or cats. The animals of the latter group can shift perspective to treat a prey from different angles—as a plaything now and as an item for food at a later moment (MacIntyre 1999).

Heidegger, as Mulhall points out, is interested in the ways in which animals appear as both within and without human modes of accessibility. Thus, the distinction between domestic and wild animals is taken to suggest that animals allow themselves to be domesticated, but they also resist domestication. The wildness of the undomesticated animals shows, for Heidegger, an aspect of animal existence that is completely oblivious to human beings. The domestication of animals, on the other hand, shows that animals can be incorporated into our forms of life, but it does not imply that the sheer alterity of the animal can be completely erased from human modes of existence. Domestic animals live with us as pets or as service animals, and so they expand the human world, but their mode of dwelling together still retains a difference from human modes of dwelling together. As Wittgenstein (1953) pointed out, when a dog looks expectantly at the door on hearing footsteps or begins to bark, we can say that it *expects* its master but hardly that it *hopes* its master will be there.

So suppose we made a small shift in our question—instead of saying that the distinction between the domestic and the wild is about asking what is animality, we ask what does this distinction say about what is it to have a human form of life? The distinction between the domestic and the wild with regard to animals and humans is fundamental to Vedic sacrifice, but I argue that this distinction is relevant precisely because it brings forward a singular aspect of humans—their propensity to deny that they are mortal or, as the texts say, our forgetfulness towards the fact that we are all born in debt to death.

The iconic story that recounts the human propensity to forget their mortality is one of the questions asked by Yaksha (a wild spirit that often guards water sources) to Yudhishthira, the protagonist hero of the great epic Mahabharata.[4] During their exile in the forest, the five Pandava brothers were once exhausted and resting, when each went in search of water but the younger four were killed by a Yaksha who was living in the form of a crane on a tree near the lake. Blinded by pride, they had refused to answer the questions he put to them. It was left to the eldest, Yudshishthira, to recognize the power of the Yaksha, to answer the questions he put to him, and to thus revive his dead brothers with the blessings of the Yaksha. One component of the last question was, 'What is it that causes the greatest wonder (*kim ashcharyam*) in the world?' Yudhshthira answered correctly that 'Day after day countless people are going to the abode of Yama (the god of death)—yet those that remain behind count themselves as immortal—what can cause greater wonder than this?'

I believe that it is to this question—the forgetfulness towards death—that the sacrificial logic of killing of certain types of animals is oriented.

Of Gods, Men and Animals as Sacrificial Beings

Wendy Doniger (2009) gives a very nice account of sacrifice in the period of the Brahmanas (800–500 BCE), when explanations about rules of sacrifice as well as folk stories around animals and humans begin to make their way into the texts. According to her, the texts begin to express greater anxiety around sacrificial acts than was registered in the Vedas. Various stories appear on the connections between humans and particular animals (e.g. the cow and the man). What is striking in these stories is not that the world of humans and the world of animals are set apart and then analogically connected, but rather that the points of disconnection are a result of particular contracts—such as the contract that humans give their skins to cows and cows give them the right to eat them. What interests me here, though, is the specific story of how the distinction between the domestic and the wild come to be enacted with reference to sacrifice.

Doniger begins her account of sacrificial animals by regarding humans as the first kind of sacrificial animals. 'Texts of this period', she says, 'regard humans as the pawns of the gods' (Doniger 2009: 151). The Vedas and the Brahmanas consider five types of animals to be sacrificial animals—bull, stallion, billy goat, ram and man.[5] These animals were all created from the first cosmic sacrifice in which the primeval man offered himself as sacrifice to the gods, therefore becoming both the object of sacrifice and the subject of sacrifice. From the primeval man's body were born all objects in the world. The sacrificial animals were crafted from the melted fat of his body, while the different body parts created the fourfold division of castes in the social world. The Brahmanas distinguish the *pashu* from the *mriga*. The latter term is derived from the verb 'to hunt'. Doniger states that the ancient Indians thus defined animals according to the manner in which they killed them, either in a hunt (*mrigas*) or in a sacrifice (*pashus*). Doniger's explanation of what it means to think of humans as sacrificial animals is interesting but falls somewhat short of confronting what might be at stake here. She says that the evidence of actual human sacrifice is sparse and thus, 'It may well be that the human sacrifice (*purusha-medha*) ["sacrifice of a man"] was simply a part of the Brahmin imagery, a fantasy of "the sacrifice to end all sacrifices"' (Doniger 2009: 152). However, she goes on to add that these texts are most likely saying that human beings are, like all other animals, fit to be sacrificed to the gods; that they are, as it were, the livestock of the gods. In such a reading, humans are to gods as animals are to human beings. In what follows, I try to provide a different reading that takes account of the euphemisms in sacrifice, its logic of substitution, and also the domestic-wild dichotomy that seems so central to the discussion.

Euphemisms

In his classic work on the religion of the Vedas, Hermann Oldenburg (1988) describes the moment of the killing of the animal by strangulation as follows:

> The sacrificial animal was killed with the expressions, common also to other people, of efforts to free oneself from the sin of a bloody deed and from impending revenge. It was told 'You are not dying, you are not harmed, you are going to the gods along beautiful paths' ... the killing was called euphemistically 'to get the consent of the animal.' The killing was effected by suffocation or strangulation without spilling blood; one tried hard to prevent the animal from crying; the main persons involved in the sacrifice turned their backs till the animal died. (Oldenburg 1988: 292)

The exact ritual term for this process was *sangyapan* (Sen 1978), which literally meant 'taking the consent'. As Émile Benveniste (1971: 266) has shown in a short essay on euphemisms, this region of linguistic expressions hinges on the paradox that one wishes to bring to mind an idea while avoiding naming it specifically. Euphemisms are distinct from taboos on speaking certain words. In the latter case, the issue is that of 'avoidance'; in the former case, words are substituted for those words that must not be uttered, thus concealing the nature of the act and yet bringing it to mind. Benveniste discusses the euphemistic character of the expressions used for certain acts; for example, saying 'snuffing the tip of the flame' instead of 'extinguishing the fire', since in popular culture, fire is given the character of a living being. He concludes his essay with this stunning observation: 'The aim of all these processes is not simply to mitigate the idea of "extinguish". Just as in the Vedic ritual of sacrifice, the victim is "appeased" (*śamayati*) or "made to consent" when in actual fact it is "strangled", so the fire that is extinguished is "appeased"' (Benveniste 1971: 270). So we are not killing the animal but only creating the beatific path for it to reach the gods, and it is the animal's desire that merges with the desire of the sacrificer.

Now what is the nature of the idea that is brought to the mind while avoiding its naming in the ritual characterization of strangulation as 'consent'? I suggest that what is at stake in the euphemistic sacred vocabulary is the question of death—not the death of the animal that is being ritually strangled but the death of the sacrificer which is being warded off. Thus the violence being done to the animal in the public (*śrauta*) ritual is an anticipation of the violence that will be done to the sacrificer in a final sacrifice that he will perform—that is, the sacrifice of the self as an offering to the gods in the final death rituals. This interpretation stems from the wider idea in the Hindu imagination of death in which each individual death repeats the sacrificial death of the primeval man (*purusha*) from which the natural and social world are said to have emanated.

Several scholars have noted that the sacrifice of the animal, in some ways, anticipates the idea of death itself as a form of sacrifice. For instance, Mariasusai Dhavamony (1973) noted that it is through sacrifice that man ransoms his being from the gods in Vedic sacrifice, and Anand Coomaraswamy (2000) explicitly drew attention to the offering of squeezed *soma* plant in sacrifice, saying that when *soma* and *agni* (fire) are united in sacrifice they jointly overcome the force of death and redeem man, since man is born in debt to death (see also Dalmiya 2001).[6] Anthropologists have shown that the structure of the cremation rituals is best understood through the vocabulary as well as the spatial and temporal organization of sacrificial rituals (see Parry 1994; Das 2012 [1977]). In his brilliant analysis of the cremation rituals, Charles Malamoud (1996) uses a culinary vocabulary to think of the transformation of the corpse through the cremation fire, which 'cooks' the corpse to make it into an oblation fit to be offered to the gods.

The implications of the euphemisms used in the sacred vocabulary pertaining to killing as well as the strict analogy between cremation and sacrifice, or rather *cremation as sacrifice,* brings death back into the realm of human consciousness not through discourse but through practice. Going beyond the analogy of 'gods are to humans as humans are to animals,' we see that death is folded into our experience of domesticity. The human as householder is joined to the animal as domesticated, and in their death, both realize their nature as sacrificial oblations. The logic here is more of a deferral than that of a strict substitution.

The *mriga* outside the sphere of domestication die as hunted prey. In the human world, it is the ascetic or renouncer who might be seen analogically as the wild animal. Before entering the mode of renunciation, the householder is required to sever all ties with the domestic and to perform his own death rituals. However, some stories in the epics speak about *rishis* (ascetics), who dwelled in the forest with their respective wives, and the modes of their death are often similar to the death of wild animals who die in hunting expeditions. The most famous story is that of King Pandu of the Mahabharata who mistook Rishi Kinidma and his wife, who were joined in copulation, to be two deer and shot them with his arrow. He was cursed by the ascetic that he would similarly die if he ever engaged in copulation with either of his two wives. Pandu then gave up his kingdom in favour of his younger brother and retired to the forest with his wives. It seems clear that the two modes of dying—one as a sacrificial oblation and the other as the hunted prey, the first reserved for domesticated beings and the second for those who inhabit wilderness—also indicate how death itself is seen as either voluntarily embraced or accidentally encountered. I cannot, however, take this contrast further on this occasion, and turn instead to the eating of animals.

Why Do Humans Eat Animals?

The Brahmanas portray reciprocity between animals and humans and create connections between the sacrificial oblations and the violence inflicted on the world when one is obliged to eat in order to live. Doniger (2009) gives two stories from the Jaimaniya Brahmana with which I open the discussion on what it means that humans eat animals.

According to the first story, in the beginning, the skin of cattle was the skin that humans have now, and the skin of a human was the skin that cattle have now. Cattle could not bear the vagaries of the weather or the pests (mosquitoes, flies) that constantly bothered humans. So they entered into a contract with humans that they would exchange their clothing and allow humans to eat them in this world. However, in the next world, cattle would eat humans. The text goes on to state that the sacrificer wears a red hide to avoid being eaten in the next world by cattle.

I will try to spell out the intriguing connections here between cattle and humans, but let me first relate the second story that spells out the sacrificial acts performed by humans and the eating of animals. According to this story, Varuna, the Vedic god of waters and of the cosmic order, was irritated by his young son Bhrigu's arrogance and contrived to send him to a world beyond this one. There Bhrigu saw a man cut another man to pieces and eat him; he then saw a man eat another man who was soundlessly screaming, and so on. Bhrigu returned to his world and told his father what he had seen. Varuna then explained to him that when people offer no oblations, cut down trees for firewood, cook animals that cry out or cook rice and barley which scream wordlessly, then those trees, animals, rice and barley take on the form of men in the other world and eat the men who had not offered any oblations.

What these stories seem to suggest is that despite the fact that men and some animals are put in the same class as 'domestic' or 'fit to be sacrificed', the difference between the eater and the eaten cannot be erased despite the promise of some kind of reciprocal justice in a future world. The significance of the domestic in bringing together sacrificial oblations and the violence entailed in obtaining food is that it shows the violent preconditions on which simple everyday acts are premised. The fact that we cannot hear the screams of the rice and the barley cannot erase the constant transactions between life and death that are taking place in everyday acts of living.

Reflections on what is entailed in the killing of animals for food continue to be engaged in later texts. Donald R. Davis (2010) gives the example from the fifth chapter in *The Laws of Manu* in which there seem to be contradictory injunctions on this issue. Thus, one of the rules states that one can never obtain meat without causing injury and therefore one should abstain from eating meat (5.48), while another rule says that there is no fault in eating meat, drinking liquor or having sex, for these are the natural activities of creatures, though abstaining from such activities carries great rewards (5.56). Davis shows how applying the notion of what is the nature of a rule in the Mimamsa, the tenth-century commentator Medhatithi argues that not all rules carry the same force since explanations and exhortations are not at the same level as the rules with injunctive force (Jha 1999). More interestingly, the text makes a distinction between what is primary and what is secondary in any act—concluding that killing the animal is secondary and eating the meat is primary (Davis 2010: 58). This is an interesting commentary precisely because it brings the intimacy between life and death so close to consciousness. Was the pleasure of the act centred on the *killing* or on the *eating*? Further, I suggest that this reflection on the everydayness of ethical acts brings into view the more profound issue of whether our motives are transparent to us—a point that has relevance for how we might understand the violence in which both life and death are enmeshed.

Why Animals?

In his famous formulation on animal symbolism in totemism, Claude Lévi-Strauss (1963, 1969) formulated his famous proposition that 'animals are good to think with.' In considering our attunement to animals as formulated in the Vedic texts, I am trying to tap into a different region of thought. I note that the term *pashu* refers to domestic animals but is also the generic term most frequently used for animals, as if the natural condition for animals was to live in domesticity and to die as a sacrificial oblation, mirroring the condition of the householder and his dharma. Yet the Vedic texts also seem to suggest that in considering what death is to an animal we might find that we are not able to inhabit its body in our imagination. I have suggested that in thinking of what is it to kill an animal in sacrifice and for food, the Vedic texts on sacrifice are struggling to find a language for depicting what is the cost of living that we pay—the violence of sacrifice is the way in which they imagine that one could redeem oneself from the debt life pays to death. Simultaneously, it signals a profound issue—the incapacity to imagine *one's own death*—to have a genuinely embodied sense of being extinguished. This is what the question by Yaksha on the greatest wonder of the world signified. This is how the god Varuna wants to tame the arrogance of his son Bhrigu who is swollen with pride about his own learning. And this is how Diamond (2008) in the register of contemporary philosophy offers her profound reflections on J. M. Coetzee's (1999) Tanner Lectures on the lives of animals, thought through the literary figure of Mrs Costello. Consider the words of Diamond:

> I want to describe Coetzee's lectures, then, as presenting a kind of woundedness or hauntedness, a terrible rawness of nerves. What wounds this woman, what haunts her mind, is what we do to animals. This, in all its horror, is there in our world. How is it possible to live in the face of it? And, in the face of the fact, that for nearly everyone, it is as nothing, as the mere accepted background of life? (Diamond 2008: 47)

I suggest that the figure of the animal is important in the Vedic texts for understanding the violence that joins life and death, precisely because in the contemplation on the killing of animals in sacrifice, it brings to the fore that accepted background of life that Diamond finds to be so wounding. If there is a glimmer of hope here, it is that we learn to live with the awareness of the way our lives are entangled with other lives and forms of suffering entailed in our living, to which we might not normally give another thought. I am not suggesting that the texts resolve these issues—just that they make us think of our forms of life as entailing the inevitability of death and the inevitable contamination of our everyday life by the violence we commit. The texts offer a mythic imagination centred on animals to give expression to this melancholy sense of how life is conjoined to death. But precisely because we are in the realm of possibilities that can only figure in very shadowy forms in our inhabitation of life with others, there are stories told with other figures that could be articulated in which life and death are conjoined through stories of ghosts and ancestors, of karma and fate or of accident and responsibility. One such path is that of learning what the texts call 'noncruelty' in inhabiting the world with animals.

Noncruelty

Despite the melancholic sense that pervades these texts, some respite is offered in adjoining texts through the notion of 'noncruelty' (*anrhamsya*). The concept of noncruelty appears in the great epic Mahabharata and according to Mukund Lath (2009: 84):

> Literally the word anrhamsya means the state, the attitude, of not being nrhamsa. The word nrhamsa is common enough in Sanskrit literature; it literally means one who injures man, from which other meanings follow such as mischievous, noxious, cruel, base,

vile, malicious. Anrshmsya would then mean an attitude where such qualities are absent. But the word has more than a negative connotation; it signifies good-will, a fellow feeling, a deep sense of the other. A word that occurs often with anrhsamsya, therefore, is anukrosha, to cry with another, to feel another's pain.

As Lath observes, the meaning of the term 'noncruelty' is not spelled out in long expositions—instead, it emerges through the stories in the text, many of which involve animals. I do not have the space to visit all the stories that would be relevant here, but let us place ourselves in the scene when Yaksha poses the questions to Yudhishthira, which I described earlier. When asked what is the highest dharma (in this context, one could translate *dharma* as 'virtue'), Yudhishthira answers that noncruelty is the highest dharma. Why noncruelty rather than, say, nonviolence? Is Yudhishthira so wounded by the wrongs that his own actions (i.e. his inability to extract himself from a game of dice in which he ends up staking his kingdom and his wife) have let loose that he cannot aspire to higher virtues? I suggest that the text is suggesting that a single-minded pursuit of dharma can itself be the cause of violence, and hence, we must look at a scale lower than that of the human.

The different stories through which a human scale or at any rate a scale lower than that of the gods might be found to speak about noncruelty do not parse out the concept into different parts—rather they allow us to circle the concept so that a swarm of ideas are generated around it. The first such idea is that of breaking the rigid law-like regularity of the relation between karma or action and its fruits, thus humanizing the force of dharma by breaking a mechanical and relentless connection between an action and its consequences. The second notion is the meaning of togetherness—thus not simply how *you* are in the world but also how you imagine *others* might live in the world. A common thread uniting these ideas is that noncruelty is generated from within the scene of intimacy and is hence perhaps to be distinguished from compassion as an impersonal virtue that is to be extended to all beings.

The story about the humanization of the relentless force of karma goes as follows. A great Brahmin ascetic, Mandavya, was performing strict austerities in his hermitage when a bunch of thieves hid their loot there. Pursued by the royal guards, they were caught, and the loot was found in the hermitage. Mandavya could not answer any questions since he was bound by a vow of silence during his austerities and was then mistakenly punished by the king to be strung on a stake. Mandavya was released when the king overheard two birds discussing what bad karmas the innocent Mandavya might have committed in his past life for which he was being punished. After his death, Mandavya questioned the god Dharma as to why he was punished. He learnt about a childhood prank he had played on some flying insects in his last life, sticking a stake into them. This led to the punishment he received. Enraged that he was punished for a childhood prank, the ascetic cursed Dharma to be born of a Shudra woman (the lowest rank in the caste hierarchy).[7] He also established that henceforth the laws of karma will not apply to childhood deeds. Alf Hiltebeitel

(2001) summarizes the import of this story, saying that the impersonal Dharma, the god of righteousness and of death, is 'humanized' here by having to take birth in human form. More importantly, the frailties of humans are acknowledged so that we are not held responsible for actions we might have committed as children. For Hiltebeitel, Dharma learns compassion. I agree that the relentless force of an impersonal logic of action and its consequences is loosened by the modality of noncruelty. We are asked to accept the power of intimacy through which we are called to inhabit the world with the animal other, even if the being of this other is not transparent within our form of life. This is what emerges in the animal stories that follow.

The scene of the first story is the evening when Bhishma, the eldest of the lineage, is lying in the battlefield, mortally wounded, and the two warring sides have come there to listen to his parting words. Yudhishthira asks Bhishma to explain the meaning of noncruelty. Bhishma explains this concept through the story of the parrot and the tree. A fowler from the famed city of Kashi went hunting antelopes but mistakenly lodged a poisonous arrow in a tree. The tree withered and died, and all the birds left it to find nests in other trees, but one parrot remained. It too began to wither with the tree. Indra, the lord of heaven, was amazed at the capacity of the parrot to take both happiness and suffering with such equanimity. He asked, how can a bird experience *anrhamsya* (noncruelty)—is that not impossible for animals? He goes disguised as a Brahmin and tries to persuade the parrot to leave for a tree with leafy foliage and fruits. The parrot says that he was born there and grew up and received protection from the tree, and so out of noncruelty and sympathy, he will not leave the tree. Indra then restores the tree and the parrot back to health.

Contrasting the qualities of nonviolence and noncruelty, Hiltebeitel (2001: 213) interprets this story to say 'While ahimsa tightens the great chain of beings, anrhamsya softens it with a cry for a *human* creature-feeling across the great divides.' Dalmiya, interpreting the same story, sees it as parable of the relational. 'Just as experience of relationality is not rule bound, the relationality itself is also not contractual. The parrot was *born* in that particular tree and *found* itself in a context that it did not actively choose' (Dalmiya 2001: 297). In both Hiltebeitel and Dalmiya, the force of a concept such as noncruelty comes from the fact that a disposition is generated through the experience of togetherness—if the parrot had gone to a different tree, no one would have termed it as 'betrayal'.

The second scene, regarded as the iconic moment for illustrating the virtue of noncruelty, is that of the final journey of Pandavas (the five brothers) with their wife, Draupadi. Since only those who are free of any sin can ascend to heaven in bodily form, everyone except Yudhishthira gets eliminated on the way. Yudhishthira continues along the path with a stray dog who had attached himself to the group. Indra, the lord of heaven, comes in his celestial chariot to take Yudhishthira to heaven, but on condition that he abandons the dog. Yudhishthira is not swayed by any argument in favour of abandoning the dog and is accused of becoming snared by the *moha* (attachment) to a dog when he was able to renounce everything else—love of kingdom, love of wife and love of brothers. In the end, the dog is revealed to be none other than Dharma, his father, who is submitting him to a final test. Yudhishthira passes this test since he has developed the qualities of noncruelty and sympathy.

How is one to understand the two features of these animal stories? First, the quality of noncruelty is demonstrated across species and at precisely those moments in which it is not through appeals to distant moral concepts such as 'obligation' or 'rule-following', but through a sense of togetherness developed by the sheer contingency of having been brought together—the fated circumstances of togetherness—that beings develop this feeling of noncruelty towards each other. Second, that it is from within a scene of intimacy that dispositions towards noncruelty develop, but in no case can either men or gods come up with reasons for the actions of the animals. The parrot simply displays the force of intimacy—Yudhishthira simply accepts the dog's attachment and the claim it lays on him. Is this a satisfactory resolution to the kinds of problems with regard to killing and eating that we encountered earlier? The answer would have to be a resounding 'no', but then that is precisely the point of the stories.

Concluding Thoughts

The recent moves in anthropology that claim that there is no single undivided world of 'nature' that all human societies simply represent in different ways has opened exciting possibilities for an expansion of thought on the being of animals. More particularly, the idea that the way of thinking about nature in the Western (Christian?) cosmologies offers just one possibility is a salutary reminder that different cosmologies pertain not only to issues of differences in cultural representations but also to the fact that different ontologies might be at stake. In many societies (such as those in Amazonia), the being of humans and animals is not seen as distinct but rather as realization of different possibilities of having both bodies and interiorities. Viveiros de Castro refers to the positional quality of some Amerindian cosmologies; in such cosmologies

> humans, in normal conditions, see humans as humans, the animals as animals and the spirits (when they see them) as spirits; the (predatory) animals and the spirits see humans as animals (preys), while the (game) animals see humans as spirits or as (predatory) animals. By contrast, animals and spirits see themselves as humans. (As cited in Descola 2006: 5)

Philippe Descola calls this positional perspectivism, a particular instance of animism. In his words:

> It boils down to a simple matter of logical possibility: if humans see themselves with a human form and see non-humans with a non human form, then non-humans who see themselves with a human form should see humans with a non human form. However this inversion of the points of view which properly characterizes perspectivism is far from

being a general feature of all animic systems (it is, for example, conspicuously absent among the Jivaroan Achuar who triggered my initial interest for animism). The most common situation in standard animic regime is one in which humans just say that non-humans see themselves as humans. But how do non-humans see humans if perspectivism is not operative? The answer that can be inferred from ethnographic accounts is that they see them as humans. This stems from the fact that animals (and the spirits who act as their representatives) generally adopt a human appearance when they want to establish a relationship with humans, an attitude that they certainly would not adopt if they thought that humans were predatory animals. (Descola 2006: 5)

In contrast to the idea that 'It boils down to a simple matter of logical possibility,' the texts I have been examining constantly run up against the fact that in the end they are fenced out from a genuinely embodied sense of what it is to be animal—and take that experience itself as a fact of human life—namely, that humans live on the generosity of animals and plants and that they do not have any route to understand from where this generosity stems. What worries me in the accounts given by Viveiros de Castro and Descola is the assumption that if humans can imagine that animals have *this* kind of being, then they are entitled to take the 'logical possibilities' of inversion or positionality as an insight into the *being* of animals. Others, such as Penelope Dransart (2002), have argued that some communities, such as Isluga, attach separate values to men and women and also to human beings and their herd animals. In the case of Isluga people, Dransart argues, human beings and their herd animals are both seen to be in need of spiritual nourishment so that the killing of a herd animal selected from the ritual merging of human and animals cannot be regarded as substituting an animal for a human but rather as sustaining both animal and human life by providing spiritual nourishment. In fact, Dransart seems to be suggesting that the context of Isluga people is a cross-cultural context in which different ontologies are simultaneously present, raising the interesting issue as to which ontologies for the Isluga would be seen as well made and which badly made in providing the spiritual nourishment that both humans and animals need?

I take Heidegger to be saying that even in the case of animals that seem closest to us we can only say that though we live with them, this 'living' might entail very different things for humans and animals. Humans are capable of internalizing animal modes of being within their own worlds, yet they cannot assimilate these forms completely. In contrast, it is the absence of any scepticism and doubt regarding the mode of being of an animal inferred purely from logical possibilities or from mythic and ritual practices that seems to me to reinstate a completely human-centric understanding of the world in the so-called ontological turn in anthropology. As Heidegger says:

We keep domestic pets in the house, they *'live' with us.* But we do not live with them if living means: being in an animal kind of way ... Through this being with animals we enable them to move within our world ... [The dog] eats with us—and yet it does not 'eat.' Nevertheless it is with us. (As cited in Mulhall 2007: 27)

The texts I analysed seem to say that if this kind of being with is all that is granted to the human, then we can still express our gratitude to animals (and to death) for enabling some kind of life for us, humans.

Notes

1. I am very grateful to Penelope Dransart for her brief but astute comments that proved to be incredibly important for fine-tuning the paper. I also want to thank the organizing committee of the Association of Social Anthropologists of the UK and Commonwealth for their generous hospitality during the conference on 'Vital Powers and Politics' in September 2011 and to the participants for the opportunity to listen to so many stimulating papers. I thank the anonymous reviewer for the comments that helped clarify some of the more obscure Vedic terms.
2. Dasein is 'human mode of being' (Mulhall 2007: 46).
3. This is not to say that the experience of being fenced out of that which seems close and even intimate is the same for the case of death and for animality, respectively, but rather that both constitute a limit to our understanding of the other within a human form of life.
4. Known as 'Yaksha Prashna' (The Questions of Yaksha), this episode occurs in the Aranya Parva (Chapter 296) of the Mahabharata. The Mahabharata consists of 75,000 stanzas and is divided into eighteen books. The English translation of the epic is in progress under the superb editorial stewardship of James Fitzgerald.
5. In some verses, the fifth animal is the donkey.
6. The *soma* plant used in Vedic sacrifice was supposed to grant immortality. Coomaraswamy interprets this as the redeeming of man from his debt to death.
7. Thus the famous character Vidura, in the Mahabharata, is known for his wisdom but is often constrained by the fact that he was born of a low-caste woman in service of the princesses. It may be useful to clarify that gods might take birth on Earth to redeem mankind, but they might also be cursed to do so since both gods and humans strive to be freed from the cycles of birth, death and rebirth.

References

Benveniste, É. 1971. 'Euphemisms, Ancient and Modern'. In M. E. Meek, trans., *Problems in General Linguistics*. Coral Gables, FL: University of Miami Press, 265–71.

Coetzee, J. M. 1999. *The Lives of Animals,* ed. A. Gutmann. Princeton, NJ: Princeton University Press.

Coomaraswamy, A. 2000. *Perceptions of the Vedas,* ed. V. Misra. New Delhi: Indira Gandhi National Center for the Arts.

Dalmiya, V. 2001. 'Dogged Loyalties: A Classic Indian Intervention in Care Ethics'. In J. Runzo and N. M. Martin, eds, *Ethics in the World Religions.* Oxford: One World, 293–306.

Das, V. 1983. 'The Language of Sacrifice'. *Man, New Series* 18(3): 445–62.

Das, V. 2012 [1977]. *Structure and Cognition: Aspects of Hindu Caste and Ritual.* Delhi: Oxford University Press, Perennial Books.

Davis, D. R. 2010. *The Spirit of Hindu Law.* Cambridge: Cambridge University Press.

Descola, P. 2006. 'Beyond Nature and Culture'. *Proceedings of the British Academy* 139: 137–55. Available at: http://old.eu.spb.ru/news/files2007/descola.pdf.

Dhavamony, M. 1973. *Phenomenology of Religion.* Rome: Universita Geregoriana Editrice.

Diamond, C. 2008. 'The Difficulty of Reality and the Difficulty of Philosophy'. In S. Cavell, C. Diamond, J. McDowell, I. Hacking, and C. Wolfe, *Philosophy and Animal Life.* New York: Columbia University Press, 43–91.

Doniger, W. 2009. *The Hindus: An Alternative History.* New York: Penguin Press.

Dransart, P. 2002. 'Concepts of Spiritual Nourishment in the Andes and Europe: Rosaries in Cross-cultural Contexts'. *Journal of the Royal Anthropological Institute* 8(1): 1–21.

Heidegger, M. 1995. *The Fundamental Concepts of Metaphysics: World, Finitude, Solitude,* trans. W. McNeill and N. Walker. Bloomington: Indiana University Press.

Hiltebeitel, A. 2001. *Rethinking the Mahabharata: A Reader's Guide to the Education of the Dharma King.* Chicago: University of Chicago Press.

Hubert, H., and M. Mauss. 1964. *Sacrifice: Its Nature and Functions,* trans. W. D. Halls. Chicago: University of Chicago Press.

Jha, G. 1999. *Manusmrti: With Manubhashya of Medhatithi.* 2nd ed. Vol. 10. Delhi: Motilal Banarisidas.

Lath, M. 2009. 'The Concept of Anrshamsya in the Mahabharata'. In T.R.S. Sharma, ed., *Reflections and Variations on the Mahabharata.* Delhi: Sahitya Academy, 82–9.

Lévi-Strauss, C. 1963. *Totemism.* New York: Beacon Press.

Lévi-Strauss, C. 1969. *The Savage Mind.* Chicago: University of Chicago Press.

MacIntyre, A. 1999. *Dependent Rational Animal: Why Human Beings Need the Virtues.* Chicago: Carus.

Malamoud, C. 1996. *Cooking the World: Ritual and Thought in Ancient India.* New York: Oxford University Press.

Mulhall, S. 2007. *Philosophical Myths of the Fall.* Princeton, NJ: Princeton University Press.

Oldenburg, H. 1988. *Religion of the Vedas.* Delhi: Motilal Banarisidas.

Parry, J. 1994. *Death in Banaras.* Chicago: University of Chicago Press.

Sen, C. 1978. *A Dictionary of the Vedic Rituals: Based on the Srauta and the Grihya.* Delhi: Concept.

Wittgenstein, L. 1953. *Philosophical Investigations,* trans. G.E.M. Anscombe. Oxford: Blackwell.

–3–

The Nature of Nature in Ramon Llull

Sarah Jane Boss

Introduction

In 1288 or 1289, during a visit to Paris, the Mallorcan philosopher Ramon Llull (1232–1316) wrote *The Book of Wonders,* which narrates the adventures of a man named Felix, who travelled the world in search of an answer to the question of why people 'no longer love and know God' (Llull 1931–4).[1] This book summarizes Llull's understanding of the whole world, including plants, animals, humans and the relationships among them. Felix's travels lead him to discover the mystery of God and creation, and *The Book of Wonders* is constructed, in ten short books, according to the pattern of the order of being. Thus, Book 1 concerns God, who created all things; Book 2 concerns angels, who are the noblest of God's creatures; Book 3 concerns the heavenly bodies, which are next in perfection to the angels. Book 4 then breaks with this pattern of hierarchical descent and treats the subject of the elements. This is because, after the creation of the angels and Heaven, God's next creation was the chaotic and elemental material out of which the bodily world (which is most of what we call the 'natural', or 'physical', world) is formed. The subsequent books then follow an ascending order of creation, with Book 5 being concerned with plants, Book 6 with 'metals', or minerals, Book 7 with animals and Book 8 with humanity. After this, there are two more books—Book 9 on the subject of Paradise and Book 10 on the subject of Hell—which explain the final destiny of the human person. The subject of humanity occupies by far the largest section of the work, but the ten books together describe the interconnections and integrity of all being. Indeed, a conviction that God's presence can be found in every aspect of creation was stated in one of Llull's earliest works, the *Book of Contemplation in God* (1274), and remained a governing assumption of his work until his death in 1316:

> God our Father, lord of all that is! If the man who finds a precious stone rejoices greatly at his discovery, since he sees that it is beautiful and knows that it is very good, then there is good reason for us, who know that you are in being itself, to rejoice in your being, because it is in being and it is not in privation. Since someone may rejoice at finding

things that are finite, it would be really amazing if they did not rejoice at finding that which is infinite. (Llull 1906: 7; see also Vega 2003: 139)

Lord, even though your creatures manifest your goodness and nobility so well, yet we do not know how to rejoice in it; and this is because of our frivolity and meanness, for we do not want to become acquainted with that which we might. (Llull 1906: 9; see also Vega 2003: 140)

In another fictional narrative, *The Romance of Evast and Blanquerna* (1283), a wealthy married couple, Evast and Aloma, decide to take up the monastic life, leaving their worldly goods to their son Blanquerna. Blanquerna, however, also wishes to leave the world in order to become a hermit in the wild. His parents, intending that he should take over his father's estate, make various protestations in their attempt to dissuade him from his desired course of action. Amongst these, Blanquerna's mother objects that he will have no proper comforts, such as clothing and shelter (Llull 2009: 109; Llull n.d.: 57). Eventually, Blanquerna's sweetheart says that if he is going to live as a hermit in the wild, then she will join him there, to which he replies:

No company will I have save that of God, and of trees, grass, birds, wild beasts, fountains and streams, banks and meadows, sun, moon and stars; for none of these things may hinder the soul from contemplating God. (Llull 2009: 114; Llull n.d.: 66)

The notion that wild places are not suitable for human habitation, and are even to be feared, has been a common one in the history of Western civilization. But, by that very token, it has often been seen as the ideal retreat for the man or woman who wishes to renounce 'the world' and to live a life of holiness. Robert Pogue Harrison, in his study of the place of forests in the Western literary imagination, writes of the Middle Ages:

While the Christian attitude toward forests was generally hostile, hagiography tells of many devout souls who took to the wilderness and lived as hermits far from the corruption of human society. There in the forests' asylum, they lived in the intimate presence of their God. Their holy bewilderment helped them purge the soul of sin and make it saintly. (Harrison 1992: 62)[2]

In a world that values the 'cooked' over the 'raw', the ascetic who renounces the world must choose the raw over the cooked. Blanquerna's desire for the wilderness may thus be taken as a sincere token of the desire to lead a holy life; however, Llull's delight in plants, animals, water and the heavens—both here and elsewhere—suggests that Blanquerna's desire to be in a wilderness expresses a genuine pleasure in the nonhuman creation.

Llull led an eventful life, but he is at least as well known in legend as in history. From the fourteenth century onwards, it was widely believed that he was an alchemist, and one tradition maintains that he made gold for the king of England

(Pereira 1989: 38–49). John Masefield's story, *The Box of Delights,* presents Llull as a magician who has discovered the elixir of life and, thus, the secret of immortality (Masefield 2012 [1935]). Llull did indeed write about medicine (Llull 1969), and it is not beyond the bounds of plausibility that he should be associated with medical alchemy. But, unless we read these tales in a purely allegorical manner, the lie is given to them in the quotations cited previously, for Llull tells us that the treasure of the natural world lies not specifically in its rare minerals, but in every part of it and in its very existence, which reveals the goodness of the infinite God. Yet Llull taught clearly that it was only in God—and not by purely earthly means—that one could find the key to eternal life.[3] Later authors may have believed that Llull's work might help them to gain power over nature, but Llull himself taught the opposite—that to know nature properly was to know and love God, and so to put all worldly ambition aside.

Furthermore, as we have already seen, it is in the very nature of God's creation that it will assist the human mind in contemplating the creator. In his *Book of St. Mary* (1290), when the allegorical figures of Praise, Prayer and Intention meet a holy hermit in the woods, they too favour a remote setting for their conversation on sacred matters:

So on these words all four were unanimously agreed: that in that place, in the shade of a lovely tree, near a clear fountain, they would talk of Our Lady. (Llull 1915: 27 [my own translation])

But the aspect of the natural world that seems to inspire the greatest devotion among Llull's fictional characters is the heavens, as is exemplified again by Blanquerna:

Blanquerna rose daily at midnight, and opened the windows of his cell, that he might behold the heavens and the stars, and began his prayer as devoutly as he might, to the end that his whole soul should be with God, and his eyes in weeping and tears. (Llull 2009: 424; Llull n.d.: 407)

Llull's understanding is that the being of God and the being of all creation are fundamentally one and, in this respect, his thought stands in contrast to a particular characterization of Western intellectual culture, a characterization that was prominent in the 1970s and 1980s and continues to deserve careful consideration today. This characterization is that of those critics, especially feminists, who have charged Western civilization with dualism. This means that

[the various social] relationships of domination share a common, dyadic structure, in which the superior party, or 'master,' in the relationship perceives himself [*sic*] to be 'other' than, and in opposition to, the subordinate. At the same time, he treats all members of the subordinate group as though they were, in all significant respects, the same as one another, and thus fails to recognize their individual differences. (Boss 2000: 16–17)

In the case of Christian philosophy and theology, critics charge that it is the whole order of being—both God and all creation—that scholars have divided up into two contrasting groups of phenomena, of which one must gain mastery over the other. It is as though the drama of the *Babylonian Epic of Creation* provides the archetype for Western learned culture: before the foundation of the cosmos, the male god Marduk confronts his ancestress, Tiamat, in battle. Tiamat seems to be a chaos monster, identified with a primal abyss of ocean. But Marduk slays Tiamat and carves up her body, distributing its various parts to form the heavens and the earth (Dalley 2000: 252–74). Thus, the male destroys the female and brings order out of turbulence. According to some historians, a similar dynamic has been at work in the learned culture of Europe—in philosophy, religion and science, for example—which, over a period of at least 700 years,[4] formed an association of ideas between goodness, light, spirit, intellect, rationality, order, masculinity and activity; at the same time, it formed an opposite and corresponding association between evil, darkness, materiality (or bodiliness), feeling, emotion, chaos, femininity and passivity. The elements of the former group have all been considered to be superior to, and even to have a duty to conquer, the elements of the latter.[5] It should be noted, however, that much of the work that examines the European cultural tendency towards dualism argues that this tendency has become much more marked in the modern period than it was in the Middle Ages.

During the 1970s–1990s, when this type of analysis was common among cultural historians, anthropologists were correspondingly concerned with whether or not there was some universal tendency for human societies to associate 'nature' with women and 'culture' with men. Notably, Michelle Rosaldo and Louise Lamphere's collection of essays, *Woman, Culture and Society* (1974), and Carol MacCormack and Marilyn Strathern's *Nature, Culture and Gender* (1980) presented critical appraisals of the notion that such dualism was ubiquitous. Regardless of the extent to which dualism of this kind can reliably be attributed to non-European societies, it has often been identified as a major defect of mainstream, or learned, Western culture, and is said to have been tied, among other things, to the culture's destructive attitude towards the natural world. It is argued that human beings identify themselves with the 'good', cultural half of the duality—which is rational and spiritual, rather than bodily—and identify physical nature with the 'inferior', natural half. In this frame of mind, men and women (but especially men) seek to subdue and dominate a world that seems alien and uncontrolled and fail to recognize their own dependence upon that world and the fact that they are themselves a part of it. One aspect of this frame of mind is a fear of chaos, since chaos, being irrational, is associated with bodiliness and gross matter.

Typically, the characteristics associated with the group that is deemed superior (spirit, rationality, activity, masculinity, etc.) are attributed to God, who is the creator, whilst those of the supposedly inferior group (physicality, emotion, passivity, femininity, etc.) are exclusively properties of the creation. However, we shall see below that Llull's sense of God's presence in all things is worked out in radically unitary, and therefore nondualist, metaphysics, with a correspondingly unitary epistemology.

Life and Calling

Llull was born in 1232, of patrician Catalan parents, and grew up at the royal court of Mallorca. His father was one of the army of Catalan Christian invaders who conquered Mallorca in 1229 and drove out the island's Moorish rulers. During Llull's lifetime, about a third of the population of the island remained Muslim, and there was also a substantial Jewish community. Llull dwelt in an environment of comfort and plenty, relative to the period in which he lived, and did not have to view the countryside of his native land from the standpoint of, say, the Muslim peasants whose property had been seized by their Catholic conquerors. At various times in his life, however, he did freely choose to make retreats in places where he lived in more austere conditions.[6]

As a young man, Llull was tutor to the crown prince, and when the boy acceded to the throne of Mallorca as James II, Llull became seneschal at the royal court. He married Blanca Picany, and they had two children, a son and a daughter. According to his own account, he lived the typical life of a courtier until he was about thirty years old, when everything changed for him. He was in his chamber one evening, writing a poem for a lady with whom he was passionately in love, when, out of the corner of his eye, he saw Christ hanging on the cross. Being alarmed by this vision, he put away his pen and went to bed. The next night, however, the vision occurred again, and again, he preferred to ignore it. This vision returned on three further nights, and finally, Llull realized that he could ignore it no longer and must attend to the vision's meaning. He understood that he was being called to dedicate his life to God and in particular to convert 'unbelievers'—that is, Muslims and Jews—to Christianity. He was to do this by two principal means: one was to write a book, 'the best in the world', to bring about the work of conversion; the other was to persuade princes and bishops to establish religious houses for the teaching of 'the languages of unbelievers', with a view to improving the communication of the Christian faith to non-Christians. In practice, this meant principally the teaching of Arabic, but also of Hebrew. Llull's own conversion was reinforced some time afterwards by a sermon that he heard preached in the Franciscan church of the City of Mallorca (now Palma). Llull then gave up his life as a courtier and husband in order to live a spiritual life and made pilgrimages to the shrines of Our Lady of Rocamadour and Santiago de Compostella (Llull 2010: 30–7).

On his return, he learnt Latin and Arabic (Llull 2010: 38–9) and, at some time, must also have studied some philosophy and theology. After about ten years of study and writing, in which he produced his first major work, the *Book of Contemplation in God,* Llull made a retreat in a cave on Mount Randa, on the south side of Mallorca. While he was staying there, he received what he believed to be a divine illumination in which he was shown the method that he should use for explaining the Christian faith to unbelievers and for explaining many more things besides to Christians as well as Muslims. Llull transcribed this vision as the first version of his Art (Llull 2010: 40–3), and he spent the remainder of his life in amending and promoting it.

He also wrote religious poetry and spiritual narratives and is often referred to as the 'father' of Catalan literature and as the first European Christian author to have written philosophy in a vernacular language. Llull travelled widely around the Mediterranean, also visited Paris, and died in 1316 on his return from a voyage to Tunis. After his death, there were scholars who continued to make use of his Art until the eighteenth century.[7]

Llull's Art and Approach to His Work

Llull's Art went through many recensions and changes over the decades. We cannot even begin to consider these here and will have to treat Art very briefly according to the principles that govern it throughout its development.

As we have seen, the principal motive for the writing of Art was the conversion of unbelievers to Christianity. Llull belonged to a society in which Christians, Muslims and Jews lived side by side, and it was common for Christian authorities to force Muslims and Jews to listen to Christian sermons and to expound Christian doctrine to them. Christian expositions would often be carried out in Catalan, the language used by Christians, rather than in Arabic, the language used by Muslims. At the same time, Christian apologists who wanted to show the errors of Judaism or Islam would rely on written sources but would not be aware of the ways in which living Jews and Muslims interpreted their own traditions (Hames 2000: 9; for the broader background, see the Introduction, 1–29 *passim*). Llull, by contrast, wanted Christians to engage Muslims and Jews in arguments that would convince them of the truth of the Christian faith. He considered that, if Muslims were to be converted to Christianity, then Christianity had to be explained to them in a way that they would understand; thus, it was necessary for the missionary to speak Arabic (hence Llull's campaign to establish centres for teaching 'the languages of unbelievers') and to use concepts and images that would already be familiar to his listeners. Furthermore, the non-Christian audience should be allowed to question the Christian missionary, and the missionary should be able to explain and defend the Christian faith on rational grounds. It is not surprising, then, that the Art assumes that there is a universal rationality shared by all peoples. In practice, the modes of reasoning that it uses draw heavily upon the Neoplatonic philosophy that was the common currency of Christian, Muslim and Jewish philosophers of the thirteenth century.

Llull's approach has great consequences for his understanding of the relationship between God, humanity and the rest of the natural world. He realized that an attempt to persuade Muslims and Jews of the truth of Christianity could not depend upon an appeal to the Scriptures, because the intended audience would not necessarily accept the authority of the Christian Bible, or, if they did, they would have different traditions of interpretation. Jews, for example, would not accept the authority of the New Testament, whilst the Old Testament was interpreted differently by Christians, Muslims and Jews. Similarly, the Christian missionary could not appeal to Christian authorities, such as Church fathers, in his attempt to convert the unbeliever, because the Muslim or Jew would have no reason to accept such a figure as authoritative. Nevertheless, Christians, Muslims and Jews all believed in one God, the creator of all things, and they all inhabited the cosmos that the one God created. Llull reasoned that God's creation revealed enough of its creator that, if we only understood the natural world correctly, we would see the truth about God—and that this truth would support Christian doctrine. Llull's Art accordingly presents the reader with the most intimate connections between God and nature.

We have already seen that Llull favours wild places as those which are most suited to the contemplation of, and conversation about, God. This fits well with Llull's intention to use God's creation to demonstrate truths of theology. However, Llull's desire to engage unbelievers in open discussion might make us wonder whether these wild places do not perform another, more political, function. Human geographers have used the term 'landscape of power' to designate 'a place that shows how the reconfiguration and appropriation of nature as property can be interlinked with human dispossession' (Coates 1998: 46). Thus, John Rennie Short gives an account of the English countryside as a landscape of power since its enclosed fields, with parkland surrounding great houses, embody the power of eighteenth-century landowners, who enclosed the fields and built and planted Arcadian landscapes but dispossessed the poor in the process (Short 1991: 66–74).[8] Taking account of the way in which landscapes can both express and impose economic and political power, we might wonder whether Llull's preference for the wild as a location for conversations about God is not partly governed by an awareness that this is a landscape not of power, but of powerlessness. During the thirteenth century, the Catalan rulers of Mallorca transferred the ownership of land from Muslims to Christians and forced a movement of the Muslim population, both within the island itself and from Mallorca to Muslim territories across the Mediterranean (Abulafia 1994: 8, 56–64). At the same time, there was 'a steady process of the dissociation of the Jews from the Christian community in Mallorca city' (Abulafia 1994: 83, 79–88). Against this background, any space in urban or cultivated areas would be associated with the Christian domination of Muslims and Jews, whilst a wilderness setting would provide a space of equality for Christians, Muslims and Jews within God's creation.

Now, the Art is supposed to give the answers to 'all questions'. This does not mean questions of a divinatory or historical type—not questions concerning particular times and places—but questions about the nature of God and creation. It consists of a number of basic tables whose elements can be combined to provide solutions to questions of a theological, moral or ontological kind, and that can thus be applied to every part of the created world, from the base elements to the heavens, and also to questions about God. The Art is based on the understanding that there are underlying principles that permeate all being, and that these principles can be understood by the human intellect.

Over the decades, Llull amended the Art, producing a number of different versions of it, but all of them begin with a Figure A, which remains essentially unchanged.

It consists of a circle with the letter 'A' at its centre. Around the circumference are the names of what Llull calls the Divine Dignities. These include, for example, Goodness, Greatness, Power and Wisdom and may be compared in certain respects to Pseudo-Dionysius's Divine Names (from which they may well be derived) ([Pseudo-] Dionysius 1987), John Scotus Eriugena's Primordial Causes (Carabine 2000: 53–8) or, ultimately, Plato's Forms (Plato 1997). In God the creator, the Dignities are infinite, and each is interchangeable with all the others. This is signified by straight lines across the circle; these lines join each Dignity to every other.

The Dignities, however, also constitute the created world, but with important qualifications. In creation, they are called Principles and exist in time and space.[9] The created Principles are not interchangeable but are differently distributed according to the creature in which they exist. There is thus a real continuity between God and creation, whilst the difference between the infinite and the finite maintains a concrete distinction between the Dignities in God and the Principles in creation (Pring-Mill 2008: 52–64).

This continuity is depicted in medieval manuscripts, which show Llull with a *scala naturae,* which is usually translated as the 'ladder of being', but which is more literally the 'ladder of nature'. It depicts the hierarchical order of being, with the lowliest represented on the bottom rung, and God at the top.[10] The lowest rung, for example, may be the level of the four elements. Above this, there may be the vegetative faculty, then the faculty of the senses, with the imaginative faculty above that, the rational above the imaginative, the moral on the rung above the rational and the heavenly above that. Above the heavenly comes the angelic, and finally, the divine.[11] Llull does not use the term *scala naturae,* but he frequently describes the order of being in terms of exactly this kind, usually referring not only to the order itself but also to the ability of the human mind to move up and down the graded sequence. In his book, *De Ascensu et Descensu Intellectus* (1304), the human understanding is taught to ascend and descend a scale of being that has fire at the lowest point, and then moves up through rock, plants, animals, humanity, heaven and angels, before finally reaching God at the topmost point (Llull 2002). The human mind can move between these various levels of nature to come to a better understanding of each level and of the whole. The intellectual tools for forming this understanding are given in the Art. By understanding something about rock and fire, we have the basis for understanding something about plants, or about the heavens and angels; and by the rising of the intellect to understand something about the angels, it can learn something more about the lower levels of nature, and also about God. We come to know God in part by knowing the created world, and we only know the created world properly when we know it in relation to God. The Principles, which exist first, infinitely, in God, exist in limited ways at every level of the created order and, indeed, constitute that order and all its levels.

Let us see, then, an example of how the natural world can give knowledge of God. It depends upon the assumption that 'nature' has a likeness to God, and it thus tends to undermine a strongly dualist doctrine of the relationship between Creator and creation.

The Demonstration of the Incarnation

The principal objections that Jews and Muslims raise against Christian teachings concern the doctrines of the Incarnation and the Trinity, and so Llull tried to show the 'necessary reasons' for the truth of these teachings. Let us look at the Incarnation. The Incarnation is the doctrine which states that Jesus Christ was both God and human—that God 'became flesh' in Jesus of Nazareth, being born of the Virgin Mary and dying on the cross. This is offensive to Jews and Muslims because it seems to confuse God and creation; it seems to deny that the one God is before and beyond all things in time and space and asserts that he has a created form. To say that God became human in Jesus seems to attribute the true, unimaginable God with characteristics that are similar to the gods of the pagans, who, like humans, are born, get married and have children. Llull, then, wanted to show positively why the Incarnation was at least more likely to be true than not.

He began by asking, 'What is the purpose for which the world was made?' His answer to this falls into two parts, the first of which we have already seen: the Principles, which as Dignities may perhaps be regarded as attributes of God, also constitute creation, and so they exist here in a limited, finite way. The second part of the argument begins with the assumption that all things tend towards their own perfection, and by asking what that perfection would consist of for the whole creation. Well, the world's likeness to its perfect creator suggests that it is in the nature of the world that it should be conformed ever more closely to that creator, and the greatest possible conformity to God would come about in an act of union with him. This, indeed, is the greatest perfection that creation could attain.[12] This means that the world was made in order to be perfected by union with God. Llull contends that this union between God and creation is realized in the Incarnation. 'That God should be human and that he should thus commune naturally with all creatures is in fact the end that is most eminent' (Llull 1989: 163 [my translation from French]).

The argument for the Incarnation thus depends upon there being a true correspondence between the intrinsic activity of God and God's action in the creation. 'God and creation' may also be termed 'God and nature', but, as we have seen, God and creation may both be regarded as 'nature'.

Llull's Cosmology: A Summary

As well as the many versions of the Art proper, Llull wrote works that express the philosophy of the Art in a less technical manner. *The Book of Wonders* is an example of this, as are *Ascensu et Descensu Intellectus* and *Llibre de Santa Maria,* which were written for lay audiences. The first two of these three make explicit Llull's metaphysics and cosmology and reveal them to be rather different from modern systems of knowledge. It must be understood that Llull is not writing a theory of agency, but an ontology and epistemology. So Llull's system is not a theological version of, say, Actor-Network Theory (Latour 2007; Ingold 2011). Rather, he is writing about the nature and purpose of the world's being, and how men and women can come to know these things.

The whole system is teleological, and not in the limited sense in which a functionalist social theory, which refers only to the order of society, is teleological. Rather, everything has both its origin and its end in God: the cosmos and all its parts are directed to attain their natural end in the God who made them. Moreover, the system is entirely hierarchical. Everything is ordered to that which is above it in the cosmic hierarchy, and it is by serving that which is above it that each element can come to its own fulfilment. Human beings have a key role in this system because God made the world in order that he should be known and loved by humanity (see, for example, 'The Book of the Beasts' [Book 7 of *The Book of Wonders*] in Llull 1993: 239–88, at 248); so those things that are below human beings in the order of creation, such as plants and animals, are meant to serve men and women, but human beings, correspondingly, must lead morally good lives in order to attain their own proper end, which is happiness in God. Creatures that are below humanity in the hierarchy will attain salvation by serving human beings *who themselves act well,* that is, who strive to know and love God. So although Llull, along with most other medieval authors, thinks that all bodily creatures in some way exist for the sake of human beings, he nonetheless complains that 'the Earth suffers the "dishonour" of lodging people who are ignorant of the one who created it' (Vega 2003: 37–8).

To the modern reader, Llull's strongly hierarchical view of the cosmos may appear to undermine a true sense of the sanctity of all things since it accords superiority to certain aspects of the created world over others. But this would be to take too simple a view. The late Robert Pring-Mill pointed out that, in Llull's understanding, hierarchical orders coexist in such a way that a being that is superior to another in one respect may be inferior in some other respect. So, for example, spiritual beings as such are superior to bodily ones; yet the heavenly bodies, which, as we have seen, are made of the elements, are superior to men and women, who are spiritual as well as bodily, in so far as the stars and planets move according to regular patterns (Pring-Mill 2008: 73–7). In fact, this complex understanding of the relationship between different hierarchical orders is common to many philosophers of this period, but Llull's fluid and organic system lends itself particularly well to the subtlety of the relationships at issue.

Not only is the hierarchy itself quite complicated, but Llull shows sympathy for the inferior, nonhuman creation in its trials with the human race. For example, Book 7 of *The Book of Wonders* is concerned with the animal kingdom—which is quite literally a 'kingdom', in this account. The book is a parable in which animals act out a political drama that is intended to serve as instruction for human princes. At one point in the story, the ox and the horse, both of which have been mistreated by their king, the lion, decide to offer themselves into the service of human beings, but this does not work out well for them:

> One day it came to pass that the horse and the ox met, and each asked the other about his situation. The horse said that he was very overworked in the service of his master, for every day he was ridden and made to gallop up hill and down hill, and was in harness day and night. The horse desired greatly to be free of his servitude to his master...
>
> After the horse had told him about his situation, the ox replied that he too was very overworked, every day, from plowing, and that his master would not let him eat the wheat grown on the land he plowed, but instead, when he was finished with his plowing and exhausted from it, he was sent to graze on the grass the sheep and goats had been eating while he was out plowing...
>
> While the ox and the horse were conversing in this way, a butcher came to see if the ox was fat, for the ox's master had offered him up for sale. The ox said to the horse that his master wanted to sell him to be killed and given to man to eat. The horse said this was a poor reward for the service he had rendered. For a long time the horse and the ox wept, and the horse advised the ox to flee and return to his native land. (Llull 1993: 250)

If the presence of God is to be found in all things, then a failure to show proper respect for any aspect of the world must be a failure to recognize the God who made it. The Neoplatonic doctrine of *participation* underlies Llull's thinking in this regard. Everything that exists is participated by the Principles, which coexist infinitely in God as the divine Dignities, and it is by recognizing this that one can recognize the presence of God in the created world. By learning the principles embodied in the Art, a man or woman will learn the proper order of the physical and moral world and will order their lives accordingly. By this means, humanity and all creation will be brought to the final heavenly state that God intends for all beings.

God, Nature and Human Understanding

Not only do we learn about God from examining God's creation, but we understand the creation only by knowing something about God. In a now famous essay, the late Frances Yates showed how, in Llull's *Tractate on Astronomy,* the techniques of the Art are applied to the heavens (Yates 1982). Fundamentally, the argument of the *Tractate* is that the movements of the stars and planets can influence life on Earth because earthly creatures are made up of the four elements—earth, air, fire and water—and the heavenly bodies likewise have distinctive elemental complexions. This means that there is a natural sympathy between the heavens and the Earth, and the heavens, which are superior, exercise an influence on the Earth. However, the heavenly bodies have the power that they do only because they are 'informed' by the Principles, which are the created continuation of the divine Dignities. The Principles govern the elements, and 'it is possible to say that the terrestrial elements have greater concordance with the heaven through their mutual *bonitas* [goodness], *magnitudo* [greatness], etc., than through their elemental affinities' (Yates 1982: 21).

Medieval thinkers in general regarded the heavens as superior to the Earth because the stars and planets move in a manner that is regular and clearly ordered. On Earth, by contrast, and especially in human life, things seem chaotic and unpredictable. On this matter, Llull is typical of his era; however, he emphasizes the physical connection that exists between Earth and the heavens. He also emphasizes the spiritual connection that underlies that physical connection and that ties both Earth and Heaven to God. This sheds light on why it is that gazing at the night sky facilitates Blanquerna in directing 'his whole soul to be with God'.

In fact, one or two claims that Llull makes about the character of created beings are claims that most philosophers held to be true only of God. For example, all philosophers agreed that God could not be defined in terms of anything other than himself. Llull, however, contends that this is true of creatures as well. Contrary to Aristotle's teaching that the definition of a thing cannot be made in terms of the thing itself, but only by reference to other things, Llull thinks it is demonstrable that one can never know what a thing is except precisely by reference to itself. For example, a human being was classically defined as a 'rational animal'; but an angel is a rational being and a lion is an animal, yet a human being is not a hybrid between a lion and an angel. Hence, the only way of properly defining a human being is by reference to humanity. Taking account of the active nature of every being, as explained above, Llull states that a human being is a 'homifying being and the end of all bodily beings' (i.e. the end to which they are directed) (Bonner and Ripoll Perelló 2002: 190).

Similarly, whilst other philosophers taught that it was impossible to know the essence of God, Llull taught that it was impossible to know the essence of anything at all. We can know what a thing does (as with the examples of the star or the human being, given above), but not what it is in itself (Domínguez Reboiras 2001: 286; for precedents, see Bertin's references in Érigène 1995: 198n8).

A governing principle of Llull's Art is that every aspect of the order of being must be understood in relation to every other aspect, and in relation to the whole. One does not come to know the universe by taking the parts and putting them together; one comes to know the universe by grasping it as a whole and then seeing how the parts are connected to that whole and to one another. It is not by chance that the revelation, or illumination, by which Llull received the Art was given in a single vision, for the Art is concerned with an integral understanding of all being. Likewise, when Llull's pupil, Thomas le Myésier, wrote an account of the Art, he began by explaining the underlying principles by which eternal substances are connected to the world of time and space, so that the assumption that all things are interconnected would be understood from the outset (Le Myésier 1990).[13] However, this does not mean that the practitioner of the Art—the 'Artist'—is in any sense outside the universe that he or she is seeking to understand. On the contrary: when Llull received his illumination, it was given finally by an exceptional grace of God, and I shall go on to suggest that Llull assumes that the Artist always requires some measure of divine enlightenment in order to practise the Art fully. Within the Art as it is presented, the human understanding comes to knowledge of the whole system partly by moving around the various levels and modes of being and so comes to know their interconnections and integrity through experience.

Llull often claims that the arguments presented by the Art provide 'necessary reasons' for their conclusions, and it seems that what he means by 'necessary reasons' involves a notion of reason as something that not only draws on logic and inductive argument but also makes use of an awareness of specifically spiritual reality. In an early version of the Art, Llull writes about what he calls 'transcendent points'. As the mind moves upwards within a single level of being, it reaches a point at which the understanding proper to that level is no longer sufficient, and one moves into a higher mode of understanding (Llull 1725: 47–61). For example, the sensory contemplation of an object may have to give way to the imagination, which moves beyond the object that is before the senses and constructs a mental representation of something that is completely dependent upon, but different from, sensory objects. Beyond the imagination lies the intellect, which can understand how the true nature of a phenomenon may differ from that which is presented to the senses. The highest such point is that which the understanding attains when it moves above its normal intellectual activity, to the plane on which matters pertaining specifically to God may be considered. We shall take one of Llull's own examples of such a transcendent point—one which illustrates Llull's radically unitary understanding of the relationship between God and creation.

Llull considers the transcendent point that the intellect attains as it contemplates God's creating the world. He states, in accordance with Christian doctrine, that God created the world 'out of nothing', and he then poses a puzzle. If God is infinite and yet creates something out of nothing, then it seems as if the act of creation must bring about some change, or alteration, in God. Yet God is unchanging, so the intellect has run up against a contradiction. Llull's solution to this—which, he claims, involves the attainment of a transcendent point—is to say that 'in himself, God is unchangeable, but in his effects, he is changeable' (Llull 1725: 61). Thus, the subject of both the unchangeable and the changeable is God, so that the two are fundamentally a unity, whilst the precise distinction between God and creation is maintained. And this is understood by the intellect's grasping of an extraordinary paradox.

Llull's reasoning here seems to be modelled on the traditional Christian understanding of the Incarnation (literally, the 'enfleshing'), whereby the Word of God—who is God—is said to be human in Jesus Christ. In the early Church, there were those who objected to such phrases as 'the Word of God died on the cross' or 'the Word of God was born of Mary' because God has no beginning and no end. However, the Church's eventual ruling was that these expressions were indeed legitimate. This is because, although the Word of God was not born and did not die in his divinity, nevertheless, in his humanity, the Word of God was indeed born and truly died. That is to say, the subject of both Christ's divinity and his humanity is the Word of God, and so it is true to say both that the Word is eternal and that the Word was born and died. Thus, Llull seems to have taken the pattern established in the paradox of the Incarnation and applied it to the work of creation.[14] Now, this way of reasoning is likely to be persuasive only to those who are seeking to understand Christian teaching with what some early Christians called 'the eye of faith'. It requires a movement of the soul that amounts to a kind of initiation, and it will not be convincing to those who consider reason to be an activity that can be conducted without an engagement with God. In practice, the term 'transcendent point' tends to be reserved for this highest level of understanding (Bonner and Ripoll Perelló 2002: 257). For Llull, then, the fullest understanding of the world—and the most compelling of 'necessary reasons' for anything that one can know about it—comes with the attainment of this highest transcendent point. Llull's understanding of the term 'necessary reason' includes a way of reasoning that, in many cases, entails the employment of this faculty of transcendence. So this movement of the understanding between its different levels, taken together with its movement up and down a ladder that includes both the whole created order and its divine Creator, gives a synoptic view of all being.

We might understand this better by contrasting Llull's epistemology with that of his contemporary, Thomas Aquinas. Aquinas allows that each branch of learning has its own subject matter and methods of study and states that natural philosophy considers created things in themselves, whilst theology considers them in their relationship to God the Creator (*Summa contra Gentiles,* Bk. 2, Ch. 4). So, although all things should be understood ultimately in relation to God, Aquinas allows that it is also legitimate for created things to be studied 'in their own right', as it were. He also thinks that the truths of faith cannot be properly demonstrated by human reason—only that they can be shown to be not incompatible with human reason. Llull's Art, on the other hand, is a single system for treating both knowledge of God and knowledge of creation, and for understanding the one by reference to the other. Thus, it is not only his approach to metaphysics that is unitary but also his theory of human understanding, or epistemology.[15] As we have seen, Llull wrote works on medicine, law and astrology in which he employed the principles of the Art to these different areas of human learning. So not only is there a coherent unity between God and creation (as most thirteenth-century scholars would have agreed), but the human mind can gain some understanding of God, as well as of creation, and, although there is a distinction, there is no separation between the proper knowledge of the one and of the other. The tendency of Llull's work is to show how things which are dissimilar are really integrated, and how boundaries can be crossed without rupture.

Nondualism

Let us return, then, to the concern with which this chapter began: dualism. We have already seen that Llull argues strongly for the unity of the whole creation and the unity of that creation with God. Against the background of the feminist criticism that was cited above, Llull evidently does not conform to type, and his short work entitled *Liber Chaos* (Book of Chaos) stands out strikingly in this regard (Llull 1722).[16] *Liber Chaos* is an addition to the *Ars Demonstrativa* (Demonstrative Art) and is intended to explain one of the figures that is given in that version of the Art—namely, the Second Elemental Figure, which is a figure showing relationships between the four elements.[17]

Llull says that Chaos was God's first creation, and that, in it, the form and matter of the four elements are all mixed up together, so that what he calls 'fieryness' coexists with 'wateriness', and both with 'airiness' and 'earthiness'. He says that, in Chaos, 'all is difference'. Now, when we think of 'difference', we think of discrete things that have their own identities and that differ from one another; but Llull says that, in Chaos, there are no discrete identities—only difference. Chaos is a state of being that is not, properly speaking, disordered, but in which even the barest minimum of order has never existed. So the state that Llull describes is literally unimaginable. Gradually, each element is formed by a process of attraction to its proper state, and out of the elements, the first rocks, plants, animals and so on are formed. Their generations then continue, but always with the assistance of Chaos. For Chaos is not something that was once present and has now disappeared, or been overcome; rather, every time a new being comes into existence—for example, a human embryo—it is generated from the 'substance and accidents' of the mother and father. 'Here, whatever was infused by the father and mother into the offspring is restored to the same parents by the prime Chaos as they partake of food' (Llull 1722: 43).[18] Chaos flows continuously into what we would call the physical world, in order to maintain it.

If we allow the correctness of the phrase 'ladder of nature', then Llull's understanding of nature could scarcely be of anything more unified. God, the angels, the heavenly and earthly realms and Chaos itself are all bound together in a single universe of being, and the structure of the world finds a correspondence in the structure of human understanding. And, at the place where a human being stands, God and Chaos are both constantly present. However, it should by now be clear that Llull does not identify God with the creation. He is not a pantheist. We can see this clearly if we return to *The Book of the Gentile and the Three Wise Men*. Here, we are told the story of a pagan (the 'gentile' of the title) who 'had no knowledge of God, nor did he believe in the Resurrection, nor did he think anything existed after death' (*The Book of the Gentile and the Three Wise Men,* in Llull 1993: 73–171 at 86). The thought that, at death, he would be reduced to nothing caused him immense sorrow and distress. The greater part of the book is then taken up with a dialogue in which a Jew, a Christian and a Muslim (the 'three wise men') explain their respective religions to the pagan so that he will learn of God and be put out of his misery. The pagan can then judge between the three religions.

Near the beginning of the narrative, before he meets the wise men, the unhappy pagan finds himself in a wood, and he thinks that perhaps the beauty of the natural world will alleviate his suffering. There are birds, flowers, river banks, meadows, animals and fruit; but whenever the pagan tries to find consolation in the sight, sound, smell and taste of these things, he remembers death, and he is again overcome with pain and sadness (Llull 1993: 86–7). Now, the man's failed attempts to be cheered by even this paradisiacal woodland surely serve to underline the intensity of his despair. So the fact that even the delights of the woodland cannot turn away the man's sorrow surely tells us that Llull considers that these things are usually sources of great joy. Yet it turns out that the beauty of the earth cannot, in and of itself, convey knowledge of the only thing that could console the pagan—that is, knowledge of God. Rather, it is only when one already has some knowledge of the true God that one can find that God's presence in his creation. God is its beginning and its end and, being infinite, is not confined even by the cosmos.

So Llull's vision of the world is a radically unitary one. The unity is founded in the one God, and it is only through knowledge of that God that the complexity and integrity of God's world can be understood. From the point of view of the analysis of Llull's rhetoric, we might say that this vision of unity emerges out of a desire to convert Muslims and Jews to Christianity. We may nevertheless suspect that there are other, and older, forces at work here—but that would be the material for another paper.

Notes

1. The University of Barcelona has a database of manuscripts and editions of Llull's works, some of which are available online. See http://orbita.bib.ub.edu/ramon.
2. For the whole section on forests in medieval Christian narrative, see Harrison (1992: 61–91).
3. See the consideration of *The Book of the Gentile and the Three Wise Men* at the end of this chapter. See also Boss (2011: especially 47–9).
4. Some theorists date the history of this dualism to a much earlier period, often starting with Plato. It seems to me that this attribution can only be defended by making a very selective reading of ancient texts, and that the main culprits do not appear until the early modern period. See the references in note 5.
5. The relevant scholarship includes, in the history of science, Jordanova (1989), Keller (1985, 1992), Moscucci (1990), Schiebinger (1987) and Weinreich-Haste (1986); in the history of philosophy, Lloyd (1984) and MacLean (1983); and in theology, Bynum (1991), Graham (1995), Keller (2002) and Ruether

(1983). Keller's work addresses directly some of the concerns of the present chapter, but from a very different theological tradition.

6. An overview of Llull's life, incorporating portions of the subject's own autobiographical narrative, is given by Anthony Bonner in Llull (1993: 1–44).

7. For example, Nicholas of Cusa (see Lohr 1988: 538–56) and Gottfried Leibniz (see, for example, Maróstica 1992).

8. A corresponding analysis, but of urban landscapes, is given in Zukin (1991).

9. This is a simplification. Llull's use of the term 'principles' was extended during the development of the Art. See Bonner (2007: 125–7).

10. Eriugena, likewise, includes God under the all-embracing heading of nature. For an account of earlier philosophical uses of the term 'nature', see Érigène (1995: 190–5n1).

11. I have taken this ascending list from Llull's *Ars Inveniendi Veritatis*, although it is not shown there in diagrammatic or pictorial form (Llull 1725: 47–61).

12. This summary draws on a variety of sources, but see Domínguez Reboiras (2001). Domínguez draws quite heavily on Lohr (1988).

13. An English translation by Yanis Dambergs is available at http://www.lullianarts. net.

14. That there is an intimate connection between creation and Incarnation is a common theme in medieval writing. In Llull's *Principles and Questions of Theology*, he treats them under the same heading (Llull 1989: 58–67 and 157–74).

15. For a study of Llull's theory of knowledge in relation to the scholasticism of his own day, see Ruiz Simon (1999).

16. An English translation by Yanis Dambergs is available at http://www.lullianarts. net.

17. The *Ars Demonstrativa* was written several years before *The Book of Wonders*, and the latter also includes a section on Chaos. See Llull (1931–4, 4: 8–16). See also Sidera i Casas (2005).

18. Translation taken from Dambergs, http://www.lullianarts.net.

References

Abulafia, D. 1994. *A Mediterranean Emporium: The Catalan Kingdom of Majorca.* Cambridge: Cambridge University Press.

Bonner, A. 2007. *The Art and Logic of Ramon Llull: A User's Guide.* Leiden: Brill.

Bonner, A., and M. I. Ripoll Perelló. 2002. *Diccionari de Definicions Lul·lianes* [Dictionary of Lullian Definitions]. Barcelona: Universitat de Barcelona and Universitat de les Illes Balears.

Boss, S. J. 2000. *Empress and Handmaid: On Nature and Gender in the Cult of the Virgin Mary.* London: Cassell.

Boss, S. J. 2011. 'Ramon Llull's *Llibre de Santa Maria:* Theodicy, Ontology and Initiation'. *Studia Lulliana* 51: 25–51.

Bynum, C. W. 1991. *Fragmentation and Redemption: Essays on Gender and the Human Body in Medieval Religion.* New York: Zone Books.

Carabine, D. 2000. *John Scottus Eriugena.* Oxford: Oxford University Press.

Coates, P. 1998. *Nature: Western Atttitudes since Ancient Times.* Cambridge: Polity Press.

Dalley, S., trans. 2000. *Myths from Mesopotamia: Creation, the Flood, Gilgamesh, and Others.* Oxford: Oxford University Press.

[Pseudo-]Dionysius. 1987. *The Divine Names.* In *Pseudo-Dionysius: The Complete Works,* trans. Colm Luibheid and Paul Rorem. New York: Paulist Press, 47–131.

Domínguez Reboiras, F. 2001. 'El discurso Luliano sobre María'. In C. M. Piastra, ed., *Glie Studi di Mariologia Medievale: Bilancio storiografico.* Tavarnuzze, Firenze: SISMEL—Edizioni del Galluzzo, 277–303.

Érigène, J. S. 1995. *De la Division de la Nature,* Livres I et II, trans. and notes F. Bertin. Paris: PUF.

Graham, E. 1995. *Making the Difference: Gender, Personhood and Theology.* London: Mowbray.

Hames, H. 2000. *The Art of Conversion: Christianity and Kabbalah in the Thirteenth Century.* Leiden: Brill.

Harrison, R. P. 1992. *Forests: The Shadow of Civilization.* Chicago: University of Chicago Press.

Ingold, T. 2011. 'When ANT Meets SPIDER: Social Theory for Arthropods'. In *Being Alive: Essays on Movement, Knowledge and Description.* London: Routledge, 89–94.

Jordanova, L. 1989. *Sexual Visions: Images of Gender in Science and Medicine between the Eighteenth and Twentieth Centuries.* Hemel Hempstead: Harvester Wheatsheaf.

Keller, C. 2002. *The Face of the Deep: A Theology of Becoming.* London: Routledge.

Keller, E. F. 1985. *Reflections on Gender and Science.* New Haven, CT: Yale University Press.

Keller, E. F. 1992. Secrets of Life, Secrets of Death: *Essays on Language, Gender and Science.* London: Routledge.

Latour, B. 2007. *Reassembling the Social: An Introduction to Actor-Network-Theory.* Oxford: Oxford University Press.

Le Myésier, T. 1990. 'Praefatio'. In C. Lohr, T. Pindl-Büchel and W. Büchel, eds, *Breviculum seu Electorium Parvum,* Corpus Christianorum Continuatio Medievalis (CCCM) 77. Turnhout: Brepols, 51–67.

Lloyd, G. L. 1984. *The Man of Reason: 'Male' and 'Female' in Western Philosophy.* London: Methuen.

Llull, R. [Ramon Lull]. n.d. *Blanquerna,* trans. E. A. Peers. London: Dedalus/Hippocrene [facsimile ed.].

Llull, R. 1722. *Liber Chaos.* In I. Salzinger, ed., *Raymundi Lulli Operum.* Vol. 3. Munich: Häffner.

Llull, R. 1725. *Ars Inveniendi Veritatis*. In I. Salzinger, ed., *Raymundi Lulli Operum*. Vol. 5. Munich: Häffner.

Llull, R. 1906. *Llibre de Contemplació en Deu*. In M. Obrador y Bennassar, ed., *Obres de Ramon Lull*. Vol. 2. Palma: Comissió Editora Lulliana.

Llull, R. 1915. *Libre de Sancta Maria*. In M. S. Galmés, ed., *Obres de Ramon Lull*. Vol. 10. Palma: Comissió Editora Lulliana.

Llull, R. 1931–4. *Llibre de Meravelles*, ed. S. Galmés. 4 vols. Barcelona: Barcino.

Llull, R. [Raymundus Lullus]. 1969. *Quattuor Libri Principiorum*, Latin text (ed. 1721), intro. R. Pring-Mill. Wakefield: S. R. Publishers.

Llull, R. [Raymond Lulle]. 1989. *Principes et Question de Théologie*, ed. and trans. R. Prévost and A. Llinarès. Paris: Cerf.

Llull, R. 1993. *Doctor Illuminatus: A Ramon Llull Reader*, trans. A. Bonner and E. Bonner. Princeton, NJ: Princeton University Press.

Llull, R. 2002. *Ascenso y descenso del entendimiento*. Barcelona: Folio.

Llull, R. 2009. *Romanç d'Evast e Blanquerna*, ed. A. Soler and J. Santanach. Barcelona: Abadia de Montserrat.

Llull, R. 2010. *Ramon Llull: A Contemporary Life*, trans. A. Bonner. Barcelona: Barcino; Woodbridge: Tamesis.

Lohr, C. H. 1988. 'Metaphysics'. In C. B. Schmitt, Q. Skinner, E. Kessler and J. Kraye, eds, *The Cambridge History of Renaissance Philosophy*. Cambridge: Cambridge University Press, 537–638.

MacCormack, C., and M. Strathern, eds. 1980. *Nature, Culture and Gender*. Cambridge: Cambridge University Press.

MacLean, I. 1983. *The Renaissance Notion of Woman: A Study in the Fortunes of Scholasticism and Medical Science in European Intellectual Life*. Cambridge: Cambridge University Press.

Maróstica, A. H. 1992. 'Ars Combinatoria and Time: Llull, Leibniz and Peirce'. *Studia Lulliana* 33: 105–34.

Masefield, J. 2012 [1935]. *The Box of Delights*. London: Egmont.

Moscucci, O. 1990. *The Science of Woman: Gynaecology and Gender in England, 1800–1929*. Cambridge: Cambridge University Press.

Pereira, M. 1989. *The Alchemical Corpus Attributed to Raymond Lull*. London: Warburg Institute.

Plato. 1997. *The Parmenides*, trans. M. L. Gill and P. Ryan. In J. M. Cooper, ed., *Complete Works*. Indianapolis, IN: Hackett, 359–97.

Pring-Mill, R. 2008. *Le Microcosme Lullien*, trans. I. Atucha. Fribourg: Academic Press.

Rosaldo, M. Z., and L. Lamphere, eds. 1974. *Woman, Culture and Society*. Stanford, CA: Stanford University Press.

Ruether, R. R. 1983. *Sexism and God-Talk: Towards a Feminist Theology*. London: SCM Press.

Ruiz Simon, J. M. 1999. *L'Art de Ramon Llull i la Teoria Escolàstica de la Ciència.* Barcelona: Quaderns Crema.

Schiebinger, L. 1987. 'Skeletons in the Closet: The First Illustrations of the Female Skeleton in Eighteenth-century Anatomy'. In C. Gallagher and T. Laqueur, eds, *The Making of the Modern Body: Sexuality and Society in the Nineteenth Century.* Berkeley: University of California Press.

Short, J. R. 1991. *Imagined Country: Society, Culture and Environment.* London: Routledge.

Sidera i Casas, J. 2005. 'Origen i evolució del concepte de caos en Ramon Llull'. In M. I. Ripoll Perelló, ed., *Actes de les Jornades Internacionals Lul·lianes: «Ramon Llull al s. XXI».* Palma: Universitat de les Illes Balears, 339–45.

Vega, A. 2003. *Ramon Llull and the Secret of Life,* trans. James W. Heisig. New York: Crossroad.

Weinreich-Haste, H. 1986. 'Brother Sun, Sister Moon: Does Rationality Overcome a Dualistic World View?' In J. Harding, ed., *Perspectives on Gender and Science.* London: Falmer Press, 113–31.

Yates, F. 1982. 'The Art of Ramon Lull: An Approach through Lull's Theory of the Elements'. In *Lull and Bruno: Collected Essays.* London: Routledge and Kegan Paul, 9–77.

Zukin, S. 1991. *Landscapes of Power: From Detroit to Disney World.* Berkeley: University of California Press.

The Tree of Gernika: Political Poetics of Rootedness and Belonging

Safet HadžiMuhamedović

Human places become vividly real through dramatization.

(Tuan 2005 [1977]: 178)

Legitimation of *present* in *past* is a recurrent political practice.[1] Past confirms that the group identities and territories to which they pertain have stable roots, often stretching towards the Creation, and, implicitly, rights conferred by a transcendental being. Starting with an apocalyptic image, this chapter outlines some of the historical and anthropological aspects of a political device par excellence, the Tree of Gernika, or *Gernikako Arbola,* as it is known in Euskara.[2] Its eventful longevity, intrinsic qualities as a particular nonhuman yet anthropomorphic being and the breadth of its presence in cultural processes across time and space suggest that it *listens* and *speaks* in different capacities (Figure 4.1). Starting from the town of Gernika, this arboreal communication, which fashioned its *genius loci,* branched out into a series of wider phenomena, most notably Basque nationalism. The chapter attempts to work with this unavoidable subject largely told through the story of the Tree, but I must admit my awareness of the simplifications contained in any such brief account.[3]

On Monday, 26 April 1937, thousands of Gernika residents came out for a market day. The bells from the nearby church sounded an alarm at 4:30 p.m. What transpired in the town for the next three and a half hours left a deep mark in world history (*Manchester Guardian* 1937; Steer 1937). The aircraft of the German Condor Legion 'machine-gunned the fleeing population' (Lannon 2002: 54) and completely eviscerated the town centre. Eyewitness accounts of two British journalists drew considerable attention to the horrors of this event. Noel Monks, the first journalist to reach Gernika, recalled: 'There were flames and smoke and grit, and the smell of burning human flesh was nauseating. Houses were collapsing into the inferno' (1955: 97). The day after the attack, George L. Steer wrote in Bilbao for the *London Times* that the object was 'seemingly the demoralization of the civil population and the destruction of the cradle of the Basque race'. The agony inflicted upon this town has been famously depicted by Picasso, whose portrait of the painful event became

Figure 4.1 Glass ceiling in Casa de Juntas (Assembly House), Gernika, courtesy of Jordi Payà, 2011-CC BY-SA 2.0.

the main image associated with the word *Guernica* worldwide. As a sort of 'modernist critique' of a violent modern age, the dismembered and scattered body parts on Picasso's canvas echo the disintegration of place. Franco denied his involvement in the destruction, yet it was widely understood to be an execution of his political goals (Alvarez-Piner 2005: 86; Lecours 2007: 71). The reports note how the air raid disregarded 'a small munitions factory' outside the town (Monks 1955: 97), which implies that the reasons for the bombing may not be found in 'strategic warfare', but rather in Gernika as 'a space of great symbolic significance' (Lecours 2007: 71). To understand how Basque identity came to be epitomized by this small town, let us now turn towards the central motif of this chapter, a story told through the many lives of one oak tree.

The medieval economic, political and legal existence of the Basque traditional regions was governed by the institution of *fueros*—'collections of local laws and customs' (Heiberg 1989: 20).[4] While the Castilian and later Spanish royalty granted these rights to many parts of their kingdom, Basque *fueros* have been locally and traditionally understood as 'charters of liberty' (Strong 1893: 317–18) because, unlike in other regions, they survived until the nineteenth century and the Carlist Wars in Spain (Peers 1936: 531) and the end of the eighteenth century in France (Douglass and Bilbao 2005: 63). It was Juan I, the Castilian king, who took an oath in Gernika that 'he and his successors would maintain the "fueros, customs, franchises and liberties" of the land' (Strong 1893: 326). In 1476 and 1483, the same loyalty to Gernika was promised by Ferdinand II of Aragon and Isabella I of Castile, the pair notable for commencing the unification of Spain but also for the sponsorship of Columbus and the expulsions and conversions of Jews and Muslims. Their pledge was given under a particular tree in Gernika, an oak tree that was the historical meeting place of the town elders (Raento and Watson 2000: 711).

So why did this particular tree stand out amongst other trees? There had been meeting-oaks in various towns, but as the sessions in Gernika were longest, representatives were gradually sent there from other towns, with 'trumpets sounded and bonfires lit on the nearby mountaintops' (Kurlansky 1999: 86).[5] Also, this oak tree distinguished itself mostly because it was the locus of ceremonial confirmation of the *fueros* by royalty, which signified regional liberties and autonomy to a certain extent. *The Royal Audience,* a seventeenth-century painting by Francisco de Mendieta, depicts King Ferdinand giving an oath before Gernikako Arbola in 1476 (Quintela 2004: 38). For Basques, the recognition of *fueros* implied several exemptions. They were not subject to arbitrary arrest, use of torture, mandatory army service or taxation. In the nineteenth century, this tax exemption was seen as an important element to defend from the liberals in the Carlist Wars who sought to abolish that particular legal system (Heiberg 1989: 23; Raento and Watson 2000: 712). W. T. Strong (1893: 327) mentioned that the reaction to the imposition of taxes in 1804 by Manuel de Godoy, the Spanish Prime Minister of the time, was the burning of the tax stamps 'by the common hangman under the tree of Guernica'. It was really the case of one legal document being refuted by another. *Fueros* have remained highly symbolic of Basque rights and liberties that centred nationalist programmes (Heiberg 1989: 20). In these demands, Gernika and the Tree have been used as the emblem of Basque historic liberties, and they attained an aura of sacredness (Trembath 2007: 3). At the outset of the nineteenth century, English Romantic poet William Wordsworth wrote 'The Oak of Guernica' (1815: 250) referencing its social and legal role:

> OAK of Guernica! Tree of holier power
> Than that which in Dodona did enshrine
> (So faith too fondly deemed) a voice divine
> Heard from the depths of its aerial bower—
> How canst thou flourish at this blighting hour?
>
> [...]
>
> Those lofty-minded Lawgivers shall meet,
> Peasant and lord, in their appointed seat,
> Guardians of Biscay's ancient liberty.

Romanticizing of medieval history is a common theme to many nationalist productions. What this chapter explores is the interaction of landscape with history, the agentive quality of nonhumans in proliferations of identity. The poetics of identity politics in the formation of places, as expressed through language, images and a nonhuman entity, provide a fertile ground for the analysis of Basque history. In the words of Raento and Watson (2000: 721), such poetics are perpetuated by 'a living organism' in 'the bringing together of past and present in the same space and the same time'. This impregnation of the tree with political meaning, indeed an equation of the local laws and political ambitions with the miraculous eternal Tree is a social construct, which reminds us of Bourdieu's (1984) analysis of the judgement of taste. It is a lived abstraction which reinvents the social norms. It classifies, and it classifies the classifiers as those who are legitimized by it, which corresponds to Anderson's (2006 [1983]: 6) definition of nations as communities imagined 'both inherently limited and sovereign'. In Wordsworth's poem, the Tree of Gernika is simultaneously an instrument of the gods (holy, divine) and society (lawgiver, guardian of liberty). These two characteristics legitimize each other. Seen as an image of a direct connection, through ancestors to the very Creation, the age of a tree perhaps best determines its significance to humans (Jones and Cloke 2002: 33). When the 300-year-old tree died in 1860, it was housed in a 'temple', and a new one was planted with the use of acorns from what became known as the 'old Tree'. The 'Father Tree' was supposedly from the fourteenth century. In 2004, after 144 years of political life, the death of the third tree was officially mourned, but not before it was made sure that its acorns would produce further replications (Kurlansky 1999: 161; BBC News 2004; Nash 2004). The tree does not die to be substituted by another, nor does the community.

Rather, the tree is always the same Tree, the community always the same Community and the values, laws, customs and liberties reflect their perdurable nature. They simply extend their existence through regeneration. In the words of the Basque journalist Gorka Landaburu: 'The tree has died, long live the tree' (Nash 2004: 1).

'Gernikako Arbola', frequently called the 'Basque hymn', a song from 1853 by José María Iparraguirre, 'a Carlist volunteer in the first war at the age of thirteen' (Kurlansky 1999: 161), which eventually got him arrested and expelled from the Basque Country, further imbued the tree with human, social, metaphysical and perennial nature. Aulestia (1981: 48) notes that the song violates syntax in the first line but compensates with direct language and emotional content. The Tree is spoken to and has the ability to answer, it is 'planted by God', its corporeal 'fresh veins' will live 'now and forever', but it is also equated with the destiny of the community: 'If you fall we will perish easily.' However, there is an intelligent catch: the Tree never really falls. In fact, the seeds of Gernikako Arbola have been planted throughout the Basque diaspora, making it a 'focal point of this international allegiance' (Raento and Watson 2000: 719). Basque life, a thoroughly imagined yet palpable process, is symbolically and politically ensured through the association with a tree. It can exist as *the* Tree across time and space. 'Objects anchor time,' Tuan noted (2005 [1977]: 187), but, as we see here, it is rather that they invite a multiplicity of temporal and spatial connections.

Gernikako Arbola is 'full of agency', not least because the roles 'embedded into it' semiautonomously enter a spectacle of communication with humans—a spectacle that creates bilateral imprints. 'Embedded' is in quotation marks because the Tree is not a mere tabula rasa or a palimpsest, but a complex and versatile actor even when apparently inscribed with meaning. Its roles are played out within social networks and are intricately woven into the lives of humans, which makes segregated research of 'subjects' and 'objects' implausible. Marx (1973 [1939]: 265) held that society, rather than consisting of individuals (or actors in our case), expresses the sum of their interrelations. So, perhaps I can deflect from his famous sentence, as Penny Dransart insightfully suggested in our personal correspondence:

> [Trees] make their own history, but they do not make it as they please; they do not make it under self-selected circumstances, but under circumstances existing already, given and transmitted from the past. (Marx 2008 [1852]: 15).

Like 'men', Gernikako Arbola is not in a casual but rather a *causal* relationship with other actors in the society. The question of what the Tree *is* cannot be answered without a morphology of its relationships. Finding elements of the social and *social agency* is exactly that, a matter of looking into the positions within these interrelations (Gell 1998: 121–6).[6] Gell (1998: 19–23) downgrades this causal quality of 'things' to the mere reflection of the vicinity of another, true agent. Agency seems to always depend on its origins in human conceptualization. Gell accepts only primary and secondary agents, both of which are inescapably linked with intention. The former hold intention; they are 'intentional beings'. This allows them a strong (primary) grip on agency. Secondary agents serve themselves to the distributed agency of these 'intentional beings', only to emanate it back to them. Gell offers a complex argument, but, like the trees that he mentions in passing (Gell 1998: 121–2), it ultimately rests upon human intention. All nonhumans, whether nonliving or biologically alive, can only be animated; they are given symbolic errands but remain separate categories, forever second in line to the social throne.

Nonhumans are always social, or at least they are as soon as we imagine them. Of something outside of what we know, we simply cannot speak. In fact, to stretch this argument further, Gernikako Arbola may only nominally be distinguished as 'nonhuman'. The term offers itself as a heuristic device to think of the complications to the 'obvious' separations. We could say that what is imagined is produced and what is produced imagines. So when we, nominally human, imagine in some way that which already exists outside of us, are we not imagining ourselves through this reiterative process? Are we not really *made* of those 'nonhumans'? This, along with a bulk of historical infrastructure, could be the most basic explanation of how Gernikako Arbola manages to equal Gernika, Javier from Bilbao or any sense of the Self.

Moving away from the structuralists, Bourdieu (1990b: 9–12) wanted to reintroduce social agents. His notion of *habitus* speaks to the practices and strategies, dispositions based on experience, which are open for variation, or improvisation without being necessarily tied into rational decision making. Bourdieu rather spoke of 'cognition without consciousness, intentionality without intention' (Bourdieu 1990b: 12). When a particular landscape belongs to the *habitus*-producing structure of one community (Bourdieu 1984, 1990a), then the community, which belongs to the same structure, also produces the *habitus* of the landscape. The social dispositions of landscape are equally affected. This idea of 'full circle impact' has also been discussed within cultural ecology (Steward 1955; Sutton and Anderson 2010) in terms of interdependent processes. Such indivisibilities suggest that research of cultural identities should be a holistic study that includes habitat, but also the practices and narratives pertaining to it. Latour complicates this Bourdieusian argument of 'structured structures predisposed to function as structuring structures' (Bourdieu 1990a: 53) by suggesting that we acknowledge varieties and ambiguities in action as 'a conglomerate of many surprising sets of agencies that have to be slowly disentangled' (Latour 2005: 44). Rather than *objects* and *subjects,* to bridge this divide, he speaks of humans and nonhumans through their relationships (Latour 2005: 72) and *actants* instead of anthropomorphic *actors,* to imply all which 'acts or shifts action' (Akrich and Latour 1992: 259; Latour 2004: 75). In what he termed Actor-Network Theory, nonhumans have an active role and are not 'the hapless bearers of symbolic projection' (Latour 2005: 10). Agency is dispersed in the networks rather than originating from a specific source. That the actors in this network are 'possessed by the action', as Ingold (2011: 214) suggested, should not imply a disregard for the useful analytical concept of agency as mere 'magical mind-dust'. Agency is not what sets into activity, as some spiritual or intellectual force behind the curtain, but the very quality of inducing action. Perhaps the puzzling allure of the Basque Tree–centred relationships stems from their anomalous manifestation in the alienation into well-defined categories that structure the lives we live.

Nationalizing the Tree

> As one of the interviewed moderate nationalists cynically remarked in 1995, referring to the importance addressed to, and to the conversation concerning, Gernika: 'Today, it is not possible to be Basque without doing your árbol laboral, without spending some time under the Tree, even if it was only ten minutes per year.'
>
> (Raento and Watson 2000: 730)

Real, not imagined, lives were subjected to the oppression of nation-state homogenization in Spain. Images of Basque culture threatened with disappearance were amplified to the extent of myth—grounds for yet another nationalism. First to formulate this sentiment were troubadour poets like Iparraguirre and Arrese Beitia who established the main elements for a later, more systematic approach (Aulestia 1981: 48). The Basque fable featuring an anthropomorphic tree was further developed to include a moral message of uncanny political resistance after Gernikako Arbola survived the attack in 1937. News reports informed about the miraculously untouched church, parliament and the Sacred Tree, 'the dried old stump of 600 years and the new shoots of this century' (Steer 1937; Monks 1955: 97), thereby solidifying the legend of Gernika[7] and 'creating a myth that they can never be eliminated' (Totori-cagüena 2004: 40).

Shortly after the annihilation of Gernika, survivors had gathered under their Venerable Oak (Kurlansky 1999: 204). The *real* and the *imagined* place of safety intertwined at that moment into a singular multilayered experience. Such palpable events fed into collective memory of the Basque Country, argued Lecours (2007: 70). History is thus perceived both in relation to human eyewitness experiences and the transgenerational life of the Tree to which they contribute. Pérez-Agote (2006: xxii) argued that Franco's regime aided the 'radicalization of [Basque] nationalist consciousness' through its persecutions of Basque culture. Euskara, the Basque language, was declining because it was not used in schools or any other public spaces. Even personal names were rewritten in registries and on tombstones (Da Silva 1975: 230; Raento and Watson 2000: 725). The Carlist Wars had already abolished the *fueros* (Peers 1936: 531), which led Sabino Arana, the fin de siècle father of so-called proper Basque nationalism, to promote sovereignty as 'an innate attribute of Basques' symbolized by Gernikako Arbola (Heiberg 1989: 55).

Lecours (2007: 72–82) noted that the idea of the Basque nation was legitimized in the resistance to the dictatorship, but also that radical nationalism and its violence have 'outlived the political and institutional circumstances that led to its birth'. Nationalism fashioned in opposition to another nationalism is a frequent occurrence. This oxymoronic posttraumatic disorder is not just Basque but also Israeli, Bosnian and Kosovar. The threat of disappearance seems to be most easily constructed into the politics of one dominant identity.

Ritual, especially commemorative ceremony, is nearly always a closed form, a repetitive performance of utterances, postures and gestures, which give rhythm to social memory (Connerton 1989: 58–61). When José Antonio Aguirre was elected the first *lehendakari,* leader of the Basque government, in October 1936 (De Meneses 2001: 122; Mees 2003: 20), he made an oath under Gernikako Arbola (Kurlansky 1999: 189):

> Humble before God
> Standing on Basque soil
> In remembrance of Basque ancestors
> Under the tree of Guernica, I swear
> to faithfully fulfill my commission.

The same pledge at the same place was given by Garaikoetxea, the next *lehendakari,* in 1980. He reclaimed Gernika, the legendary Tree, and Euskara, the language he was not taught in Franco's Spain, as Basque national symbols par excellence (Kurlansky 1999: 275–6). The ritualized performance of the pledge seems to be unavoidable in political ceremonies today, even though different programmes are legitimized through slight changes in the wording. So, Paxti Lopez, who is the first socialist *lehendakari,* omitted the word 'God' in his address under the Tree and swore upon the Statute of Autonomy of the Basque Country rather than the Bible (Euronews 2009). Nevertheless, the centrality of the Tree in the emotional geography of the Basques was both confirmed and exploited, as politicians continue to be elected upon the presumption that 'Gernika's identity remained rooted in a mythological past' (Raento and Watson 2000: 714).[8] The power of a single nonhuman entity to the feelings of belonging has branched out onto wider levels of abstraction. As Tuan (2005 [1977]: 150) noted, 'Cosmic views can be adjusted to suit new circumstances.' Yet, the very fact that the main elements of the legendary oath before the Tree are ritually reenacted (Connerton 1989: 61) makes them successful, not so much as mnemonic devices, but rather as political devices infiltrated into the mnemonic power of ritual.

Ritual recitations of myths are often performed by specialists of some kind (Goody 2010: 55). In its role as a myth, which has been adapted to a specific age, Gernikako Arbola is tied to a *lehendakari* as a particular sort of secular shaman. The hermeneutic role of a *lehendakari* is limited by networks of agencies. Shorter (1989: 68) argued that myths, which articulate archetypal truths, are never completely lived.

They are rather felt as relevant by people in their daily lives. By imputing a certain agency to the Tree as an actor in the myth (a sort of 'social arrangement' that I previously described as full of nominal humans and nonhumans), I do not wish to exclude the human cognitive process of decision making, although the agency of the Tree is a disclaimer to its limitlessness. The Myth of the Tree is a reproduced disposition, which may adopt more layers or be completely rejected in particular group or individual experiences. However, as soon as any actor enters into a relationship with the Tree, there is a situation of at least two agentive entities of the social. To induce a division between the social and the nonsocial is, as Latour (2005: 47) says, possible 'precisely once the overall society disappears'.

Images of the Tree and oak leaf also continue to permeate Basque political and cultural arenas. The flag and the coat of arms of the Biscay province are adorned with depictions of the Tree and a wreath of oak leaves, which have also been used by nationalist parties and radical groups, as well as on Basque police badges (Mansvelt Beck 2005: 159). The same symbols are present in the coat of arms of the Basque Country, but also in posters, paintings and sculptures of the Basque diaspora (Totoricagüena 2004: 40). This omnipresence relies on the notion that the Tree somehow 'soaked up the complex social constructions' (Jones and Cloke 2002: 93) and it speaks for itself. Tourism is also feeding into these trademarks of *Euskaltasuna,* an actual word meaning 'Basqueness' or 'the quality of being Basque', according to the website of the North American Basque Organizations. Visitors are invited to '[l]earn about the importance and the symbolism of the Tree of Gernika' and '[s]tand in the place of a Lehendakari, swear the oath of office, and take home a commemorative souvenir scroll' (Gernika-Lumo Town Council n.d.). Merely to perform the ceremony and actually to understand what the performance signifies to those who live by it are two completely different experiences (Turner 1991 [1969]: 7). This invitation to the (presumed) international visitor to engage in a quick performance of history begins a parallel, yet a completely different life of the Tree. Executing performances and being habituated to them implies not only incommensurable relationships (Connerton 1989: 71) but also discrepant discourses. Heritage tourism operates through outsider appreciation at best and does not engender a sense of belonging and placedness.

A monument named 'My Father's House', referring to Gabriel Aresti's (1963) poem of the same title made famous by Basque nationalists, has been built near the Tree (Raento and Watson 2000: 721). Placing the 'Father tree' next to the 'Father's house', which will, the song proclaims, remain standing after everything is lost, extends the symbolic capital of the Tree as the embodiment of unbreakable kinship to the domain of exclusive memory. This juxtaposition is a political mnemonic technique. Remembering implies an associative process. New information is 'deposited' together with new images (Butler 1989: 19). However, the power of association is not exclusive to human agency. While Gernikako Arbola has proved useful to a proliferation of nationalist sentiment, it has taken on a life (or rather lives) of its own. It is an organic image that may, with or without the public performance associated with it, speak to different, even conflicting claims. It has already exploded geographically. A monument's definitive meaning, what is inscribed in or out of it, is progressively difficult to control. Is the Tree socialist, nationalist, touristic? Which version of history does it uphold—Franco's version, the Basque nationalist version, a diasporic version or a more intimately human one? Why did the Condor Legion spare it after all? Wondering about the same question, Kurlansky (1999: 205) wrote: 'Maybe the Germans, not knowing Basque history, thought it was just a tree.'

The Nature of Nature

> But this is not just any tree. For one thing, it draws the entire landscape around it into a unique focus: in other words, by its presence it constitutes a particular place. The place was not there before the tree, but came into being with it.
>
> (Ingold 1993: 167)

How does *organic* become *political,* and why? It would be much easier to discuss the many positions of Gernikako Arbola in the forming of identities without the complications of nationalism—the imperative 'false consciousness'. Violence invested in identity politics favouring homogeneity acts to smooth out the multiplicity of meanings. How can the more subtle relationships with landscape, including those that are widely termed political, surface under such essentializing forces?

By relating the Basque example to research on *miyoomb* trees from southwest Congo (De Boeck 1998), Athapaskan and Tlingit glaciers (Cruikshank 2005) and my ethnographic research on Bosnian sacral geography, I would, if only briefly, like to look at another possible aspect in the appropriation of the Tree as the Basque political tool par excellence. An intricate relationship with the image and meaning of *miyoomb* trees as living shrines allows aLuund to 'replant' their sense of home in another space (De Boeck 1998: 26). Basqueness, as told through oak trees—and every oak *is* in theory a potential Gernikako Arbola—has secured the regeneration of Basque communities (or political programmes) wherever and whenever there is at least one acorn left. The basic formula in the 'legend of Gernika', the preservation of placedness through the symbolic lives of nonhuman beings, works similarly in De Boeck's example: 'What turns a space into a place for the aLuund of southwestern Congo is, literally, its rootedness in the past and its capacity to constitute, and conjure up, a living spatialized memory and link between past and present' (De Boeck 1998: 25). Thus, locality can always be reached anew through the growing of new trees, which are representational of the community, its past and the human bodies in multitudes of their 'biological and social' experiences. In the geographically wider Basque case, diasporic communities render *space* into concrete *place* by seeding the symbol into the soil, and one can 'travel the Americas from south to north by way of the Gernikako Arbola' (Raento and Watson 2000: 719).

The Basque Tree, much like *miyoomb* trees, is a listener and a speaker, with the ability to both embody processes of life and to 'perpetuate the ideal cultural order' (De Boeck 1998: 42). The world is both constituted and elucidated through the relationship with the landscape.

A combination of anthropomorphic and arboreal qualities of Gernikako Arbola suggests various kinship strategies, most of all the insistence on durability and continuation. Cruikshank (2005: 11) noticed that Tlingit and Athapaskan communities traditionally understood glaciers as intensely social spaces with characteristics normally attributed to persons, such as gender. Many toponyms in the sacral Bosnian geography are also gendered, reflecting their symbolic power. 'Maiden's Cave' (*Djevojačka Pećina*), a monumental crevice near the village of Brateljevići, is regularly visited by thousands of Muslim pilgrims who enter *Earth's womb* to pray for the soul of the legendary woman who was not afraid to enter and eventually die there. The spring called 'Male Water' (Muška Voda), a renowned aphrodisiac, is in close proximity to the cave.[9]

Basque community, traditionally Catholic and patriarchal, as well as the older natural archetypes are thus similarly reflected in the naming of the oldest stump as the 'Father tree'. Russel (1979: 223–4) argued from a folklorist perspective that the equation of tree with kinship lineage may be traced to the Neolithic and that the metaphor has been variously ritualized around the world since then. In her view, the archetypal tree 'is the kinship symbol par excellence, and since kinship has always been at the centre of social life in every society, it is natural to find a cosmic tree (kinship) at the centre of the cosmos (society), and we do indeed find cosmic trees in many societies' (Russel 1979: 228).

Sacred trees are often involved in communication with humans, which implies their agency in processes of listening and speaking. For example, enquirers heard replies from Prussian oak trees inhabited by gods, near which they held their religious and political assemblies (Chadwick 1900: 31–2). A parallel with the Gernikako Arbola is obvious—it is a place of political and religious congregation which imparts sacred knowledge. Its designation as the Venerable Oak might be a starting point for researchers of European 'pre-Christian' pantheons, which seem to have revolved around the agency of what Europeans now call 'nature'. Cruikshank's (2005: 10) argument that the 'Western material and cultural world' rejects the possibility of landscape being the listener is perhaps best denounced by one of the verses in Iparraguirre's national hymn after the Basques ask it to *live forever*:

> The tree answered
> that we should live carefully
> and in our hearts
> ask the Lord:
> We do not want wars
> [but] peace forever,
> to love here
> our fair laws.

The symbolic is communicated from and to the tree, but the content must be in a way 'confirmed' by its intrinsic organic qualities, as 'nature "pushes back" with its own vitality' (Jones and Cloke 2002: 6). Political and otherwise socialized poetics of organic nonhuman life act as a sort of human heuristic device in the very basic formation of identities.

But why would Basques relate to this specific species of tree? The use of oak-related imagery in Europe was abundant throughout its history. Oak leaf crowns were regularly used in Roman crowns as symbols of divine sanction because oak was sacred to Jupiter the thunder god, but they were also used in civic wreaths as a sign of military achievement (Riccardi 2000: 105–6). A thunder god is a pan-European deity, the only one in common to all the Indo-Germanic-speaking communities of the continent (Chadwick 1900: 42). The old oak sanctuary at Dodona was related to the thunder god Zeus, who was sometimes seen as a deity dwelling in a sacred oak (Cook 1903: 403). Chadwick (1900) also mentioned that Perkuno or Perkunas, the Prussian and Baltic thunder god, inhabited oaks, and his symbol was a perpetual oak-wood fire.[10] The establishment of a cognitive relationship between thunder, the 'thunderer' and large oaks seems almost logical. Wouldn't such a tree be first to attract thunder in an open space? These divine oak inhabitants, it may be argued, are just another conception of the agency of nonhumans that are so thoroughly examined in modern scholarship.

Across time and space, oaks have been understood as symbols of freedom, strength and refuge (Jones and Cloke 2002: 35). Although the stories contain some resemblances, Gernikako Arbola is markedly different from the Royal Oak, the tree in which King Charles II was supposedly hidden after the battle of Worcester (Scott 2011: 284), or the Charter Oak in Connecticut, where in 1662 the Colonial Charter was safeguarded from King James II according to the legend and which grew into a symbol of American liberties (Corrigan 2008). The Basque Tree has not only been featured in several important historical episodes rather than one, but was also socialized into the 'magical drama of human agency' (Kwon 2006: 102) and reworked into the process of constituting different places through the memorialization of an imagined temporal, moral and geographical stillness.

With the case of Bosnia, which, like Gernika, had experienced destruction and suppression of culture, alternative memory becomes embedded in narratives and landscape, as a way of distancing itself from official interpretations. Equating the Basque community and its values with the Tree and then imagining the Tree as miraculously perennial has developed through stages of local custom, political resistance, formation of nationalism and towards the many contemporary claims to the symbol. Observing that 'Gernika embodies various geographical, historical, and political scales of conflict,' Raento and Watson (2000: 708) considered another form of embodiment in relation to struggles against the state when they added that 'Gernika reflects competing interests within Basque nationalism.'

How does a tree sustain particular kinds of memory? Mnemonic methods are 'ways of organizing information to make it easier to remember, typically by using codes, visual imagery or rhymes' (Foster 2009: 117). Some of the best known methods, like the *method of loci* and *mental mapping,* entail a possibility to remember particular events, people and stories through their association with place and correlating them to other places and one's own position in the world (Foster 2009: 123). This process of memory depends upon the repetitive inscription of bodies and nature into one another (Lovell 1998: 11) but may take the form of both remembering and memorialization feeding on remembrance, which makes landscaped memory apt to answer the changing circumstances of the lived present in the form of political claims inter alia.

In their analysis of trees as markers of 'changing places', Jones and Cloke (2002: 95–6) do not consider the elements of *active silence* and *symbolic mirroring* of human lives, which Gernikako Arbola exudes concomitantly. Combined, these two characteristics allow Gernika not only to change as place but also simultaneously to exist as more than one place. When I say *active silence,* I am implying that the agency of a tree is (perhaps frustratingly for some) stubborn in a particular kind of stillness. It doesn't side with any of its histories. This adds to its versatility as a symbol. Basso's (2007) account of silence in Western Apache culture is of a (human) response to unpredictability in social situations. Silence is not empty, but a form of communication. Gernikako Arbola's act of 'withholding' may be experienced as a hierarchical arrangement, discipline and punishment, a sign of respect, age, a lament over unfortunate circumstances, contemplation or reflection. It extends the minute of silence over the loss of Gernika lives but works altogether differently in another social situation.

But how is this idea of *active silence* different from 'simple passivity of objects' as a support for human symbolic projections? Firstly, even if imagined somehow detached from the world of humans, trees might only be considered silent in terms of human vocal and sign languages. The spatial and temporal presence of trees, some more than others, is powerful. They grow, rupture and affect soil, produce and reproduce. They make sounds turn, and grow towards water and sun. They suffer from hunger, thirst and sickness; they fall and die. They are independent of human action but have a mutually beneficial relationship with much of what is around them. Can we really assume that annual rings of trees, as a cross-species (human and nonhuman if you will) measurement of time, are symbolic projections? Or is dendrochronology just a matter of multiple reflexes? A tree reflects periods of rain and sun, a human reflects the tree, the tree reflects the human, the periods of sun and rain reflect the tree and so forth. Claiming agency for humans really implies a claim to the intentionality of action, yet intention on its own affects nothing outside of the given actor directly.

Trees are also a good start for the questioning of boundaries between activity and passivity. Passivity performs. It is a way of action, a modus operandi. It may accept or reject content, communication and intervention. Passivity as a decontextualized concept is not very informative, however. To say that subjects or objects, humans or nonhumans, are passive contains no information about the quality of their existence. To what are they passive? What conditions their passivity? There is no more simplicity to the passivity of Gernikako Arbola than there is to the passivity of humans.

Clearly, there is an entanglement of people and trees. People are affected by trees as organic beings, symbols and objects, and trees are affected by people in much the same way. The first two effects of this reverse process should be rather self-explanatory, but how are trees affected by people as symbols? Rather than imputing them with some kind of appreciation for symbolism, it is clear that their lives with people are affected by symbolic anthropomorphic comparisons. The life of Gernikako Arbola is shaped by important instances of human–nonhuman encounters. Was not the pledge of Isabella under the Tree just an assembly of two symbolic living beings who are affected by and affecting the networks through which they operate?

An easy presumption would be that the whole story of agentive trees rests on vivid anthropomorphism, but a closer observation reveals that humans are just as often arboreomorphic in their mirroring of the many qualities and life stories of trees: 'Trees can construct places and vice versa' (Jones and Cloke 2002: 86). To ask who started this process of mutual affection would be similar to the pointless dilemma of what was first, a chicken or an egg.

Genius Loci

> A place is, therefore, a qualitative, 'total' phenomenon, which we cannot reduce to any of its properties, such as spatial relationships, without losing its concrete nature out of sight.
>
> (Norberg-Shulz 1980: 7)

The idea of 'unchanging landscape' has been successfully dispelled, not least by anthropologists. We are now able to understand it as a 'cultural process' (Hirsch 1995: 23). Building upon Veena Das's notion of 'critical events', Frances Pine (2003: 281) concluded that 'moments of shifting ideologies must be taken into account when considering how meanings, land and personhood transform over time and, conversely, how core ideas remain consistent despite changes.' Gernikako Arbola defines the *genius loci* of Gernika, 'the concrete reality man has to face and come to terms with in his daily life' (Norberg-Shulz 1980: 5), the spirit of place which encapsulates both desirable and undesirable history and speaks from the complex intersection of the lived and the imagined. Rendered as the human mirror, synchronically and diachronically, and socialized into a range of roles, from the legal document to the cathedral of pure *Basqueness,* from a kinship symbol to the stumbling block for one and a foundational pillar for another nation, from the shelter of the frightened to the tourist playground, from the call for freedom to the justification for violence, the Venerable Oak, once just a tree, grows with agency that transcends each of the particularities associated with it.

The ethos of Gernikako Arbola, however, has always remained political, from the medieval *fueros* to the contemporary Basque nationalist claims. It should be understood as a performed organic history, layers of which cannot otherwise be conveyed. The 'common oak' is the most frequent and versatile type of tree to enter the process of culture (Jones and Cloke 2002: 35). The Oak of Gernika engages dialectically with ideological processes within its reach. It sustains Gernika as the place of destruction but also contradicts it, as it embodies survival, life and liberty. Raento and Watson (2000) observe that there have been at least two different places *Guernica* and *Gernika* imagined side by side. There are political attempts to merge them into a single symbolic place, which the request to move Picasso's painting from Madrid to the Guggenheim Museum in Bilbao also implies (Lecours 2007: 71). The masterpiece reminds of a dreadful event but, curiously, invites hope through light bulbs that shine upon the shattered town. Was it in rootedness and regeneration that Picasso predicted a cultural reconstruction? It would have been more appropriate, it seems to me, to simply paint an oak tree as the organic image which encapsulates the different dimensions of Basque history, but '[w]e make time and place, just as we are made by them' (Bender 2001: 4) and the painting-tree-town-nation signified by Gernika operates under many, if sometimes contradictory, meanings.

Notes

1. For a wide-ranging analysis of social memory, see Paul Connerton's *How Societies Remember* (1989).
2. I have decided to use the Basque spelling *Gernika,* rather than the Spanish *Guernica* in this chapter. It is the official name of the town, but a variation in the spelling of this toponym is also pertinent to the existing identity politics. Note that Raento and Watson (2000: 709, 710) use *Gernika* 'as a means of distancing the place from the painting [by Picasso]'.
3. I would like to express my gratitude to Vanja Hamzić, whose readings and comments have, so many times, been detailed and constructive. I also thank Sari Wastell for introducing me to Gernikako Arbola during her fieldwork in the Bosnian town of Stolac, and Penny Dransart for her insightful editing. I would also like to thank the anonymous reviewer. Shortcomings of this chapter are solely mine.
4. The seven traditional regions include Bizkaia, Gipuzkoa and Araba (which form the Basque Autonomous Community or the 'historical territories'), Navarra/Nafarroa, and Labourd, Basse Navarre and Soule in France (Douglass and Bilbao 2005: 14, 62; Facaros and Pauls 2012: 24). *Fueros* are also known as *foruak* in Basque and *fors* in French.
5. For a discussion of dendrolatry in a wider context, other important Basque trees and a map with the most famous examples, see Julio C. Baroja's *Ritos i Mitos Equivocos* (1989: 339–88).

6. For an insightful discussion of these distinctions, see *Thinking through Things* (Henare, Holbraad and Wastell 2007).
7. On the history of discussions about whether the news reports contributed to the 'legend of Guernica', see Herbert Routledge Southworth's *Guernica! Guernica! A Study of Journalism, Diplomacy, Propaganda and History* (1977) and Armin Paul Frank's *Off-canon Pleasures: A Case Study and a Perspective* (2011: 92–108).
8. In his very detailed analysis of *The Social Roots of Basque Nationalism* (2006), sociologist Alfonso Pérez-Agote succeeds in not mentioning either Guernica or its famous oak tree which are so central to the formation of historical and contemporary perception and self-perception of the Basque existence. A similar observation can be made with some other volumes which offer insights into the Spanish Civil War and Basque nationalism (Da Silva 1975; Ben-Ami 1991; De Meneses 2001; Seidman 2002; Ealham and Richards 2005). There is no Gerni-kako Arbola in these accounts.
9. This relates to my ongoing research and fieldwork in 2012–2013.
10. Chadwick (1900) explained that Perkuno is etymologically related to the Latin word *quercus,* while druid is related to the Greek word *druidēs,* both denoting oak. Druids, according to Pliny the Elder (c. AD 77–79) held 'nothing more sacred than the mistletoe and a tree on which it is growing, provided it is Valo-nia Oak'.

References

Akrich, M., and B. Latour, 1992. 'A Summary of a Convenient Vocabulary for the Semiotics of Human and Nonhuman Assemblies'. In W. Bijker and J. Law, eds, *Shaping Technology, Building Society: Studies in Sociotechnical Change.* Cambridge, MA: MIT Press, 259–64.

Alvarez-Piner, C. M. 2005. 'Guernica'. In K. W. Estes and D. Kowalsky, eds, *History in Dispute.* Vol. 18, *The Spanish Civil War.* London: Gale, 81–6.

Anderson, B. 2006 [1983]. *Imagined Communities: Reflections on the Origin and Spread of Nationalism.* New York: Verso.

Aulestia, G. 1981. 'Poetry and Politics: Basque Poetry as an Instrument of National Revival'. *World Literature Today* 55(1): 48–52.

Baroja, J. C. 1989. *Ritos y Mitos Equivocos.* Madrid: Ediciones Istmo.

Basso, K. 2007. 'To Give Up on Words: Silence in Western Apache Culture'. In L. Monaghan and J. E. Goodman, eds, *A Cultural Approach to Interpersonal Communication: Essential Readings.* Oxford: Blackwell, 77–87.

BBC News. 2004. 'Basques Mourn Symbolic Oak Tree'. 22 April. Available at: http://news.bbc.co.uk/2/hi/europe/3649397.stm. Accessed 17 July 2012.

Ben-Ami, S. 1991. 'Basque Nationalism between Archaism and Modernity'. *Journal of Contemporary History* 26(3/4): 493–521.

Bender, B. 2001. 'Landscapes on the Move'. *Journal of Social Archaeology* 1: 75–89.

Bourdieu, P. 1984. *Distinction: A Social Critique of the Judgment of Taste.* Cambridge, MA: Harvard University Press.

Bourdieu, P. 1990a. *The Logic of Practice.* Cambridge: Polity Press.

Bourdieu, P. 1990b. *In Other Words: Essays towards a Reflexive Sociology.* Stanford, CA: Stanford University Press.

Butler, T. 1989. 'Memory: A Mixed Blessing'. In T. Butler, ed., *Memory: History, Culture and the Mind.* Oxford: Basil Blackwell, 1–31.

Chadwick, M. H. 1900. 'The Oak and the Thunder-God'. *Journal of the Anthropological Institute of Great Britain and Ireland* 30: 22–44.

Connerton, P. 1989. *How Societies Remember.* Cambridge: Cambridge University Press.

Cook, A. B. 1903. 'Zeus, Jupiter and the Oak'. *Classical Review* 17(8): 403–21.

Corrigan, D. J. 2008. 'Exploiting the Legend of the Charter Oak'. *Hog River Journal* (Winter 2007–8). Available at: http://connecticutexplored.org/issues/v06n01/CharterOak.pdf. Accessed 10 August 2012.

Cruikshank, J. 2005. *Do Glaciers Listen? Local Knowledge, Colonial Encounters, and Social Imagination.* Toronto: University of British Columbia Press.

Da Silva, M. M. 1975. 'Modernization and Ethnic Conflict: The Case of the Basques'. *Comparative Politics* 7(2): 227–51.

De Boeck, F. 1998. 'The Rootedness of Trees: Place as Cultural and Natural Texture in Rural Southwest Congo'. In N. Lovell, ed., *Locality and Belonging.* London: Routledge, 25–52.

De Meneses, F. R. 2001. *Franco and the Spanish Civil War.* London: Routledge.

Douglass, W. A., and J. Bilbao. 2005. *Amerikanuak: Basques in the Modern World.* Reno: University of Nevada Press.

Ealham, C., and M. Richards. 2005. *The Splintering of Spain: Cultural History and the Spanish Civil War, 1936–1939.* Cambridge: Cambridge University Press.

Euronews. 2009. 'The First Ever Non-nationalist Leader in the Basque Country'. 5 July. Available at: http://www.euronews.com/2009/05/07/first-ever-non-nationalist-leader-in-basque-country/. Accessed 25 July 2012.

Facaros, D., and M. Pauls. 2012. *Bilbao and the Basque Lands.* London: New Holland.

Foster, J. K. 2009. *Memory: A Very Short Introduction.* Oxford: Oxford University Press.

Frank, A. P. 2011. *Off-canon Pleasures: A Case Study and a Perspective.* Göttingen: Universitätsverlag Göttingen.

Gell, A. 1998. *Art and Agency: An Anthropological Theory.* Oxford: Clarendon Press.

Gernika-Lumo Town Council. n.d. 'Experience: Basque Country's roots: Gernika'. Available at: http://www.gernika-lumo.net/en-US/Tourism/Visit-Gernika/Pages/notelopierdas2_3ExperienciaGernikaRaicesdeEuskadi.aspx. Accessed 10 August 2012.

Goody, J. 2010. *Myth, Ritual and the Oral.* Cambridge: Cambridge University Press.

Heiberg, M. 1989. *The Making of the Basque Nation.* Cambridge: Cambridge University Press.

Henare, A., M. Holbraad and S. Wastell, eds. 2007. *Thinking through Things: Theorising Artifacts Ethnographically.* Cambridge: Cambridge University Press.

Hirsch, E. 1995. 'Introduction: Landscape—between Place and Space'. In E. Hirsch and M. O'Hanlon, eds, *The Anthropology of Landscape: Perspectives on Place and Space.* Oxford: Clarendon, 1–30.

Ingold, T. 1993. 'The Temporality and Landscape'. *World Archaeology* 25(2): 152–74.

Ingold, T. 2011. *Being Alive: Essays on Movement, Knowledge and Description.* London: Routledge.

Jones, O., and P. Cloke. 2002. *Tree Cultures: The Place of Trees and Trees in Their Place.* Oxford: Berg.

Kurlansky, M. 1999. *The Basque History of the World.* New York: Walker.

Kwon, H. 2006. *After the Massacre: Commemoration and Consolation in Ha My and My Lai.* London: University of California Press.

Lannon, F. 2002. *The Spanish Civil War: 1936–1939.* Oxford: Osprey.

Latour, B. 2004. *Politics of Nature: How to Bring the Sciences into Democracy.* Cambridge, MA: Harvard University Press.

Latour, B. 2005. *Reassembling the Social: An Introduction to Actor-Network-Theory.* Oxford: Oxford University Press.

Lecours, A. 2007. *Basque Nationalism and the Spanish State.* Reno: University of Nevada Press.

Lovell, N. 1998. 'Introduction: Belonging in Need of Emplacement'. In N. Lovell, ed., *Locality and Belonging.* London: Routledge, 1–22.

Manchester Guardian. 1937. 'Basque Town Wiped Out by Rebel Planes'. 28 April. Available at: http://www.guardian.co.uk/theguardian/1937/apr/28/fromthearchive?INTCMP=SRCH. Accessed 8 March 2013.

Mansvelt Beck, J. 2005. *Territory and Terror: Conflicting Nationalisms in the Basque Country.* London: Routledge.

Marx, K. 1973 [1939]. *Grundrisse: Foundations of the Critique of Political Economy.* London: Penguin Books.

Marx, K. 2008 [1852]. *The 18th Brumaire of Louis Bonaparte.* Rockville, MD: Wildside Press.

Mees, L. 2003. *Nationalism, Violence and Democracy: The Basque Clash of Identities.* New York: Palgrave Macmillan.

Monks, N. 1955. *Eyewitness.* London: Frederick Muller.

Nash, E. 2004. 'Pride and Prejudice'. *The Independent.* 11 May. Available at: http://www.independent.co.uk/news/world/europe/pride-and-prejudice-562891.html. Accessed 17 July 2012.

Norberg-Shulz, C. 1980. *Genius Loci: Towards a Phenomenology of Architecture.* London: Academy Editions.

North American Basque Organizations. Available at: http://www.nabasque.org/. Accessed 1 August 2012.

Peers, E. A. 1936. 'The Basques and the Spanish Civil War'. *Irish Quarterly Review* 25(100): 529–44.

Pérez-Agote, A. 2006. *The Social Roots of Basque Nationalism.* Reno: University of Nevada Press.

Pine, F. 2003. 'Reproducing the House: Kinship, Inheritance, and Property Relations in Highland Poland'. In H. Grandits and P. Heady, eds, *Distinct Inheritances: Property, Family and Community in a Changing Europe.* Münster: Lit Verlag, 279–95.

Pliny the Elder. c. AD 77–79. *The Historie of the World,* trans. P. Holland [1601]. Available at: http://penelope.uchicago.edu/holland/index.html. Accessed 15 August 2012.

Quintela, M. G. 2004. *Mitos hispanicos II: Folclore e ideologia desde la Edad Media hasta nuestros dias.* Madrid: Akal Ediciones.

Raento, P., and C. J. Watson. 2000. 'Gernika, Guernica, *Guernica*? Contested Meanings of a Basque Place'. *Political Geography* 19: 707–36.

Riccardi, L. A. 2000. 'Uncanonical Imperial Portraits in the Eastern Roman Provinces: The Case of the Kanellopoulus Emperor'. *Hesperia* 69: 105–32.

Russel, C. 1979. 'The Tree as a Kinship Symbol'. *Folklore* 90(2): 217–33.

Scott, H. 2011. 'Review of Matikkala Antti's "The Orders of Knighthood and the Formation of the British Honours System, 1660–1760"'. *Journal of Interdisciplinary History* 42(2): 284–5.

Seidman, M. 2002. *Republic of Egos: A Social History of the Spanish Civil War.* Madison: University of Wisconsin Press.

Shorter, B. 1989. 'Memory in Service of Psyche: The Collective Unconscious in Myth, Dream and Ritual'. In T. Butler, ed., *Memory: History, Culture and the Mind.* Oxford: Basil Blackwell, 61–76.

Southworth, H. R. 1977. *Guernica! Guernica! A Study of Journalism, Diplomacy, Propaganda and History.* Berkeley: University of California Press.

Steer, G. L. 1937. 'The Tragedy of Guernica: Town Destroyed in Air Attack'. *Times of London.* 27 April.

Steward, J. H. 1955. *Theory of Culture Change.* Urbana: University of Illinois Press.

Strong, W. T. 1893. 'The Fueros of Northern Spain'. *Political Science Quarterly* 8(2): 317–34.

Sutton, M. Q., and E. N. Anderson. 2010. *Introduction to Cultural Ecology.* Plymouth: Altamira Press.

Totoricagüena, G. P. 2004. *Identity, Culture and Politics in the Basque Diaspora.* Reno: University of Nevada Press.

Trembath, R. 2007. 'Guernica and After: Australian War Correspondents and the Spanish Civil War'. In M. Van Heekeren, ed., *Australian Media Traditions.* Available at: http://www.csu.edu.au/special/amt/publication/trembath.pdf. Accessed 15 July 2012.

Tuan, Y. 2005 [1977]. *Space and Place: The Perspective of Experience.* London: University of Minnesota Press.

Turner, V. 1991 [1969]. *The Ritual Process: Structure and Anti-Structure.* Ithaca, NY: Cornell University Press.

Wordsworth, W. 1815. *Poems.* London: Longman.

−5−

Bringing the Forest to the City: Spaces Imagined in Israeli Sacred Song Circles

Ronit Grossman-Horesh

Introduction

This chapter is part of a comprehensive, multisite ethnographic study on new spaces and places created by contemporary spiritual seeking. The spiritual practice I explore here is prominent in contemporary spiritual renewal: sacred song circles. According to their promoters, these practices create a connection between diverse individuals on a spiritual path. Sacred song circles are mainly held at New Age movement festivals, popular among consumers of spiritual tourism. Most participants are people searching for spiritual experiences who travel to various sites around the world to take part in workshops and shamanic and neoshamanic ceremonies (Shanon 2002: 1–13; Luna 2003: 20–23; Holman 2011: 90–93).

In recent years, sacred song circles have also been held monthly in urban settings outside the festival venue, and some of them also apart from shamanic ceremonies. The institutionalization of sacred song circles in Tel Aviv has given rise to songbook collections of more than 300 prayers—songs of gratitude and praises to nature in general and the forest in particular—from various spiritual traditions and languages in English, Sanskrit and Portuguese, as well as original Hebrew songs.

I focused my observations of sacred song circles on an urban environment, the Yoga Center in Tel Aviv, where monthly sacred song circle evenings are held for the general public. Many yoga centres exist throughout the city of Tel Aviv; however, the Yoga Center is different. Aside from providing a place to practise various styles of yoga, it functions like other urban spiritual centres, offering a range of activities, including meditation workshops, lectures on healthy nutrition, and community events, such as ecological Sabbath ceremonies, women's clothing evenings (for clothing exchanges to reduce consumption) and, once a month, sacred song circles on Saturday evenings. A weekly newsletter advertises the centre's upcoming activities along with pertinent articles. Although its founders deny any connection to politics, they did support the Green Party in the national election (10 February 2009), while avoiding involvement altogether in the municipal elections.

The sacred song circles are the largest gatherings of all the varied activities supported by the centre. More than fifty men and women aged twenty-five to fifty attend the sacred song circle evenings at the Yoga Center. Many of the regular participants have vocations in the therapeutic professions, such as spiritual mentors working in hospitals, old age homes and hospices, or are social workers and therapists in various alternative methods. Their singing is heard throughout the building and even in the streets. More than 500 people participate regularly in such circles and in shamanic ceremonies in various locations in Israel and abroad. Thousands participate in sacred song circles at the various New Age festivals and gatherings of the Rainbow Family of Living Light, an international community that has its roots in the US counterculture of the early 1970s and adopted in Israel in the 1990s (Tavory 2007: 95; Tavory and Goodman 2009: 263). Most participants are urban dwellers, although the music circle leaders, without exception, live close to nature in rural communities in Israel, and some of them are members of groups that immigrated to the forest in Costa Rica and only come to Israel for visits.

After following the participants and promoters for two years (since January 2009), I was invited to join song circles outside the city where I could make additional observations in rural and nature sites in Israel. As shown below, invitations to participate in sacred song circles held both in and out of the city that are provided by the Yoga Center contain latent social and spatial imaginaries that are generally found on the margins of political discourse.

I shall focus on the spiritual work of one group, Vision of the Forest, which invites the public at large to the urban Yoga Center to experience the 'magical green energy of the forest through sacred songs' (Yoga Center, newsletters, 2009–2011). From 2010, members of this circle (approximately 100 regular participants) have invited others to join the alternative spiritual community in Costa Rica.

Vision of the Forest members present the sacred song circle as a unification, many voices as one voice to open the heart and enable the individual to forge a simultaneous connection inwards and outwards, to himself or herself and to the circle. According to the circle leaders, dissolving feelings of separation creates a sense of unity and partnership experience. They report that this feeling is fully achieved within the community activities in the forest of Costa Rica.

This discussion will focus on the significance of one particular path among the song circles—bringing the forest to the city and bringing people to the forest. Analysis of the songs and messages transmitted in these circles reveals the imageries of three places and the connection between them: urban, rural and forest. Additional analysis considers the movement of participants between the various sites, which creates experiences that influence the subjective authenticity of the spiritual event.

My assertion is that sacred song circles create a connection between urban and rural spheres. For the leaders of Vision of the Forest, bringing the forest to the city through sacred song circles is a way to spread the vision of a community that lives on spiritual hospitality beyond national space. For them, the spirit of the forest exists beyond words, beyond national borders, outside specific social context and separate from political and moral questions. This vision can only be fully attained in one place: the forest. For many urban and rural song circle participants, who among other things seek spiritual growth and a sense of community in the city, the forest vision is a fantasy that most do not actualize through action. Many are satisfied with what is considered by the leaders of the song circles as simulations of forest life—the urban and rural song circles. In these contexts, Vision of the Forest groups actively participate in the creation and maintenance of urban spiritual enclaves that produce intimacy and agreement between familiar strangers.

Forest, City, Spirituality and Their Imaginaries

Thoughts of place linked to social imaginaries are not a new theme in the theoretical literature. Doreen Massey (1994: 154–5) suggests that:

> Instead of thinking of places as areas with boundaries around, they can be imagined as articulated moments in networks of social relations and understanding, but where a large proportion of those relations, experiences and understandings are constructed on a far larger scale than what we happen to define for that moment as the place itself ... And this in turn allows a sense of place which is extroverted, which includes a consciousness of its links with the wider world.

This perception is particularly relevant to the understanding of those places created as an idea and a feeling by the contemporary movement of 'the forest'.

The focus on places created by spiritual seeking and the interchange between them raises queries as to the manner in which spiritual practices are used to create and spread social imaginaries as well as sociospatial imaginaries (Hervieu-Léger 2002: 100) and urban imaginaries (Hancock and Srinivas 2008: 617–30). In their everyday urban lives, people actively participate in production, consumption and distribution of cultural ideas. The different ways groups remember and imagine places influence their urban activities. In this way, collective imagination is the flip-side complement to the collective memory. Both are dynamic, and their creation often involves linkage between physical space and time. The collective imagination, however, has a future orientation. Thus, when people invest in various urban activities—be it time, participation, financial support or granting significance and emotional value—fantasy or wishes for future life in the city are also included (Borer 2010: 97–9). Another possibility I present here in an analysis of sacred song circles concerns a search for alternative experiences to city life altogether.

The research literature abounds with studies linking spiritual experiences with the sacredness of nature in general and the forest's sacredness in particular (Williams and Harvey 2001: 249–51; Trigger and Mulcock 2005: 308–9; Ivakhiv 2007: 265; Sharpley and Jepson 2011: 57–8). In similar fashion, multidisciplinary research on contemporary spirituality in Israel places emphasis on the creation of temporary sites (some institutionalized) in nature environments. By this I refer to various festivals which have a given time frame that create places and specific social imaginaries to facilitate an alternative social experience for the participants. Among the prominent simulations in these places in Israel are the following: 'egalitarian society' (Tavory and Goodman 2009: 273), a society where 'peace, freedom, brotherhood, harmony, and love reign' (Simchai 2009: 41–2), as well as 'a world without women' (Shiva festivals), 'a world without men' (Shakti festivals), 'a world without clothing' (Simple festivals) and more. These initiatives are kept relatively separate from populated areas, with locations situated in various natural settings and rural areas of Israel. When the simulation is terminated, most participants return to their urban lives and continue to learn and practise in urban spiritual centres, such as the Yoga Center.

In contrast, modern urban environments are perceived as lacking inspiration for spiritual experiences (Sharpley and Jepson 2011: 57–8). This also holds true for the image of Tel Aviv. In the literature, this city is perceived as a cosmopolitan bastion of secularity, materialism and worldliness (Vinitzky-Seroussi 1998: 185–6; Sznaider 2000: 308–9; Ram 2007: 5; Ram 2008: 70); seemingly, it is the antithesis to a site for spiritual seeking. In this context, the urban environment is not a trivial choice for research on contemporary spiritual practices. However, empirical observation into the Israeli quest for spiritual experiences reveals that the turn towards spirituality creates a variety of new places—urban spiritual centres and spiritual centres in nature. Furthermore, there is much movement between them through various initiatives, many of which are tourist oriented. As I shall show, a similar experience in the city demands a new definition of the place of activity and fairly precise control of the social imaginaries.

Sacred Song: Not Performance or Songfest Sing-alongs

Creating a space that facilitates individual introspection and the communal connection of a random group at one event is achieved through means aiming at all the senses while rigidly framing the event. Holding the circles on Saturday evenings is significant. It is a time where even nonobservant Jews complete a day of rest and get ready for a new week. The sacred song circles set at this liminal time, however, make no reference to Orthodox Judaism.

At the entrance to the building, the visitor is met with the smell of incense; several times I have heard new participants say: 'It reminds me of India.' Furthermore, many participants dress in the fashion attributed to Israeli tourists in India. A tray with candles is placed in the centre of the room. Pillows are scattered in a circle on the floor to sit on. The musicians are not separate from the circle. Faint music fills the background, and the lighting is dim. Many of the participants are regulars and dress in white, which symbolizes an exception to routine. The white dress, symbolizing purity, is also a sign to the other participants: a declaration that they are on a spiritual path. One of the regular participants who was not wearing white said to me: 'Don't think that everyone who wears white clothing is spiritual or enlightened. There are many people here wearing white who don't do any spiritual work at all. I don't feel worthy yet to wear white ... this inner work, is personal, complex, and long.'

Other places echo this atmosphere, the most prominent being enclaves created by Israelis, especially in India. Studies focusing on Israeli backpackers in India (Noy and Cohen 2005: 1–37; Maoz 2007: 128–33; Cohen 2008: 268–73) are instructive with respect to their touring and characteristic behaviour patterns. There is a prominent tendency to tour in large groups to defined destinations and along fixed trails. These patterns create Israeli enclaves, populated by Israelis for extended periods of time. Common features in these places are the creation of 'momentary communities' and the sense of solidarity between 'familiar strangers' (Enoch and Grossman 2010: 527–9).

The leaders of the song circles, without exception, all went on extended journeys, experienced the life in the forest and gathered the songs from their journeys. The prominent destinations among the Vision of the Forest group are India and Brazil, which is conveyed through the Sanskrit and Portuguese songs. In contrast, the participants of the urban song circles I spoke with represent a wider variation. Some travelled for extended periods and are familiar with the atmosphere of life in the Israeli enclaves of India; others, primarily women, travelled to India in the framework of organized tours. I also spoke with regular song circle participants who never went on an extended tour but participated in many festivals all over Israel, some in forests (in northern Israel and the Jerusalem hills). The forests in Israel (planted and natural) constitute approximately 9 per cent of the total land area (Statistical Abstract of Israel 2012: Table 19.7). Aside from temporary experiences through venues of festivals, vacation and recreation in Israeli forests, life in the forest is foreign to most Israeli residents, most of whom live in urban areas. In addition, for the regular ceremony participants, the atmosphere in urban song circles resembles more intimate song circles that have taken place in recent years in Israeli rural and nature areas.

As mentioned, the monthly song circles are open to the public at large. Although the circle leaders are acquainted with the inner circle of regular participants, the event is intentionally open to the public (for a small entrance fee) to broaden participation. The design and framing of each gathering begins with the circle leader's opening remarks, which identify the gathering as 'spiritual work'. The behaviour of the regulars, wandering between one song circle and the next throughout Israel, dominates and supports this definition. Typical behaviours include silence between songs, closing eyes during mantras, ecstatic dancing during some of the songs and holding hands at the end of gatherings. New participants in the urban circles may have different interpretations of the event that threaten the definition of song circles as reality-altering, spiritual experiences. The first is the perception that they are performances.

This definition undermines the desire to shatter hierarchies between musicians and participants. The second perception sees these events as songfest sing-alongs.

Gathering to sing together is still common practice in Israel and among Israeli communities abroad (Shokeid 1988: 104–25). In these instances, the songs are all in Hebrew, defined as 'songs of the Land of Israel', directly connected to kibbutz culture and perceived as the sacred reservoir of authentic, deep-rooted, Israeli music (Regev 2001: 845). When present in the circle, these two social imaginaries are explicitly rejected by the leaders. Participants are expected to be silent between songs and are encouraged to sing and play instruments.

Moreover, the opening statement concerning the spiritual intentions, given by the leader of the circle, is not associated with a particularly Israeli experience. Also, the songs are mainly not sung in the Hebrew language. New participants sometimes chatter between songs and laugh at the sound of songs in Portuguese or Sanskrit. Some commented that they didn't connect to the songs or that they prefer Hebrew songs. In these exceptional cases, the circle leader broke the silence between songs to repeat the intentions of the circle. On occasion when several participants conversed out loud between the songs, the response was more precise and longer: 'There are people who go to pubs or clubs; there are those who go to songfests and performances. Here we are trying to do something different and between songs there is silence.' Shortly after that, these participants left the circle.

In another exceptional case, I sat next to a couple in their fifties who participated. They both seemed distant and sat outside the song circle. While the woman was silent most of the time and behaved according to the expectations of the circle leaders, her partner joked a lot, whispering and offering interpretations that undermined the definition of the gathering as 'spiritual activity'. For example, when the leader was silent between songs and just announced the number of the song in the songbook to direct participants to sing the next song, this participant laughed quietly and whispered: 'Bingo! I don't connect to this. I want to sleep.' Those sitting near him smiled but continued to sing. Later on, he lay on his back outside the circle and closed his eyes.

Negating sing-alongs contests the national culture that was dominant in Israel for many decades and is still prominent in the Israeli cultural space. Its sounds are heard especially on national memorial days. The Vision of the Forest group's rejection of national imaginaries is absolute. These imaginaries are not present in the songs' content and are explicitly dismissed by the circle leader. Denying the definition as a performance rejects the passivity of the audience and expresses the intention to blur hierarchies. This mission is nonexistent in the urban venue, contrary to the more intimate frameworks of rural locales and natural settings.

Despite sitting in a circle, which emphasizes equality, and inviting the participants to join the singing and playing of instruments, in the city song circle, the circle leader chooses the songs from a songbook distributed to the participants and announces the song number. Moreover, sharing a participant's personal experience after the song choice, although common in rural locations, is absent in the urban song circles of Vision of the Forest. Furthermore, when opening the circle, the Vision of the Forest circle leaders who have actualized their spiritual work in the forest emphasize that 'we bring the sounds of the forest to enlighten this place, so that the sound can go forth from here and spread to other places to change the vibrational frequency.' On occasions when neighbours complained about the volume of the singing, the leader of the song circle said, 'It's good to create cracks in Babylon.'

In the Rainbow Gatherings that have taken place in Israel since 1992, the ambition is to create a temporary, egalitarian, cooperative community that is differentiated from the world outside of it. This external world is identified by those in the gathering by the generic name of 'Babylon'. Its conceptual meaning is a dominating, hierarchical social space, which is in complete opposition to Rainbow values, where the tone of harmony, community and communion in nature prevail (Tavory 2007: 89–90). From discussions with regular participants and the words of the song circle leader, the city of Tel Aviv is given the nickname 'Babylon', symbolizing negative qualities like avarice, overconsumption, alienation and materialism. In one of my conversations with a regular participant of the urban song circles, a student studying psychology, I asked if the Yoga Center is also considered 'Babylon'. The answer was absolutely negative: 'The Yoga Center is not Babylon. My friends are there.' In another instance a circle leader, who emigrated with his family to Costa Rica from Israel but was now visiting, opened his address by saying: 'In the forest there is no need to sing loudly. There is quiet and the flow of water. In the city, loud voices are called for. There is a need to overcome the noise of the city.' In a conversation with one of the circle leaders, I was told: 'Everything is one with nature. We forgot this and we separated. The connection we have in the forest cannot be realized in the city; certainly not in Tel Aviv reeking of ego, money, and sex.' In separate sessions of song circles, circle members who emigrated to Costa Rica and now visit Israel talk about the life in a forest farm and offer this alternative to regular participants of the urban song circles. As such, the forest is a real and metaphorical substitute for urban existence suggested by these circle members.

Along with their activities for spiritual maintenance in the city, these circle members living in Costa Rica are a reminder that this activity exists outside its natural place, and thus urban circles do not facilitate authentic spiritual experience when compared to spiritual experiences in nature. The message is clear—the spirit of the forest can be fully realized only in the forest and within the framework of community life in nature itself. As I shall show below, initiators and participants are not in agreement regarding the hierarchy of authenticity in spiritual experience as structured into the urban sacred song circle.

The Spirit of the Forest: Music beyond Words

> It doesn't matter if you practise yoga, tai chi, tantra, mantra or Kabbalah, every path leads
> to light, awareness ... which is very important at this time ... when there is war. An aware
> person cannot make war ... It is especially important here in Tel Aviv to change the col-
> lective mind, with the stress of everything that is happening here.

These words were spoken by a song circle leader at the time of the Operation Cast
Lead ceasefire (17 January 2009). Contrary to Israeli public opinion regarding the
fighting in Gaza (Ben-Meir 2009), the participants in the song circles cheered the circle leader. This was my first observation, and I was shocked by the response of the
people inside the room because it was completely contrary to opinions heard outside
of it. When the song circle ended, I spoke with a young woman, a graphic designer,
who sat next to me. She shared the deep feeling of loneliness she felt at work since
the war began: 'I don't share my opinions with my colleagues. Everyone speaks of
the war as being a just one and I don't dare bring forth my different views. I am so
happy that I came here today.'

Direct reference to political aspects was absent from the sacred song circles and
was not present in conversations among participants before or after the song circles.
Before the general elections of 2009, the Green Party's election propaganda could be
found in the entranceway to the Yoga Center alongside information about workshops
and calling cards of therapists of various methods. However, this propaganda was not
given any special attention by the participants, and the Yoga Center did not hold political gatherings. In my conversations with various participants, issues were raised that
primarily expressed the personal support that they derive from their participation in
urban song circles, especially in situations of great difficulty. Thus, for example, one of
the regular participants told me that a building next to her residence in the city went up
in flames. She shared the anxiety she experienced during the night but did not continue
to describe her emotions, rather she immediately added: 'I came here. I am taking care
of myself. I feel that there will be something very strong here [in the circle] today.'

When I first was introduced to song circles, I was surprised at the variety of languages sung in the Vision of the Forest circles. Is it possible that a random crowd
would know Portuguese and Sanskrit in addition to English? It took a year of monthly
participant observations to understand that very few understand the words of the songs,
which are only partially translated to English. Perhaps more important was the process of understanding and feeling the message restated at the beginning of each circle,
which echoed in my mind: 'The words are not important, the vibrational frequency is
the core.' 'Raising the vibration' or touching 'higher energies', in this context, means
that the group action creates a change in the collective consciousness towards a reality
of peace and tranquillity. According to its leaders, the spirit of the forest reminds city
dwellers of the quiet, simplicity and confidence of the earth through its song circles.

Many of the participants of the urban song circles sing with their eyes closed, focusing their attention on the singing and the sounds of the varied instruments around them: guitars, bongo drums, flutes, rain sticks (a cylinder with various granules inside) and wind chimes. Reminiscent of flowing water and wind, the tones suit the circle leader's ideas of bringing the sounds of the forest to the city. A young man participated in one of the urban meetings by playing whistles and imitating bird calls throughout the songs. At the other meetings, the involvement was primarily with singing, and there was less instrumental music.

The forest is the source of inspiration for original musical creations and is present in many of the songs that transmit messages of simplicity and connection to the earth. The song that opens most of the urban song circles is a well-known Rainbow song: 'Humble'. Its last verse is sung in the cities with very intense power:

> Humble yourself to the spirit of the forest
> You gotta bend down low
> Humble yourself to the spirit of the forest
> Don't be afraid to let go
> And We, we shall lift each other up
> Higher and higher
> We, we shall lift each other up

Another Rainbow song that is sung at most of the urban circles is 'I Find My Joy':

> I find my joy in the simple things
> coming from the earth
> I find my joy in the sun that shines
> and the water that sings to me
> listen to the wind and listen to the water
> hear what they say
> singing
> Heya Heya Heya Heya Heya Heya Ho

Most of the songs transmit simple messages of love of nature and harmony among all of life's creatures. The song that closed many of the Vision of the Forest's song circles is the song 'United':

> Sisters and Brothers
> We are united
> We are One
> Change the face of the world out there
> Give respect to Mother Earth
> See the Spirit inside ourselves
> Know what we are really worth

The participants are already standing in a circle, holding hands, breathing deeply and smiling. Moreover, at the end of the song, the leader of the circle expresses the wish that all the participants will take the spirit of the forest with them throughout the next week: 'Pass on the frequency and what you feel here to every encounter with people.'

Regular participants of circles of the Vision of the Forest group also listen to the circle's songs during the week. Recordings of these songs are on the Internet, and for a nominal sum, a CD of the recordings of song circles can be purchased at the Yoga Center. One of the regular participants of the urban song circles said to me: 'I listen to the songs at home, and while travelling. These songs flow in my body; they are in my veins.'

In its urban circles, the Vision of the Forest group sings hit songs from festivals and other song circles. They seldom sing songs in Portuguese. In the more intimate circles, which are not open to the public at large, the songs have a greater focus on the forest, where the group attains its vision. Then most of the songs are in Portuguese and connect to shamanic ceremonies, which originate from Brazil. The only case in which a participant disclosed difficulty in singing was at an intimate song circle gathering of fifteen circle members at a participant's home in a rural area. The difficulty was due to an external event in March 2011—the earthquake in Japan and the huge tsunami that followed causing many deaths. Shaken by the event, he chose to share his difficulty in the circle: 'I am angry. Right now I find it hard to sing songs to nature, to the forest, to mother earth when so much damage and suffering fills Japan today.' As is the way in intimate circles, after the sharing, a song was chosen, the circle continued and after that the participants listened to the sharing of another participant. Even the most intimate circle is not a discussion group or a therapy group, but it does enable its members to share a central issue for them during the circle. The messages transmitted by the participants are not unified around common themes. Many of the messages are coded in the idiosyncratic language of the participants. But each message is received without judgement or criticism, generally to cries of 'Aho' and, in the forest songs finale, there are cries of 'Viva Floresta!' This atmosphere is reflected at the urban circles and is frequently referred to by the circle leader, who said: 'What happens here (in the Yoga Center) between us is reality. This is the real world, not the race outside.'

Simulation of Forest Life?

Aside from aforementioned messages of the leader of the circle that emphasize the unique atmosphere created at the Yoga Center song circles, and expressing the wish for collective, consciousness change, especially in the city, there is an emphasis on the hierarchy between various physical spaces in which song circles are held. For the leader of the circle and for many of the members, a full spiritual life can be experienced in the framework of the spiritual community in the forest of Costa Rica. Once a leader of the circle defined the Yoga Center as 'our home in the city', as well as the 'display window' for their activities. In the same vein, a regular participant in urban sacred song circles and in other places throughout Israel told me: 'What you see here at the Yoga Center is just the tip of the iceberg.' The real experience is at the ceremonies in nature. However, in conversations with regular urban song circle participants, I was exposed to various views regarding the actual implementation of the Vision of the Forest and to various opinions regarding the proposals to join the Vision of the Forest community in Costa Rica. I found a range of views from being distant and avoiding the inner circle to admiration of those who implement the fantasy of living in the forest. When the leaders of the Vision of the Forest invited the urban song circle to join them in a song circle and shamanic ceremony in a rural area of Israel, I asked one participant if I could attend with my family. She looked at me surprised and said resolutely, 'This is really not an event for children.' In another instance, I asked a participant if she is considering joining them in the Costa Rican forest. Her answer was: 'Are you crazy?! They have nothing there! They live like pioneers lived here 100 years ago. That kind of life doesn't suit me.'

In a conversation on this issue with members of the inner circle, it was claimed that life's constraints prevented them from joining life in the forest. Thus, for example, a student and regular participant in song circles said to me: 'I wish I could; I can't travel there at the moment, but maybe after I finish my studies.' So it was for many urban song circle participants; the forest in Costa Rica is a fantasy that most do not bring to fruition. Many are satisfied with slight involvement in the 'momentary community' and solidarity among strangers, enabling personal memories to find momentary continuity in the representations of forest life through the urban song circles.

In addition, I discovered that the inner circle group knew very little about Costa Rica, the land for enacting their vision. To them the forest is an unlimited, infinite space, beyond specific social and historical context. In a conversation with one of the circle leaders I said, 'You know, Costa Rica is a country without an army.' He responded in wonder: 'Really?' I didn't know that.' I added: 'There are quite a few Israelis and Israeli spiritual centres in Costa Rica.' To that he replied: 'What others are doing doesn't interest me. There is room for everyone.' When I expressed concern that the success of the Vision of the Forest community will mark the destruction of the forest as hundreds of Israelis and others put it on their touring maps, he responded: 'Excellent! Let everyone come and we'll make money! The forest has nothing to worry about, everything is ecological there. The forests are huge; it isn't like Israeli forests.'

Regarding the specific forest site purchased by the cooperative effort of the community members, my impression is that there is great excitement about the possibility of establishing a community that lives on spiritual hospitality, ceremonies and workshops. However, metaphorically, the members of the community in the best-case scenario may nurture a tree but do not see the forest. Economic, political and moral implications of their initiative are absent from the inner group's discourse. Their interest focuses on personal spiritual work and individual journeys, their desire to live together in nature in a cooperative, spiritual community and the inability and lack of desire to implement this ambition in Israel. Furthermore, this perception of ideal community forest life opposes the Jewish-Hasidic European tradition, which is present and renewed in contemporary spiritual discourse (Garb 2009: 13–5).

According to this approach, nature is wild and is placed in contrast to the city. In this tradition, the forest has contradictory meanings. On the one hand, it is seen as a threatening, dangerous, savage place where demons and other pernicious beings dwell, and a place of blurred boundaries between human reality and the world of witches and the dead (Bar-Levav 2004: 202–4). On the other hand, the forest symbolizes a positive essence in itself. The entrance to the forest is a doorway to a world of mystical experience and spiritual ascension to another level. People can hear the music of harmonic creation only in special conditions of the forest. After a mystical encounter with nature in the forest, an individual can achieve a sense of absolute harmony in every contact with each part of nature. Yet, even with this interpretation of 'being' in the forest, and however anchoring the experience may be, this encounter is neither the aim nor the purpose. Human purpose is manifested upon one's exit from the forest and return to the city (Even-Israel 2011: 104–7).

Moreover, the Vision of the Forest circle leaders chose a cooperative model, although connections to the idea of the kibbutz are denied. The word 'commune' is also absent from the discourse as the group prefers the definition of 'community' with its positive connotation (Bauman 2001: 1–7). De facto, the group members live according to the primary idea of many communes, as well as the kibbutz at its outset: from each according to his abilities, for each according to his needs. Their negation of nationalism is naturally different from the Israeli kibbutz, which was established for the most part to realize national objectives (Yuchtman-Yaar, Ben-Rafael and Soker 2000). Still, their rejection of any connection to national culture is full of contradictions. While they aspire to establish a community cut off from nationality, they approach mostly those similar to them—Jews and Israelis—as potential additions to forest life. Indeed, an article published in an Internet newspaper described the community's activity and their vision, to which one of the talkbacks with cynical astonishment commented: 'Going to the jungle to get stuck with Israelis? That can easily be done in another place—it's called Israel.'

Despite claiming that they wish to 'just live', when asked 'How do you live in the forest?' or 'What do you do in the forest?' it appears that they do in fact rely on their nationality. Until the spiritual community tourism initiative in the Costa Rican forest succeeds, the group members make their living from selling the Israeli national food—falafel—in a local market in a Costa Rican village.

In mid-July 2011, the members of song circles—participants, those playing instruments and creators—relocated to one of the most expensive residential streets in the centre of Tel Aviv, Rothschild Blvd. They were among the first to join and support the 'tent protest'. This protest was characterized as a 'young protest'. Its leaders were young, and the main demands focused on the life of the young and their expectations, hopes and difficulties. In addition, the protest articulated the apprehension of the 'brain drain' of the young, and the worry of the parent generation for the younger generation. At its height during the month of July, the protest had the overwhelming support of the public—more than 90 per cent support among the Jewish population of Israel (Haber, Heller and Hermann 2011: 1–3).

While the central voice of the various demonstrations throughout Israel cried out its 'demand [for] social justice', 'a welfare state', and criticized the high cost of living and housing in Israel, in the tepee set up in the centre of the boulevard, where many song circle members gathered, another interpretation of the protest was offered and influenced the style of protest. It supported the dominant voice of the protest—the ambition to blur hierarchies and contain all the social sectors. A nonviolent protest including song circles open to the greater public, a common central kitchen and an attempt to have a tepee founded on ecological principles. Students of alternative medicine came with treatment tables and offered various treatments. Song circles were held every evening in the centre of the boulevard in an area with a sign near the tepee tent that read 'Sababylon'—which is a combination of Babylon and Sababa[1]—meaning 'cool' in Tel Aviv.

In the second week of the protest, circle promoters came to the city and organized singing through the night. Afterwards, one of the Vision of the Forest leaders wrote the following message on Facebook to his friends throughout the world:

> For all global (non-Hebrew speakers) family [members] … an amazing consciousness shift is happening in Israel, the protest for freedom and the voice of the people is reaching a new level. So many people with tents all over the big cities, creating a Tribal Energy, connecting with a new fragrance of change and simple Love, so much music and truth in the air … may the love we share here spread its wings … viva the revolution.

One of the musicians participating in many of the song circles at the Yoga Center joined the tent and shared his view of the protest with his Facebook friends:

> This is the first time I saw the yuppie culture in Tel Aviv. Rainbow in the centre of Tel Aviv—tepee, common kitchen, sharing food free to all and there is never a lack for anyone. People coming to camp out for a week, talking about what they think, love, don't love … about how they work all the time just to pay the rent. Suddenly they think: maybe I don't have to be a slave all my life? Maybe I can live in a tent? Maybe I will find a community and join it? Why should I live in the centre of the city and pay so dearly? People are discovering now that there is another way to live. For me, this has the meaning of revolution!

The Vision of the Forest group, one of many offering their wares in the 'tent city', was actualizing a path towards consciousness change. The message of containing and the unity of all living creatures that was transmitted in festivals, song circles at the Yoga Center and in the Sababylon site integrated well with the intentions of some of the leaders of the protest—the most prominent being Daphni Leef.

At the protest with estimates of a quarter of a million participants from all over Israel, she said:

> My generation grew up with the feeling that we were alone in the world. This is us fac-
> ing the screen. That the other is our enemy, that he competes with us, we grew up with
> the feeling that we are living a race we have no chance of winning and that we cannot
> count on anyone else. We were taught that it is either you or him. That is capitalism—
> competition that never ends. The fact that this generation—the most lonely and closed
> generation—woke up and did something is not short of a miracle. The miracle of
> summer 2011. Here, everything we thought, everything we were taught, is not true! ...
> This summer, day after day, week after week, we went into the streets and made things
> clear, not just to the government, but also to ourselves, that there is something to live
> for! And the minute that we understood this, the moments that we began to think of
> tomorrow together we all were set free! ... What kind of world doesn't have a place
> for dreamers, for idealists, for poets? What kind of world disinherits them? This is a
> world of poverty, because we all dream and we all have the right to dream. To be poor
> is not only not being able to finish the month financially or to be without shelter. To
> be poor is to be bothered by these things, but to the very foundation, to the point that
> you cannot dream, think, learn, hug your children ... The fact that we all went out to
> the street we found a home. (Leef 2011)

In the city centre, the Vision of the Forest group participated in creating a place; for them it was another simulation of alternative living, but, in contrast to the other voices of protest, their vision did not relate to the struggle for 'right to the city' or the future of Israeli society. Theirs was a call to all those feeling placeless because the local place did not offer community or a sense of belonging. Their call was to live outside the city, outside a national space—living in a spiritual community in the forest. The Vision of the Forest leaders appeared on the boulevard for a moment and then, in the third week of the protests, took off for the forests of Costa Rica.

Concluding Remarks

The spiritual work of the Vision of the Forest group, whose members wander among circles in different spatial locations, creates new imaginary places—in the city, in rural areas and in the forest—and invites movement between them. This movement creates connections between various areas but, at the same time, also creates new differentiations between enclaves.

The group members bring the spirit of the forest to the city as a simulation experience of spiritual community life, harmony and cooperation. For them, the true spiritual experience is in nature, in the forest to which they immigrated. As noted above, regular members of the urban circles are sometimes invited to intimate song circles taking place in the homes of inner circle members in rural areas. But despite their differences, both urban and rural circles remind members that community life can only be fully attained in one place—the forest. This message is intended for the circle leaders and the members of the inner circle.

My ethnographic work suggests that participants use the circles to fill different, personal needs. Bringing the forest to the city through sacred song circles is a way to spread the vision of the group living in the forest to individuals who, among other things, seek spiritual growth and a sense of community in the city. Many of them draw strength from the forest as an imaginary entity that is carried with them into their work routine and placed in urban social spaces that contrast the atmosphere of the circle. Thus, despite the different concrete goals, the Vision of the Forest group actively participates in the creation and maintenance of urban spiritual enclaves that produce intimacy and agreement between familiar strangers. This atmosphere is achieved by the resolute negation of interpretations forming social imaginaries opposing the spirit of the forest (performances, sing-alongs). For the leaders of the song circles, as well as for some of the participants, the spirit of the forest is both individual and communal and inundates all the senses both at the declarative level and while singing the sacred songs. It exists beyond words, beyond national borders, outside specific social context and separate from political and moral questions. For a moment, during the protest of summer 2011, these messages were present throughout the streets of the city and integrated in the political criticism.

Notes

I wish to express my gratitude to Yael Enoch, Matat Adar-Bunis, Sigal Alon, Tamar Hermann, Adriana Kamp, Moshe Shokied and two anonymous readers for their helpful comments. The fieldwork was carried out between January 2009 and July 2011. Names of individuals and groups in this study have been changed to protect the participants' privacy.

1. In literary Arabic, the meaning is yearning for a loved one. But this meaning is not known to most Hebrew speakers who use the word as slang, meaning 'cool', excellent, wonderful. It is interesting to note that Arab speakers in Israel also use this word in the same way as Hebrew slang. I thank Ruvik Rosental and Mohammad Massalha for the clarification.

References

Bar-Levav, A. 2004. 'The Bridge to the Human: The Myth of Tantalus in the Story of the Marriage of a Man and Demon'. In C. Bin-Nun, ed., *The Cradle of*

Creativity: Shlomo Giora Shoham Jubilee Volume [in Hebrew]. Hod Ha-Sharon: Sha'arei Mishpat, 199–206.

Bauman, Z. 2001. *Community: Seeking Safety in an Insecure World.* Cambridge: Polity.

Ben-Meir, Y. 2009. 'Operation Cast Lead: Political Dimensions and Public Opinion'. *Strategic Assessment* 11(4): 29–34. The Institute for National Security Studies: Tel-Aviv University.

Borer, I. M. 2010. 'From Collective Memory to Collective Imagination; Time, and Urban Redevelopment'. *Symbolic Interaction* 33: 97–114.

Cohen, E. 2008. 'Taking Distance: Israeli Backpackers and Their Society'. In J. Brauch, A. Lipphardt and A. Nock, eds, *Jewish Topographies: Visions of Space, Traditions of Place.* Aldershot: Ashgate, 265–77.

Enoch, Y., and R. Grossman. 2010. 'Blogs of Israeli and Danish Backpackers to India'. *Annals of Tourism Research* 37: 520–36.

Even-Israel, A. 2011. *Six Stories of Rabbi Nachman of Bratzlav* [in Hebrew]. Tel-Aviv: Dvir.

Garb, J. 2009. *The Chosen Will Become Herds: Studies in Twentieth Century Kabbalah.* New Haven, CT: Yale University.

Haber, K., E. Heller and T. Hermann. 2011. 'Solidarity in Summer 2011 Protest?' [in Hebrew]. *The Israel Democracy Institute.* 1–12.

Hancock, M., and S. Srinivas. 2008. 'Symposium: Spaces of Modernity: Religion and the Urban in Asia and Africa'. *International Journal of Urban and Regional Research* 32: 617–30.

Hervieu-Léger, D. 2002. 'Space and Religion: New Approaches to Religious Spatiality in Modernity'. *International Journal of Urban and Regional Research* 26: 99–105.

Holman, C. 2011. 'Surfing for Shaman: Analyzing an Ayahuasca Website'. *Annals of Tourism Research* 38: 90–109.

Ivakhiv, J. A. 2007. 'Power Trips: Making Sacred Space in New Age Pilgrimage'. In J. Lewis and D. Kemp, eds, *Handbook of New Age Religion.* Amsterdam: Brill Academic, 263–86.

Leef, D. 2011. 'We Opened Our Eyes and They Will Not Be Closed Again' [in Hebrew]. *The Official Struggle Site.* Available at: http://j14.org.il/articles/4797. Accessed 4 September 2011.

Luna, L. E. 2003. 'Ayahuasca Shamanism Shared Across Cultures'. *Cultural Survival Quarterly* 27: 20–3.

Maoz, D. 2007. 'Backpackers' Motivations: The Role of Culture and Nationality'. *Annals of Tourism Research* 34: 122–40.

Massey, D. 1994. *Space, Place and Gender.* Minneapolis: University of Minnesota Press.

Noy, C., and E. Cohen. 2005. *Israeli Backpackers: From Tourism to Rite of Passage.* Albany: State University of New York Press.

Ram, U. 2007. *The Globalization of Israel: McWorld in Tel Aviv, Jihad in Jerusalem.* London: Routledge.

Ram, U. 2008. 'Why Secularism Fails? Secular Nationalism and Religious Revivalism in Israel'. *International Journal of Politics, Culture and Society* 21: 57–73.

Regev, M. 2001. 'Introduction to Israeli Culture'. In E. Ya'ar and Z. Shavit, eds, *Trends in Israeli Society* [in Hebrew]. Tel-Aviv: Open University Press, 823–98.

Shanon, B. 2002. *The Antipodes of the Mind: Charting the Phenomenology of the Ayahuasca Experience.* New York: Oxford University Press.

Sharpley, E. R., and D. Jepson. 2011. 'Rural Tourism: A Spiritual Experience?' *Annals of Tourism Research* 38: 52–71.

Shokeid, M. 1988. *Children of Circumstances: Israeli Immigrants in New York.* Ithaca, NY: Cornell University Press.

Simchai, D. 2009. *Flowing against the Flow* [in Hebrew]. Haifa: Pardes Press.

Statistical Abstract of Israel. (2012). 'Planted Forest Area'. The Central Bureau of Statistics. Available at: http://www.cbs.gov.il/reader/shnaton/shnatone_new.htm.

Sznaider, N. 2000. 'Consumerism as Civilizing Process: Israel and Judaism in the Second Age of Modernity'. *International Journal of Politics, Culture and Society* 14: 297–314.

Tavory, I. 2007. 'The Rainbow and "Babylon": Dynamics of Resistance and Continuity'. In I. Tavory, ed., *Dancing in a Thorn-field: The New Age Spirituality in Israel* [in Hebrew]. Tel Aviv: Hakibutz Hameuhad Press, 89–119.

Tavory, I., and Y. C. Goodman. 2009. '"A Collective of Individuals": Between Self and Solidarity in a Rainbow Gathering'. *Sociology of Religion* 70: 262–84.

Trigger, D., and J. Mulcock. 2005. 'Forests as Spiritually Significant Places: Nature, Culture and "Belonging" in Australia'. *The Australian Journal of Anthropology* 16: 306–20.

Vinitzky-Seroussi, V. 1998. 'Jerusalem Assassinated Rabin and Tel-Aviv Commemorated Him'. *City and Society* 1: 1–21.

Williams, K., and D. Harvey. 2001. 'Transcendent Experience in Forest Environment'. *Journal of Environmental Psychology* 21: 249–60.

Yuchtman-Yaar, E., E. Ben-Rafael and Z. Soker. 2000. *The Kibbutz and Israeli Society* [in Hebrew]. Tel-Aviv: Open University.

–6–

Sensuous Photographies: Living Things
Explored through Phenomenological Practice

Carole Baker

Introduction

As an artist photographer, my interest lies in exploring, through practice, experiential approaches to nature and more precisely to living things. One of the most productive and enlivening sources of inspiration for contemporary artists over the last few years, particularly in the physical arts, such as dance, theatre, interactive computing and film, has emerged from a critical reevaluation of phenomenology, which has given rise to works as diverse as Olafur Eliasson's installation 'The Weather Project' (2003) and Susan Kozel's performance 'Yellow Memory' (2009), and has expanded the whole notion of what constitutes practice. Still photography, a medium characterized by the visual, the representational and the technological, does not immediately appear to share a natural affinity with a philosophy that foregrounds firsthand *lived* bodily experience. Yet, despite these apparent dissimilarities, this productive enquiry begins to question the very nature of photographic practice. It will, in particular, encompass the *process* of making creative work and the viewer's response to it, areas which have received relatively meagre critical attention (Flusser 2000; Pettersson 2011) when compared to that given to the analysis of photographs as representations. This chapter, then, seeks to position the photographic artist within the context of phenomenological practice and to explore the possibilities of such an engagement.

My aim is to construct a conceptual framework that supports, and allows an expansion of, my personal photographic practice. This practice is, in part, a response to the lively theoretical debate that is currently being generated within the social sciences on the subject of nature, which is questioning the very basis of human positioning in the world. Semiotic cultural constructions interpret, classify, order and largely dominate nature, but nature is also experienced firsthand through lived, phenomenological being-in-the-world (Csordas 1994: 11). Nature is at the very centre of phenomenological enquiry since it entails positioning the human as a living being within the context of a living world. Photography, as a complex cultural practice, combines both representational and phenomenological characteristics. Looked at as a process, photographic practice operates on a number of levels as '[r]epresentations are embodied and drawn into a felt "doing" and knowledge in practice' (Crouch 2001: 68). The practice of photographic art, with its ability to represent the world so persuasively whilst also providing symbolic meaning, offers a potentially fertile means of exploring this complex area and bridging the gap between representation and practice.

In this chapter, I reference the work of contemporary Japanese photographers Rinko Kawauchi and Masao Yamamoto to illuminate and develop aspects of my own photographic research. These practitioners have been chosen because aspects of their process, the work itself and viewer engagement with the work (and through it, with what the work reveals about human relationships with nature), could be understood as phenomenological in some sense. Over the past few decades, Japanese photography has emerged into the global art world seemingly free from hidebound Western photographic tradition and with an expressive force and arresting visual power that has taken the medium in new directions. The work of Kawauchi and Yamamoto is, thus, a merging of Eastern and Western cultures, with strands of influence from diverse cultural sources. Japanese concepts of nature are equally complex and mutable, with traditional national values interwoven with global modernist ideologies (Thomas 2001).

Immersed in Nature

Through photographic practice I am seeking to explore our human connection with living things, a timely enquiry since nature appears to have joined the urban as the focus of contemporary cultural discourse. Over the past two decades, photographic practitioners have explored nature with renewed interest, reflecting a more widespread enquiry conducted by social scientists into 'the question of nature' (Whatmore 2002: 3). This curiosity about nature is perhaps a response to the increase in the scale of destruction of the natural environment, the rapid expansion of an urbanized and technologized world and an associated sense concerning the loss of an intrinsic aspect of humanness: 'a feared negation of materialities and those things that matter' (Rose and Tolia-Kelly 2012: 2). Or perhaps it is simply the result of intellectual curiosity in an Otherness that still retains a sense of mystery in an increasingly disenchanted world (Clark 1997). Julia Adeney Thomas offers a further explanation, arguing that the project of modernity fails to liberate the individual consciousness from the deterministic forces of biology and geography by transcending and controlling nature. This, Thomas claims, has led to the contemporary need to reinstate the human subject's relation to nature (2001: 20–6).

Certainly, the increasing distance that has grown between humans and other living things with the expansion of urbanization appears to be generating an anxiety, which is giving rise to renewed attempts to reconnect our bodies with nature and the environment. To some extent, it could be said to account for the rise in interest in the phenomenology of practices. While postmodernist anxieties portrayed a human condition caught in a web of signifying practices, preventing direct contact with the 'real' world, recent attempts to renegotiate a connection with the world are positioning humans in the midst of it. Once characterized in Western thought as a passive background to human activity, the nonhuman, including animals, plants and the inorganic, is also undergoing a reconceptualization and is emerging as a vital and dynamic force in its own right. Owain Jones and Paul Cloke, for example, describe a nature that is not merely inscribed upon by human culture and practice, but that '"pushes back" with its own vitality which is manifest in specific material processes' (2002: 6). Doreen Massey (2005: 98), characterizing a more conventional view of nature, points out that its supposed docility is frequently set against the dynamism of culture and, as such, provides a stability on which the global mobilities of technology and culture can play. Relationships with nature in the West, based on domination and exploitation and maintained by the nature-culture binary, are no longer tenable or productive. In the light of this awareness, new forms of connection are being sought, particularly those based on empathy, cooperation and participation, which Wolfe describes as escaping 'the dialectical vortex of nature-society relations' (Whatmore 2002: 2).

By choosing an apple orchard as my subject matter, my work engages with a site that could be described as a hybrid space, where nature and culture intersect (Figure 6.1). This engagement opens up many possibilities for conceptualizing a less objectifying and more reciprocal relationship with a nature that is regarded as active, creative and dynamic. I have chosen to conduct this investigation through visual, material practice (practice, according to Rose, 'is what humans do with things' [Rose and Tolia-Kelly 2012: 3]) since through visual practice we are able to realize and make apparent the interconnections that exist between our human first-person perspective and objects in the world around us. Visual practice 'considers the (geo)politics of embodied, material encounter and engagement' and 'unravels, disturbs and connects with *processes, embodied practices and technologies*' (Rose and Tolia-Kelly 2012: 3, original emphasis). It thus provides a way of investigating the world from within our situated, embodied perspective and is able to incorporate some sense of the multiplicity of positions and negotiations that living things adopt in relation to one another and to the world. Perhaps it is even possible for the process of creative practice itself to transform and deepen connections with the natural environment. By working in a holistic, empathetic and immersive way in relation to the world around us, could we begin to erode interspecies divisions and reconnect with nature? And could this experience then be shared with others through resultant artworks? These are questions that I am concerned with in my own creative photographic practice.

Figure 6.1 Orchard image 1 by Carole Baker.

The World 'Already There'

A fundamental characteristic shared by both photography and phenomenological enquiry is that both begin with the world as it is presented to us: the multispecies world
that is 'already there', before reflection begins (Merleau-Ponty 1962: vii). Painting,
in contrast, starts with a blank canvas and is more akin to Descartes's philosophical
method in the *Meditations,* which erases all beliefs in order to begin with one indubi-
table truth. The photograph replicates the inalienable presence of the physical world.
By choosing photographic materials and processes, the photographer is able to affect
how the world visually appears in the photograph but nevertheless must work *with*
the material conditions of the world. It could also be argued that a photograph does
not *capture* a fully-formed, passive world; rather, the world is an active *participant*
in the making of the photograph, for it imposes its presence upon the lens.

For the photographer who aims to compose meaningful images, the visual surplus
of the world can be problematic, for it introduces 'indefiniteness, endlessness, random arrangement', as Rudolf Arnheim puts it:

> The optically projected image ... is characterized by the visual accidents of a world that
> has not been created for the convenience of the photographer, and it would be a mis-
> take to force these unwieldy data of reality into the straitjacket of pictorial composition.
> (1974: 158)

For other photographers, the contingency, chance and accident (or alternatively, serendipity) to which photography, as a medium, gives rise is a critical component of their practice. Both photographers in my study have expressed their openness to incorporate into their work things that they encounter in the world. In a video interview, Yamamoto reveals that, '[w]hen I photograph, I start out with an open mind. If I start out with a precise idea of what I want to photograph, I might miss an interesting event or object' (Berthomé and Bosdedore 2009). And Kawauchi states that '[f]or a photographer, it's a necessity that you can shoot stuff magically. Accidents are necessary' (D'Addario 2012). This suggests an *intuitive* practice that is liberating, suspends conscious thought and establishes a direct, empathetic engagement with the world. This approach allows the body to make decisions in ways other than through conscious thought; as Merlin Donald argues, consciousness provides only a small window of awareness, while 'most of what we achieve takes place unconsciously' (2001: 25).

Kawauchi's photographs, in particular, demonstrate an exhilarating freedom in her use of the camera, her photographs being more akin to direct perceptual responses to the world than to attempts to contain or control it. The variety and immediacy of Kawauchi's photographs allow the viewer the chance to experience something of the vitality of the sensing body, which as David Abram notes 'is an open and active form, continually improvising its relation to things and to the world' (1997: 49). Kawauchi's technique, whilst highly skilled, seems almost artless and naïve, appearing to disregard the more conventional 'correct' forms of photography, with their careful control of composition, exposure, depth of field and focus. Viewed in this way, these photographs become records of the photographer's firsthand, lived experience as she engages with the world; images are unified by her unique subjectivity. On viewing the completed body of photographs, the viewer is aware of Kawauchi's subjectivity and, simultaneously, is able imaginatively to take her place as the central consciousness of the work.

The ongoing interchange that occurs between body and world has been likened to a conversation (Beneditktsson and Lund 2010: 2–4), in that it involves both attention and action, a 'dynamic blend of receptivity and creativity' (Abram 1997: 50) on the part of the human subject, and a corresponding reciprocity from the nonhuman participant. The photographer could be considered to be engaging in a form of conversation with the world in the practice of their work. Nature, as the central concern of the work of Kawauchi, Yamamoto and myself, is a realm to which we can assign an independent vitality. The metaphor of the conversation assigns active agency to both participants, thereby recognizing nonhuman agency, a notion that attempts to decentre human agency by breaking down any nature-culture divide. It also enables the material and the social to intertwine and interact in unique ways. Jones and Cloke (2002: 129) recognize the 'unique creativity of being able to produce fruit' that trees possess, making them 'purposive ... transformative and even creative' (2002: 7). This notion relies upon an openness between human and nonhuman and a reassessment of the boundaries that separate (or unite) the two. As humans we are not separate and distant from the world, but connected and porous; exchanging air, light, energy, organic materials and liquids, as well as imaginative and affective states. Abram (1997: 57) noted that in his work, Merleau-Ponty regarded perception as always involving 'the experience of an active interplay, or coupling, between the perceiving body and that which it perceives'. The self and the world are constantly renewing one another through their interaction from moment to moment and cannot be regarded as static. This dynamic emergence can also be transferred to the photograph when viewed; the meaning of the photograph then slips and shifts and refuses to solidify.

The Body of the Photographer

In using the camera as a tool, my practice involves a direct, complex and dynamic bodily engagement with living things that are equally complex and dynamic. A renewed interest in the material world and the development of theories of embodiment (Csordas 1994; Bennet 2010; Coole and Frost 2010) has provided the basis for current phenomenological thinking. This 'turn to the body' conceptualizes bodies not as fixed, material entities, but as the epitome of flux (Csordas 1994: 2). There is 'no longer such a thing as a relatively fixed and consistent person—a person with a recognizable identity—confronting a potentially predictable world, but rather two turbulences enmeshed with each other' (Phillips 1999: 20).

For Merleau-Ponty, the body is not the material mechanism of Cartesian dualism, directed by an immaterial consciousness, but is constituted by a wide range of cognitive, affective and motor activities; it is able to think, remember, imagine, feel and act in an embodied way. The body is a holistic entity, interwoven with mental and physical capacities, and positioned within the context of the world. Importantly, the body is open and extends out into the world; it is a relational mechanism that is adapted for the social.

Increasing critical attention is now centred on the concept of the social, and its possible expansion to allow it to encompass other living things (Thrift 2007: 21), in opposition to the human-centredness of much previous enquiry. David Harvey, for example, argues that 'the artificial break between "society" and "nature" must be eroded, rendered porous, and eventually dissolved' (1996: 192), while Tim Ingold (1997: 249–50) suggests that there is a need to dissolve 'the category of the social' and 'to re-embed these [human] relationships within the continuum of organic life'. Sarah Whatmore suggests that it is time for 'a re-cognition of the intimate, sensible and hectic bonds through which people and plants; devices and creatures; documents and elements take and hold their shape in relation to each other in the fabric of everyday life' (2002: 3). A photographic practice that emerges from such debates cannot simply be an observational one that documents a distant and discrete nature but must be cognizant of the fact that the photographer, and the viewer, are themselves part of nature. This acknowledgement demands a more complex and multilayered engagement on the part of the photographer and a practice that recognizes the web of connections in which humans are immersed.

The Senses as Interface

A human being interfaces the world through the senses, a process that gives rise to feelings, thoughts, emotions and imaginings. At its most basic level, our sense of sight can produce in us instinctive feelings of visual pleasure as it responds to the world around us. In Michel de Certeau's poetic response to Merleau-Ponty's *Visible and Invisible,* he describes vision as 'the bursting apart as well as the brilliance of the thing seen—a particular shade of blue, a form, a contrast' (1983: 29). He praises Merleau-Ponty's text for its unconscious, incantatory language, and de Certeau's own imagistic writing, for example in his use of metaphors of the sea, is particularly apt in exploring a vision rooted in the material that opens out towards the world in an act of 'perceptual faith' (de Certeau 1983: 24). The immediacy and vibrancy of vision is apparent in the photographic work of Kawauchi and Yamamoto, whose images strike the eye, seducing the senses and 'captivating' the viewer. In a transcribed interview, Kawauchi tells us:

> People often say that I have a child's eye. For example, I stare at ants gathering around sugar, or when I seek shelter from the rain, I gaze upon snails. These are things which you often do when you are a child aren't they? I have a very similar sensibility to that. (Mayalina 2006)

This lack of guile suggests a primitive look associated with childhood, prior to the corruption brought by knowledge. Engaging with the work of Yamamoto and Kawauchi, we can begin to access a vision that, through a heightened sensitivity to the everyday world, extends an empathy and openness to the minutiae surrounding us, creating an awareness of ourselves as organisms among the things of the world.

The more profoundly we look, the more that is revealed to us (the world is endless, limitless in this sense), and this continual process of discovery stimulates creative activity. Merleau-Ponty sees in Cézanne's intensity of looking 'the same kind of attentiveness and wonder, the same demand for awareness, the same will to seize the meaning of the world that occurs in phenomenology' (1962: xxiv). But, how can this profound looking be achieved, and is it open to everyone or merely a few visionary artists? Laura Sewall (1999: 14) believes that it is possible to cultivate our sensitivity and awaken and recover 'the fullness of our sensory, sensual, and perceptual capacities' and discover 'the very lusciousness of having senses' by developing a greater understanding of the capacity of our perception and recognizing its ability to connect us to the world through a web of relations.

What is it that makes the photographer release the shutter at a precise moment? Perhaps, as Abram argues, things in the world reach out to us, demanding our attention. He asks the question, 'Where does perception originate?' (Abram 1997: 53). For Merleau-Ponty, it is neither in the perceiver nor the perceived, but rather, perception occurs between, as body and world merge in a reciprocal and sympathetic relation:

> [M]y gaze pairs off with colour, and my hand with hardness and softness, and in this transaction between the subject of sensation and the sensible it cannot be held that one acts while the other suffers the action, or that one confers significance on the other. (1962: 214)

The use of focus and depth of field allow the photographer to manipulate the viewer's gaze, to determine what is open to detailed study and what is relegated to a generalized vision. The photographic work is a catalyst that evokes a response in viewers through the arousal of their own sensations, thoughts, emotions, memories and imagination.

Movement: The World in Flux

A nature (such as that of human beings) that is undergoing constant change cannot be considered a preexisting reality but is instead continually emerging through time. This heightens our temporal awareness, a central feature of phenomenological enquiry, as Ingold (1993: 152) affirms when he writes that '[h]uman life is a process that involves the passage of time.' There is no faculty in us that is dedicated to the calculation of time, and yet we are able, through our subjective experience, to feel that we are living through time. Paul Rodaway (1994: 125) describes touch, unless it is active and exploratory, as a more fragmentary experience than vision and asserts that the latter gives a more continuous experience of time. Virilio is more persuasive, however, arguing that our entire experience of time is subject to the vagaries and inconsistencies of our perception. In his notion of picnolepsy, our reason creates the illusion of continuity, covering the perceptual gaps—breaks, absences, dislocations—that occur in consciousness (Virilio 2009: 24–5).

The subject lives the world through its body. The body's mobility, for example, when physically travelling and as perception-in-motion (Wylie 2007: 177) confirms that living things are not static and sedentary but immersed and involved in a dynamic relationship with the flux of the world. As a creative practitioner, the photographer walks through the landscape, exploring the world with a camera, negotiating its dips and inclines, its hard and soft surfaces, its spaces and obstacles. In a 1931 essay, Husserl describes walking as the experience by which we understand our body in relation to the world (1981: 248–50). The body is our experience of what is always here, and so the body in motion experiences a unity of continuous 'heres' moving towards and through the various 'theres'. Thus the body is distinguished from, but placed in alignment with, the world: 'Walking, ideally, is a state in which the mind, body, and the world are aligned, as though they were three characters finally in conversation together' (Solnit 2006: 5).

The camera has the ability to record the shifting visual orientations that the mobile photographer experiences. Kawauchi's photographic work conveys the impression of a flowing consciousness, a restless prowling curiosity, that appears to relish the ability to see, indulging in a scopophilia of the everyday. Phenomenological accounts acknowledge that '[m]ovement then, constitutes a knowing, sensitive encounter with place and space' (Jones and Cloke 2002: 85). The world, in part, dictates our physical movement, as we manoeuvre through the objects and spaces around us. As we move through space, a myriad of different points-of-view appear, creating 'a constantly emergent perceptual and material milieu' (Wylie 2007: 177). These perspectives 'combine to create complex sensory and imaginative, dynamic, collages of being-in-this-place' (Cloke and Jones 2001: 663) and contradict 'the core fantasy of humanism's trope of vision': the conceit that perceptual space is organized around and for the looking subject; that the pure point of the eye (as agent of *ratio* and *logos*) exhausts the field of the visible; that the invisible is only—indeed, merely—that which has not yet been seen by a subject who is, in principle, capable of seeing all (Wolfe 2009: 132).

Michel Serres (2008: 304), in his description of the 'statue-like' viewer of traditional philosophy observing the dynamic world from a fixed interior position, observes that movement disrupts the objectifying gaze of vision. Vision, as de Certeau reminds us, 'organizes our ways of knowing' (1983: 25) and forms the basis of Western epistemologies that hold human knowledge of the world as analogous to visual perception. This spectator theory of knowledge depends upon a detached, observing subject who stands 'aloof from the dramas and intricacies of an objective world which lies "beyond" and "outside"' (Wylie 2007: 144). According to Wylie, 'A certain distance is established, carrying the gazing subject from the world to a position of detached epistemological authority' (2007: 147).

The world, according to traditional Western philosophy, is a single, wholly determinable, objective reality independent of human activity. This system of thought forms the basis of traditional landscape studies. Since its invention, photography was implicated in such thought, acting as the 'perfect Enlightenment tool', seemingly able to record existing reality by offering 'empirical knowledge mechanically, objectively, without thought or emotion' (Pultz 1995: 9). The photograph stills an otherwise dynamic world, enabling a studious contemplation. Bal (1993) and Houlgate (1993) have attempted to counter these arguments by proposing that vision's association with rationality and objectivity is not inherent but the result of its conceptualization and exploitation. If vision is regarded not as something that consumes and dominates, but as cooperative, generous and egalitarian, then there is potential for its rehabilitation, allowing for novel possibilities in the practice of photography.

For Serres, the *sensible* itself ('everything pertaining to the senses' [2008: x]) is the epitome of the changeable:

> our ecological niche includes a thousand movements ... The earth turns, our global look-out post has long since left stability behind, the sun itself, the giver of light, mobile, is apparently rushing toward another place in the universe. (2008: 304)

The 'mobile niche into which the body is plunged' (Serres 2008: 50) attests to the fact that we are part of nature and subject to the same entropic processes as everything in the world. Photographs, as fragments, capture the unpredictability and randomness of experience, the constant succession of images to which each ecological niche subjects its species.

In my own photographic work, time is marked by changes in weather, diurnal and nocturnal rhythms, seasonal cycles, tracks and traces of insects, animals, machinery, growth and decay (Figure 6.2). Repetitive sensing builds our knowledge of and connection with things and places over time. Time is intrinsic to photography and affects it on multiple levels, from the precision of the exposure in the making of the photograph to the photograph's apparent ability to represent the past (Barthes's intractable *noeme* 'that-has-been' [1993: 96]). By giving expression to layers of temporal experience, photographic practice can supply insights concerning the nature of lived time. By approaching photographic practice as a process that evolves through

Figure 6.2   Orchard image 2 by Carole Baker.

time, encompassing the making of the image through to the exhibiting of the work, possibilities for a more profound interrogation of the medium are opened up beyond the mere interpretation of a series of photographs.

Michel Serres regards vision as a mobile sense in itself, which connects to, rather than distances from, the world. Similarly, Michel de Certeau tells us that vision 'captivates' us because 'it is a journey toward external things,' a journey that *returns* us to the world of objects from whence we have come. In the very act of looking, then, we travel into the space of the world: 'to travel is to see, but seeing is already traveling' (de Certeau 1983: 26). Serres adopts the same metaphor, which he refers to as 'visiting'. His notion of visiting is, so to speak, vectorial vision, itinerant or excursive vision, vision on the move. The senses 'visit the world, in actions of excursion or self-exceeding' (Connor 1999):

> The subject sees, the body visits, goes beyond its place, and quits its role and speech ... The body leaves the body in all senses, the sensible ties that knot, the sensible or the body never remains in the same territory or content but plunges into and lives in a perpetual exchanger, turbulence, whirlpool ... The body exceeds the body. (Serres 2008: 306–7)

The body transcends itself in its interaction with the world. For Serres, 'the senses are nothing but the mixing of the body, the principal means whereby the body mingles with the world and with itself, overflows its borders' (2008: 3). There are challenges associated with conceiving of the body as a source of knowledge; the subjective nature of experience, its fleetingness and lack of full reproducibility make it difficult to examine. Nevertheless, it is my contention that creative photographic practice, with its combination of experiential and symbolic elements, is an expressive form that is able to communicate the experience of being-in-the-world, not in a way which replicates experience, but through evoking in the viewer a sense of their own multidimensional, complex experience.

Multisensual Experience

Despite Western preoccupations with the individual senses, they are not, in fact, discrete faculties but work together in a variety of combinations, continuously harmonizing and overlapping. Rodaway argues that vision is concerned only with surface appearances, and that some of the perceptions we associate with it come from other senses. Vision is a deductive sense that is dependent upon the information of the other senses and memory to assist in the interpretation of the images it receives (Rodaway 1994: 117). David Abram argues that the senses are inseparable from one another, and that perception is, thus, the 'concerted activity of *all* the body's senses as they function and flourish together' (1997: 59, original emphasis) in a synaesthetic experience. Merleau-Ponty argues that human estrangement from direct experience has caused synaesthesia—the overlap and blending of the senses—to be a rare occurrence. The senses *are* distinct modalities, but in their perception of the world, they participate and intertwine. According to Crouch (2001: 62), the body as 'sensuous, sensitive, agentive and expressive' encounters the world in a multidimensional way, expressing emotion and our 'relationship with it, through inter-subjective body-communication'. Similarly, Witmore (2006) advocates a multisensory approach as the most productive in manifesting something of the complexity, multidimensionality and multitemporality of the material world.

Yamamoto writes of his experience of making work by photographing what he calls *Shizuka* (translated as quiet, calm combined with summer and perfume) treasures, small and precious things that he finds in nature. These treasures are revealed to him through his own sensual responses to the signals they exude:

> 'Shizuka' transmits itself through the delicate movement of air, the smell of the earth, the faint noises of the environment, and rays of light. 'Shizuka' sends messages to all five of my senses. (Fifty One Fine Art Photography 2012)

Through Yamamoto's work, Western viewers become aware of interconnections between the senses; the world entices the senses with its multisensory messages, and a suggestion of this is perceptible in the resulting photographic work. Serres (Serres and Latour 1995: 131–2), like Merleau-Ponty, argues that a separation of the senses is impossible. In his introduction to Serres's book on the senses, Steven Connor writes that 'for Serres, the senses are not islands, or channels, that keep themselves to themselves' (Serres 2008: 7). Rather than resembling the outer, well-finished surface of *The Lady and the Unicorn* tapestry in the Cluny Museum in Paris, our senses are more akin to its underside, where the loose ends are visible and unruly, interconnected in a multitude of unique combinations (Serres 2008: 7).

A Haptic Visuality

Recent critical and creative attention has focused on a reevaluation of the nonvisual senses, particularly that of touch, in discourse and practice. In Western cultures, touch is often marginalized, being grouped as a bodily sense with taste and smell rather than with the higher, cerebral senses of sight and hearing (Rodaway 1994: 148). (However, this is not necessarily the case in non-Western cultures [Geurts 2002].) According to Yukari Sakiyama and Nana Koch (2003: 81–6), in Japanese society people are accustomed to touching and being touched; such tactile experience includes interactions between people and aesthetic interactions of people with art objects. They argue that touch behaviours are affected by the way the body is perceived overall; in the Japanese concept of *mi,* the mind and body are interrelated and have fluid boundaries which allow the body to extend into space.

Kawauchi's photo books, such as *Illuminance* of 2011, and Yamamoto's *A Box of Ku* of 1998 are presented in ways that emphasize their objectness, making them available to the viewer's sense of touch. The images in Yamamoto's *A Box of Ku,* held in the centre of the palm, proffer the illusion of possession, whilst as photographic images they signify the world's absence and thus expose the viewer's distance from it. The miniature scale of Yamamoto's images and their exquisite quality (each individually toned in tea-like shades) give them a precious and fragile aura. Being able to touch and arrange these tiny objects gives the viewer (or 'experiencer') an illicit pleasure that they are normally denied in the art gallery. To give his photographs the appearance of treasured possessions, valued for their ability to evoke memories and emotions, Yamamoto ages them by subjecting them to various forms of touch: by carrying them in his pockets, thumbing through them and rubbing them. Montagu (1971: 128) writes that touch 'is not experienced as a simple physical modality, as sensation, but affectively, as emotion'. Touch, then, is able to induce emotion. When exhibiting his photographs on gallery walls, Yamamoto does not place them behind protective glass but leaves them exposed to the contagion of the outside world, revealing the vulnerable skin of the print to the senses of the viewer.

The senses of vision and touch in Western culture appear to be at opposite ends of sensory experience; vision is culturally ascribed as cerebral, male and distant, while touch is bodily, female and proximate (Rodaway 1994: 122–3). And, unlike vision, touch is not valued epistemologically, as Vasseleu attests that '[i]nformation gathered through touch and more proximal senses is thought to provide only subjective feeling and cannot be grounds for knowledge' (1998: 12). Despite this, touch is, as Rodaway argues, associated with 'intimacy, trust and truth' (1994: 149) and, as such, is used to 'confirm other sensuous information and to affirm contact between people and between people and their environment' (1994: 149). Touch, as Montagu argues, 'is sometimes seen as "containing" all the other senses, or as a foundation upon which the subsequent sensuous experience is built' (1971: 270). Rodaway adopts the term 'haptic' in order to incorporate the sensuous experience of the whole body, including movement, orientation and temperature, in contrast to touch, which he sees as being limited to the hands. Because sight provides us only with visual representations, which are 'appearances of phenomena in light' and not 'the phenomena themselves in their fullness and depth', the 'possibility of illusion is always present' (Rodaway 1994: 117). Touch is more interactive and direct and so is a more trustworthy indicator of the nature of the world.

The alignment of touch with truth perhaps explains why the ontology of the analogue photograph has in the past been defined by its indexicality, a categorization dependent upon physical touch. As Elkins (2007: 29) explains, '[P]hotography is indexical because the silver compounds in the negative are directly affected by photons from the object.' Kawauchi's photographs and my own use analogue processes. (I can find nothing about Yamamoto's techniques, but they *appear* to be the product of an analogue process in terms of their quality and traditional appearance.)

The use of a celluloid film camera still retains appeal for artist photographers. The film is coated with emulsion on which a latent image of the scene in front of the lens is formed and then awaits the process of development to reveal it. Its enduring appeal may have something to do with the air of mystery and magic associated with the photograph's creation but may also perhaps be due to the direct physical relationship that develops between subject and image.

The analogue photograph has been described as a trace, 'something directly stenciled off the real' (Sontag 1979: 154), or an 'emanation of the referent' (Barthes 1993: 80–1), since light projected from the subject strikes the light-sensitive emulsion and physically transforms it, leaving an imprint which can then be made permanent. 'The photograph as such', writes Bazin, 'and the object in itself share a common being, after the fashion of a fingerprint' (1960: 8).

Peter Geimer questions whether light touching both object and emulsion is indeed enough to claim physical contact, or whether the skin of the object must actually have been in contact with the surface of the emulsion (as in a photogram):

> Does the appearance of a ray of light qualify as direct physical contact, even perhaps as a material 'extension' of the light source? Does light 'touch' the object upon which it shines? Is a lit surface the 'imprint' of something? (2007: 16)

He explores the notion by recounting the story of the fly caught inside Antonio Beato's nineteenth-century camera as he exposed a collodian plate to the light reflected from the pyramids of Egypt. The fly, having landed on the glass plate during

Figure 6.3 Orchard image 3 by Carole Baker.

exposure, imprinted itself upon the photograph. As 'the only object on the twenty by twenty-six centimeter albumin print that is not adjusted for perspective ... [the fly] instead appears as its actual size of a few millimeters,' creating a photogram within a photograph, simultaneously producing in one image 'two different techniques of representation' (Geimer 2007: 14–15). Geimer appreciates the complexity that this idea presents for our spatial comprehension, as '[t]he fly appears together *with* the landscape, but at the same time separated from it. It seems to occupy a space *on* the image or *in front* of it; but this "in front" itself constitutes an entirely flat surface and is thoroughly unperspectival' (2007: 14). Geimer appears to suggest that the actual physical contact of the fly on the light-sensitive surface makes it more compelling a trace than the projected light from the pyramids.

Luce Irigaray proposes that vision itself is *dependent* upon the sense of touch and 'without the sense of touch seeing would not be possible' (Vasseleu 1998: 12). Kelly Oliver explains that in Irigaray's theory, 'we are touched by, and touching, everything around us even as we see the distance between ourselves and the world or other people in the world' (2007: 125–6).

Thus, we experience a form of haptic visuality that intertwines us with everything in the world. This haptic visuality is particularly apparent in the work of Kawauchi with its strongly visceral close-ups and textural forms, which suggest no sense of hierarchy or bias in terms of subject. A haptic system creates in us our sense of self, as Yi-Fu Tuan (1993) argues; our ability to feel creates our sense of being in the world, and to lose it results in a loss of being. As well as being vital for the formation of our identity, touch is also central to our relationship with other living things. Rodaway emphasizes this sense of connection by arguing that, '[t]ouch literally concerns contact between person and world. It is participation, passive and active, and not mere juxtaposition' (1994: 44).

An Exceeding of the Senses

Our capacity to imagine, in particular, allows us to exceed our senses. A consciousness that could not imagine, writes Sartre, would be hopelessly 'bogged down in the real' (2010: 184). His theory of the imaginary offers potential for furthering our understanding of how a viewer engages with a photograph. Sartre maintains that a photographic image stimulates the imagination (a creative process involving knowledge and affectivity), allowing the viewer to experience the same affective responses they would if they were in the actual presence of the person or scene depicted. This faculty enables us to achieve a deeper understanding of the world than is provided by the senses alone. Abram describes the imagination as:

> not a separate mental faculty (as we so often assume) but ... rather the way the senses themselves have of throwing themselves beyond what is immediately given, in order to make tentative contact with ... the hidden or invisible aspects of the sensible. (1997: 58)

Drawing on present perceptual and remembered experience, imaginary objects are a 'melange of past impressions and recent knowledge' (Sartre 2010: 90) and are ascribed emotions, traits and beliefs as if they were real. Sartre adopts the term 'analogon' to describe a thing that resembles the object it represents; and by its very nature, the photograph is a ready-made analogon. The viewer's engagement with, or intention towards, the photograph brings it to life, as Sartre writes: 'We have consciousness, of some sort, of *animating* the photo, of lending life to it in order to make an image of it' (2010: 25). Our response to the photograph is dependent upon our unique knowledge and affectivity; as I look at the photograph, my 'imaging consciousness' constantly adds new details to the subject.

Conclusion

In this chapter, I have attempted to develop a conceptual framework for an innovative practice that explores the complexity of living things. I have discussed both the making of the photographic work, involving the photographer's engagement with the world, and the reception of the work by the viewer in order to challenge critical writing that focuses on the final work and isolates it from the photographic process as a whole. It is possible, therefore, to conceive of photography as a method of phenomenological enquiry, and the final work becomes not a mere reading of the image, but an expressive interface between the photographer's experience of the world and the viewer's. As Csordas suggests, representation, rather than replacing experience, gives access to a world of experience (1994: 11). Because photographic practice is both symbolic and phenomenological, and involves both representational and experiential practices, it is able to explore complex relationships between natures and culture, and self and other. I contend that viewing a creative photographic work is a dynamic experience that involves all of the senses and affective and intellectual faculties. Whilst I deal here only with vision and touch, there is further work to be done on the other senses, affective states and memory in relation to photography. I have introduced Sartre's theory of the imaginary as a way to begin to investigate the complexity of the viewing experience. Finally, I concur with Elkins' view that '[s]eeing is metamorphosis, not mechanism' (1997: 12), since we can see that the photographs of Yamamoto and Kawauchi evoke rather than document. They transform the world with their poetic sensibility rather than replicate appearances and, in so doing, they enable us to experience something of the vibrancy, richness and dynamism of firsthand, lived experience. They also provide a different way of understanding the situation of human beings *in* nature as opposed to observing nature across a human-nonhuman species divide. Creative visual practice is well suited to exploring this territory, as it is able to negotiate the space between the material and the abstract and to explore embodied experiences in relation to the world of living things.

References

Abram, D. 1997. *The Spell of the Sensuous.* New York: Vintage Books.

Arnheim, R. 1974. 'On the Nature of Photography'. *Critical Inquiry* 1(1): 149–61.

Bal, M. 1993. 'His Master's Eye'. In D. Levin, ed., *Modernity and the Hegemony of Vision.* Berkeley: University of California Press.

Barthes, R. 1993. *Camera Lucida: Reflections on Photography.* London: Vintage Books.

Bazin, A. 1960. 'The Ontology of the Photographic Image'. *Film Quarterly* 13(4): 4–9.

Benediktsson, K., and K. Lund. 2010. *Conversations with Landscape.* London: Ashgate.

Bennet, J. 2010. *Vibrant Matter: A Political Ecology of Things.* Durham, NC: Duke University Press.

Berthomé, L., and F. Bosdedore. 2009. 'Visual Haiku, Photographs by Masao Yamamoto', trans. C. Leonard. *Lens Culture* [video]. Available at: http://www. lensculture.com/yamamoto.html. Accessed 7 November 2012.

Clark, N. 1997. 'Panic Ecology: Nature in the Age of Superconductivity'. *Theory, Culture and Society* 14(1): 77–96.

Cloke, P., and O. Jones. 2001. 'Dwelling, Place and Landscape: An Orchard in Somerset'. *Environment and Planning A* 33(4): 649–66.

Connor, S. 1999. 'Michel Serres's Five Senses'. Paper presented at Michel Serres Conference, Birbeck, University of London, 29 May. Available at: http://www. bbk.ac.uk/english/skc/5senses.htm. Accessed 11 July 2012.

Coole, D. H., and S. Frost. 2010. *New Materialisms: Ontology, Agency, and Politics.* Durham, NC: Duke University Press.

Crouch, D. 2001. 'Spatialities and the Feeling of Doing'. *Social & Cultural Geography* 2(1): 61–75.

Csordas, T. J., ed. 1994. *Embodiment and Experience: The Existential Ground of Culture and Self.* Cambridge: Cambridge University Press.

D'Addario, A. 2012. Posts Tagged 'Fine Art Photography'. *Reportage Festival.* Available at: http://reportage.com.au/?tag=fine-art-photography. Accessed 11 July 2012.

de Certeau, M. 1983. 'The Madness of Vision'. *Enclitic* 7(1): 24–31.

Donald, M. 2001. *A Mind So Rare: The Evolution of Human Consciousness.* New York: W. W. Norton.

Elkins, J. 1997. *The Object Stares Back: On the Nature of Seeing.* San Diego, CA: Harvest Harcourt.

Elkins, J. 2007. 'Camera Dolorosa'. *History of Photography* 31(1): 22–30.

Fifty One Fine Art Photography. 2012. *Masao Yamamoto.* Available at: http://www. gallery51.com/index.php?navigatieid=9&fotograafid=61. Accessed 11 July 2012.

Flusser, V. 2000. *Towards a Philosophy of Photography.* London: Reaktion.

Geimer, P. 2007. 'Image as Trace: Speculations about an Undead Paradigm'. *differences: A Journal of Feminist Cultural Studies* 18(1): 7–28.

Geurts, K. L. 2002. *Culture and the Senses: Bodily Ways of Knowing in an African Community.* Berkeley: University of California Press.

Harvey, D. 1996. *Justice, Nature and the Geography of Difference.* Oxford: Blackwell.

Houlgate, S. 1993. 'Vision, Reflection, Openness'. In D. Levin, ed., *Modernity and the Hegemony of Vision.* Berkeley: University of California Press, 87–123.

Husserl, E. 1981. 'The World of the Living Present and the Constitution of the Surrounding World External to the Organism'. In P. McCormick and F. A. Elliston, eds, *Edmund Husserl Shorter Works.* Brighton: Harvester Press, 238–50.

Ingold, T. 1993. 'The Temporality of the Landscape'. *World Archaeology* 25(2): 152–74.

Ingold, T. 1997. 'Life Beyond the Edge of Nature? Or, the Mirage of Society'. In J. Greenwood, ed., *The Mark of the Social.* London: Rowman and Littlefield, 231–52.

Jones, O., and P. Cloke. 2002. *Tree Cultures: The Place of Trees and Trees in Their Place.* London: Berg.

Massey, D. 2005. *For Space.* Thousand Oaks, CA: Sage.

Mayalina. 2006. '10 Questions to Rinko Kawauchi about Photography'. *Ping Mag.* Available at: http://pingmag.jp/2006/08/11/10-questions-to-rinko-kawauchi-about-photography/. Accessed 15 March 2013.

Merleau-Ponty, M. 1962. *Phenomenology of Perception.* London: Routledge.

Montagu, A. 1971. *Touching: The Human Significance of the Skin.* New York: Columbia University Press.

Oliver, K. 2007. 'Vision, Recognition, and a Passion for the Elements'. In M. Cimitile and E. Miller, eds, *Returning to Irigaray.* Albany: State University of New York Press, 121–36.

Pettersson, M. 2011. 'Depictive Traces: On the Phenomenology of Photography'. *Journal of Aesthetics and Art Criticism* 69(2): 185–96.

Phillips, A. 1999. *Darwin's Worms.* London: Faber & Faber.

Pultz, J. 1995. *Photography and the Body.* London: Weidenfeld & Nicolson.

Rodaway, P. 1994. *Sensuous Geographies: Body, Sense, and Place.* London: Routledge.

Rose, G., and D. Tolia-Kelly, eds. 2012. *Visuality/Materiality: Images, Objects and Practices.* Farnham: Ashgate.

Sakiyama, Y., and N. Koch. 2003. 'Touch in Dance Therapy in Japan'. *American Journal of Dance Therapy* 25(2): 79–95.

Sartre, J.-P. 2010. *The Imaginary: A Phenomenological Psychology of the Imagination.* London: Routledge.

Serres, M. 2008. *The Five Senses: A Philosophy of Mingled Bodies.* London: Continuum.

Serres, M., and B. Latour. 1995. *Conversations on Science, Culture and Time.* Ann Arbor: University of Michigan Press.

Sewall, L. 1999. *Sight and Sensibility: The Ecopsychology of Perception.* Los Angeles: Jeremy P. Tarcher.

Solnit, R. 2006. *Wanderlust: A History of Walking.* London: Verso.

Sontag, S. 1979. *On Photography.* London: Penguin.

Thomas, J. A. 2001. *Reconfiguring Modernity: Concepts of Nature in Japanese Political Ideology.* Berkeley: University of California Press.

Thrift, N. 2007. *Non Representational Theory.* London: Routledge.

Tuan, Y. 1993. *Passing Strange and Wonderful: Aesthetics Nature and Culture.* Washington, DC: Island Press.

Vasseleu, C. 1998. *Textures of Light: Vision and Touch in Irigaray, Levinas and Merleau-Ponty.* London: Routledge.

Virilio, P. 2009. *The Aesthetics of Disappearance.* Cambridge, MA: MIT Press.

Whatmore, S. 2002. *Hybrid Geographies: Natures, Cultures, Spaces.* Thousand Oaks, CA: Sage.

Witmore, C. 2006. 'Vision, Media, Noise and the Percolation of Time: Symmetrical Approaches to the Mediation of the Material World'. *Journal of Material Culture* 11(3): 267–92.

Wolfe, C. 2009. *What Is Posthumanism?* Minneapolis: Minnesota University Press.

Wylie, J. 2007. *Landscape.* London: Routledge.

7

The Field: An Art Experiment in Levinasian Ethics

Alana Jelinek, with Juliette Brown

Foreword

Juliette Brown: This piece describes *The Field,* an artwork by Alana Jelinek, and its relationship to the philosophy of Emmanuel Levinas. For reasons described below, the description of *The Field* as artwork will be undertaken by myself, Juliette Brown, and the philosophical basis of the project will be described by Alana Jelinek.

The Field is a complex and subtle artwork that expresses some of the difficulties of negotiating theory and practice. It is concerned with difference as a positive force and with an ethical engagement with Otherness.

Why I will be describing *The Field* as artwork derives from debates on the classification of art as such, settled in some sense by philosopher George Dickie's (1974, 1984, 2001) institutional definition of art. Dickie contends that that which is proposed as art must be accepted as such by an art world. He doesn't explain what constitutes the art world.

Not a practising artist, I have been an observer of Jelinek's work and involved in the production and dissemination of contemporary artwork through the terra incognita art organization for fifteen years. This means I have worked with numerous artists and arts institutions and write about art. As the institutional definition deems, the artist is incapable of legitimating their work. This role falls to me, as part of the wider art world. Subsequently, references to *The Field* relate to a field and the objects and activities therein which are the proposed artwork. *The Field* includes both physical space (12.9 acres, Essex field and woodland) and a series of encounters which take place in and in relation to the site.

Conceptually difficult for some may be the notion that both a space and the activities taking place there, including those that take place without human involvement, can constitute art. My understanding is that these aspects form the material of the work, which stems from and generates thought and understanding in the participant or observer. As a conceptual piece, the artwork itself resides in referencing a wealth of ideas and a history of thought, even in a brief experience of it. Each aspect of the artwork, *The Field,* demands that we consider the negotiation of different subjectivities, be it the group who come together to 'conserve' the natural world, those who aim to grow food together and separately, those who debate ideas or the human individual confronting unwanted wildlife.

The idea, the concept behind this conceptual piece, is that as individuals we struggle to contend with other subjectivities, or that which is outside of us, and not only in the ways we usually imagine. An ethical engagement with the Other (through Levinas) involves examining false assumptions on which we have built a culture of the same. This means we have suppressed difference. We can attempt a more ethical engagement, a face-to-face engagement, by recognizing the ignorance, prejudice, assumptions, desire to repress difference, ill-considered notions, cultural heritage, personal demons, systemic biases, defended anxieties and desires that constitute our usual approach to that which is not us. In a conceptual piece such as this, these contestations will be clear in some sense from even a brief engagement.

The development of the work is important, as is its place in the history of the discipline of art. Jelinek has written that the discipline of art includes a knowledge of and reference to art history (Jelinek 2013). *The Field* sits in relation to a number of reference points, particularly Land Art, as manifested in the United Kingdom (for example, Richard Long and Hamish Fulton), 'microtopian' practices (Bourriaud 2002 [1998]) and Conceptual Art (Osborne 2002).

Jelinek's work has for some time considered relationships between individual subjectivities mediated by preexisting, often contradictory narratives (*you-me-them* 2001–4; *Tall Stories: Cannibal Forks* 2010, 2011; *The Fork's Tale* 2013). Some of her work with the Museum of Archaeology and Anthropology, University of Cambridge, sites itself in a form of institutional critique, which challenges orthodoxy from within.[1] As with *The Field*, in her museum work she allows herself to range in scope from the minutiae to the entirety of the museum and also what takes place there. The work also alludes to ideas about how knowledge is constituted.

As an artist whose intellectual interests and training lie in philosophy, Jelinek is disposed to discuss ideas, sometimes directly, with others as part of her work, for example in Moot Point, described below, which forms part of *The Field.* Of note, Jelinek also proposed the first moot on utopias. While interaction with others is an important part of this work, it is not to my mind in the sense of relational aesthetics (Bourriaud 2002 [1998]), which is more interested in the quantity of shared experience generated than in the quality of debate and communication. Some of the practices described within relational aesthetics have modelled politically inspired utopias. Methodologically, *The Field* tends to expect the failure of its many experiments rather than attempting to satisfy a desire for utopian models. In this aspect, it also contrasts with antecedents found within Conceptual Art of the 1960s and 1970s. Again, this follows the philosophical intentions of the artwork, the point being that failure generates opportunities for reflection and reflexivity.

Both Land Art and Conceptual Art grew from notions of active refusal of market ideologies of their time. Heir to this tradition, Jelinek's work with *The Field* refuses commodification by privileging concept. One of the pivotal concepts is the idea of rules-as-art. *The Field* operates with a set of rules, drawing on the work of artists On Kawara, Hanne Darboven and Sol Lewitt. In contrast to the fixity and intentionally random or trivial aspect of the rules maintained by these artists, often over many years and common to the *modus* of 1960s Conceptual Art, the rules of *The Field* are reflexive, and practice can inform and change theory. Finding Conceptual Art now also subject to commodification through the sale of ephemera and documentation, the strategy Jelinek employs is to avoid documentation wherever possible, maintaining the work as an ongoing process without end in sight, and generating many momentary, minimal, unmediated encounters.

One of the most striking aspects of *The Field* as an artwork—its site, its location in the natural world—would suggest some relationship to Land Art. The British tradition of Land Art, in particular, recognizes and quietly reflects on the artist's impact on the land (e.g. in the art of Richard Long and Hamish Fulton) as distinct from the US tradition, which is generally monumental in scale and grandiose. It is the subtlety of the British tradition that is an antecedent to *The Field.* There is more to be said on this subject, beyond the scope of this chapter. Truly, nature can never *not* be political, but in the case of *The Field,* nature both represents a set of challenges that demand collective action and generates all of the difficulties inherent in collectivity.

What is important to note here is that, as an artist, it is not Jelinek's duty to substantiate a claim to any particular tradition or worth but to propose and, if so desired, to discuss her work.

Introduction

The Field is a location for art, conservation and outreach projects, but it is more than the mere physical host for such activities. In itself, *The Field* is a long-term, collaborative, interspecies art project. It is a physical, geographical location at a specific moment in time with a set of ethical and aesthetic propositions attached. It is hoped that *The Field* affords the opportunity to engage mindfully and reflexively in relationships with other humans and other nonhuman species, both plant and animal, making a contribution to a history of such art practices.

Behind this project lies the philosophy of Emmanuel Levinas, who observed that Western knowledge (philosophy) has been based on an assumption, and an alarming paradox, that knowledge is universal, while knowledge stems from, and is confined to, the particularity of the Graeco-European experience and tradition. Levinas understands that knowledge, based on this *philia,* a system of likeness, on the exchange of the same with the same, is a system of knowledge, of thought, of culture that inherently has a horror of the Other. This horror can only be minimized when the Other is assimilated as part of the same. The Other is not allowed to be other; it must be an extension of the self or the same (Critchley 1999 [1992]: 31). Orientalism, primitivism and, in the case of animals, anthropomorphism can be understood as cultural manifestations of the extension of the self.

The Field was purchased in 2008 by Alana Jelinek and Juliette Brown of terra incognita, a small arts organization based in London, generating exhibitions, catalogues, publications and educational or outreach events since 1997. It was Jelinek who initiated *The Field* as an artwork in Levinasian terms and set up the 'rules' of the artwork. It is also just a field, and some participants are not aware that the field is viewed as part of an artwork. While this is understood by us as positive and pluralistic, in that anyone can engage with *The Field* according to their own educational and cultural backgrounds, needs and desires, for Jelinek, in order to consider certain questions and values pertaining to the experience of *The Field,* it must be understood as art, in dialogue with other artworks and created with a history of art practice in mind. In other words, because certain values and precepts are attached to the experience, and participants or audiences are invited to understand the experience through these values and precepts, it is art.

From the beginning, *The Field* was understood as an opportunity for those who generally have restricted access to the outside or 'natural world', and particularly those in inner London who live in flats with little or no access to gardens or allotments.[2] Activities include monthly conservation days at which hedge-laying, coppicing, creating dead hedges, scything and fence-building occur. These activities are performed solely with hand tools both as a strategy for minimizing fossil fuel use and as a strategy for understanding our impact on the environment through the extension of bodies with hand tools, understood as the more responsive, communicative technologies. These technologies are contrasted with the insensitivities and disconnection seemingly inherent in power tool use.[3]

The Field was conceived in naïve terms, symbolically as 'bees and trees': a shortcut for the predominately urban paradigm of endangered, subjugated nature requiring human action against destructive human exploitation. Most of the initial participants had a background in ecoactivism or other forms of activism and an interest either in gardening or food sustainability. These ideas were from a decidedly idealistic point of view as none had access to land in any form, none owned property in any form and none had educational expertise in these areas. Some of us had been girl guides or scouts.

Physical Aspects of *The Field* and Encounters Therein

The Field once formed part of an estate owned by the landed gentry, and this history has to a large extent determined its current composition, although there is evidence that the woodland is ancient and therefore predating the estate. When it was sold to Broadland Properties Limited in 1973,[4] the adjoining Elsenham Hall was divided into flats, and the area of *The Field* was divided into four gated areas: field one is pasture or meadowland with a broad border of mostly indigenous or naturalized 'amenity' trees, including ash, lime, oak, beech, sweet chestnut, holly and, more recently, sycamore; field two is woodland including birch and overgrown hornbeam coppice with oak standards; field three is a meadow with ancient anthills enriched by overgrazing so that it subsequently lost some of its character; field four is woodland with a strip of cherry laurel planted by the Hall as ground cover for game birds, dividing it into two distinct areas. To the south there is a continuation of the neglected hornbeam coppice with oak standards, and to the north there is an area with mature oaks and a great profusion of young sycamores (less than twenty years old). The woodland area has been neglected for at least fifty to seventy years, and since 1987, the meadowland was used to keep horses with the erection of stables at its western edge. The stables now form an art studio and sometime meeting room, a shed to store our communal tools, plus a relatively undefined general storage area shared with swallows in the summer when we remember to open it up in time.

With its conceptual transformation into *The Field,* allotments were introduced to field one plus an apiary, an orchard, a compost toilet and a green wood working area. Immediately, certain precepts were put in place. *The Field* was to be shared with as wide a range of people as possible; it was going to be an environmentally-friendly engagement which, given our idealism tempered by ignorance, meant we were going to be organic, and have bees and work broadly from permaculture principles. We collected a range of books on what is termed 'self-sufficiency'. *The Field* was also to be a continuation of the projects and values that informed our work through terra incognita arts organization. Diversity, a value at the heart of our projects, continued to be a central value for *The Field,* both in terms of biodiversity and human diversity.

The value of diversity was enacted initially in ways already familiar within terra incognita projects. We knew from the outset that we'd host outreach projects for those who don't ordinarily have access to the countryside, both physical and psychological; that those offered allotments would, at least to some extent, reflect the diversity of our chosen neighbourhoods in London as distinct from the local Essex norm; that we would host at least one contemporary art event per year that engaged across academic and practice disciplines: making and thinking, arts, humanities, social science and science. These early goals were easily achieved. It was familiar territory: staging moments of diversity, as we had done through other terra incognita projects, though without the box-ticking cynicism that New Labour policies for the arts had fostered (Wallinger and Warnock 2000; Jelinek 2013). Having said this, the eight allotmenteers reflect age, gender, sexuality and ethnic diversity in a way that any publicly funded body could proudly boast and at times this mix was somewhat forced: at one stage, it seemed all too easy to ask yet another woman to have an allotment but, instead, and slightly self-consciously, we chose the apparently riskier option of inviting a (white, heterosexual) man into our fold.

Outreach projects have included projects with young mothers from Coram Fields Trust, London, Bangladeshi young people from London Borough of Tower Hamlets and members of London Borough of Newham Mental Health Trust user groups.

Each of these projects, in their own ways, were not only appreciated by the participants as instances of access to ordinarily restricted or unattainable experiences but, more importantly, from our point of view, each of the projects did something new and innovative within their type. For example, the Bengali young people were a group of Bollywood dance students, and our project, *Bolly-woods,* brought them in contact with ideas of environmentalism and ignited reflection, memory and discussion with their own families about an agricultural heritage 'back home'. This then fed into a new dance choreographed and performed at a local arts centre.[5]

A different type of diversity is enacted and explored at the annual event Moot Point. Moot Point focuses on process, on being there, in that space, with those people, at that time. Different people, largely strangers to each other, are invited each year to propose a subject to 'moot'. The subject is then interrogated through a variety of practices and disciplines. There are practical engagements and discussions on the subject; different people lead the discussions, 'mooting' for ten minutes, after which time discussion is opened up to the group as a whole and the mooter is gently interrogated. In 2009, through Moot Point we interrogated the idea of utopia; in 2010, it was string theory or 'difficult science'; in 2011, revolution; in 2012, failure. Moot Point in particular is the project that most overtly brings together making and thinking, foregrounding methodologies common to contemporary art practice. It typically involves academics and nonacademics, scientists and artists, in an attempt at a type of interdisciplinary dialogue and operating within the rules of art practice.

The main inclusive event to facilitate human-nonhuman engagement is the monthly conservation days, although less mediated, more personal engagements also occur when engaging via the allotments. The monthly conservation days, to which a wider range of people and theoretically the general public are invited, are advertised on a few websites, including the Trust of Conservation Volunteers and the BBC's 'Things to do' activities. The days usually involve encounters with plant species, and usually we are chopping them down or digging them up, and sometimes, more rarely, we plant them. For many in our group with our previous ideas fixed from road-protest activism and antilogging protest, where cutting down trees is seen as an aggressive and destructive act, this type of engagement with nature seemed brutal and contrary to our core values in attempting ethical engagements. It took many practical conservation courses and a leap of faith to believe in coppicing (which seems like chopping down whole swathes of trees). It was even harder to believe in the ethics of digging up whole species just because they were alien or invasive. The racist or xenophobic rhetorical overtone of this practice is apparent, and it has been described by social scientists (Warren 2007) and scientists (Carlton 1996) and explored by artists such as Erika Tan (*In-Situ,* 2003: site-specific artwork in which an 'invasive' bamboo species was introduced to the English 'native' environment of the Forest of Dean, Gloucestershire).

These shifting understandings are present within scholarly communities concerned with ecology (Simberloff 2003) and debated internally within the project.

There are no simple answers and no 'good practice' that is always already 'good'. We have reconsidered herbicide use, cutting down trees, using piped clean water for uses in addition to human consumption and even the use of hydrocarbons as fuels. Lines drawn in the sand have blown away with the winds of new knowledge and experience, and, yet, we remember that they existed and where they were. We have beliefs, values and standards that we are trying to achieve, and no question is settled for all time. We are not travelling in a direction from bad to good, from complete ignorance to outright knowledge; instead it is a continuing dialogue where uneasy, temporary settlements are made.

Anthropologists Bhatti and Church write that gardens permit 'opportunities and possibilities in relation to nature that may not exist elsewhere either in the rest of the home or in public spaces' (2001: 380). For those without gardens in the urban environment, opportunities for engaging with nonhuman others, both flora and fauna, are mediated through authorities, or they are passive, occurring through parks or zoos for example. In the city, there are also unexpected and unwanted encounters with nonhuman others, with what must be perceived as pests given the conditions of city living: rats, mice, flies, bedbugs, fleas. Because all of the allotment holders live in flats in central London with little or no outside area, for each of us, the allotments at *The Field* fulfil those opportunities for relations with nature that are active, unmediated and not entirely dominated by those feelings of intrusion, trespass and threat that pests inspire. Pests also occur in the context of gardening, and, similar to anthropologist Cathrine Degnen's informants (2009), most of us who have allotments at *The Field* speak about the allotment experience using human tropes including demonizing the unwanted, nurturing the desirable and attributing intentionality and sentience to plants and other nonhuman animals including spiders, ants, slugs and snails. Even those who have read permaculture tracts and agree with its principles or who have a self-consciousness about any tendency towards 'purification' tend to view some plants and animals favourably and others as destructive aliens, unwanted interlopers or, more charitably, as vagabonds. Some admire or curse these animals and plants for what we perceive is their nature.

One rule is that we garden our allotments organically. As far as we're aware that means that no one uses pesticides or fertilizer except for compost, made onsite or bought, although other choices could be made within the letter of organic law. Organic pesticides exist, including the universally acceptable liquid soap formulations and sticky insect traps, particularly for fruit trees, and, at the more contentious end of the spectrum, Monsanto's glyphosate has been understood as a permissible herbicide in some circumstances by some parts of the organic industry. The lack of herbicide and pesticide use is thus far an unexamined consensus across the allotmenteers, although in early 2012, consequent of some hot discussion, a paraffin-burning flame-thrower was bought and used twice against some of our abundant nettles (and everything else living within the nettles). This attempt at controlling certain species was unsuccessful, but it was successful as a team sport and a treat for visitors. It may be repeated again next year as the issue of 'weed control' hasn't shifted for those who understand allotment-gardening in these terms.

Horticulturally, there are distinct differences between the allotmenteers. Some seek advice from traditional authorities including television experts, some have been on Royal Horticultural Society courses and others have an active interest in permaculture principles. Most maintain an uneasy admixture while balancing principle with the practicalities of gardening approximately thirty-five miles away from home. The rules of the artwork state that each participant is autonomous and can make free choices within the confines of their allotment while also abiding by the overarching rule that each must engage ethically with the other, which is generally glossed by all as 'organic'. Tensions have arisen not only in discussions about how to treat the communal areas and areas around each individual allotment, but simply because there is a tendency for each of us to feel our understanding of gardening, food, and nature is the right one. To state the obvious: an ethical engagement with the Other is easiest when there are no tensions. When there is no palpable tension, when the Other is no longer other in a contested way, we are released to imagine they are the same, if temporarily. It is when the Other asserts his or her Otherness that the project's Levinasian ideals are tested.

Levinas and an Ethical Engagement with the Other

Simon Critchely, Levinas scholar, explicates the issue at the heart of the problem of knowledge, ethics and engagement with others:

> [P]hilosophy tells itself a story which affirms the link between individuality and universality by embodying that link either in the person of Socrates or by defining the (European) philosopher as 'the functionary of humanity,' but where at the same time universality is delimited or confined within one particular tradition, namely the Greco-European. (Critchley 1999 [1992]: 128)

We Europeans cannot appreciate, even see, the face of the Other because our entire knowledge base is built on Greek *philia,* on 'the exchange of the Same with the Same' (Critchley 1999 [1992]: 260). In practice, our horror of the Other is transformed into Orientalist and primitivist fantasy, where the Other is understood and engaged with within the terms (positive and negative) of the same.

In limited space we cannot possibly do justice to Levinas's philosophy, let alone point out where the aims of *The Field* project and the engagements fostered through it veer from his ideas, but the following is a point to note. Levinas does not use the term 'Other' in the ways that disciplines like gender studies, queer theory, art and anthropology tend to use it. 'Other' does not here refer to everyone who is not European, male, heterosexual and so forth—that is, the dominant or privileged side of an existing dichotomy. Other is everyone who is not the self, irrespective of social tagging or apparent proximity. His philosophy describes the difficulties of engagement even on this level, between two selves—that is, the self and the one who is not the self—and this difficulty is irrespective of custom, culture, language or position in an existing hierarchy.

The discipline of philosophy in the Anglo-American tradition has, at its conditions of knowledge production, the imperative to abstract ideas from their social context. This is done because, as Levinas (1981) points out, the test for the philosophical knowledge or truth lies in its universal validity. A thing can only be true in philosophy if it is true at all times and in all spaces, and today many philosophers approach this disciplinary value with great degrees of subtlety. In this sense, philosophy seems to be the polar opposite of anthropology. Social anthropology embeds knowledge in the local, in social relations that are manifested in particular places and times. Extrapolations are treated with caution in social anthropology, while in philosophy extrapolation within the rules of logic is the very foundation for knowledge. *The Field* is an attempt at combining these modes of knowledge within the rules of contemporary art making by both interrogating ideas in abstraction and with their local manifestation as it is experienced. Our project's methodology can be phrased as 'philosophical praxis' (while acknowledging that philosophers would likely find this paradoxical): we act on ideas, values or perceptions that are true in a philosophical sense, in that they must stand up to a salvo of hypothetical and theoretical assaults, but the values, ideas or perceptions are also only true if there is empirical, lived evidence, as fraught and contingent as this necessarily is. We navigate these values with knowledge of the history of art and in reference to other art experiments.

Explaining the Levinasian Other

Alana Jelinek: My aim for *The Field* is to understand just how embedded is the preponderance for hierarchy within a culture of the same: ideas of inferiority and superiority, better and worse, one species instead of another, one being preferred over another, one human or culture over another, one time period over another. Levinasian ideas that 'we are born into a world of social relationships which we have not chosen and which we cannot ignore' (Hutchens 2004: 19) underpin this project not just because Levinas's observations are interesting philosophically, but because they are empirically true.

When I read a piece by Marilyn Strathern, I was struck by how well it seemed to demonstrate Levinas's point about European or Western knowledge and its presumptions to universality with all its subsequent, inevitable unethical engagements. It concerns a negotiation between a mining company in Papua New Guinea and a local pressure group (PPG).

One side acknowledged that the knowledge set of the other existed even though they did not believe in it: '[L]ocal people for their part "don't believe in science."' The other side, rooted in Graeco-European systems of thought, 'found there was no scientific case to answer'. The disagreement from the point of view of the Western mining company could only be resolved by a universal truth: either there was damage to the local environment, or there was not. The Papuans, by contrast, were able to countenance a different type of negotiation, not dependent on agreeing or on demolishing disagreements. Strathern goes on to observe:

> [T]he kind of 'accountability' to which the Papua New Guineans [PPG] subscribed does not require agreement about what each side wants from the transaction; each may have their agenda. But the PPG did wish to make that lack of agreement explicit. And if they were forced to accept the CM [mining company] story, then it should be acknowledged that they were going along with it for the sake of a settlement, not because they had been convinced. (Strathern 2004: 94)

Each of us within *The Field* project, like the mining company, understand ourselves and our engagement with each other unthinkingly from within our own paradigm. We know that other people know different things, but we act without reference to those other paradigms, both known and unknown, and cannot imagine a form of negotiation that can account for more than one truth.

Each of us has suffered from an inability to negotiate across differences in values and culture. We demonstrate an inability to negotiate different horticultural knowledges and priorities, which has meant that we successfully ignore differences in maintaining autonomous zones, despite the knowledge of interconnectedness of each allotment and with wider field environment. This imagined truce enacted through imagined autonomy breaks down when we argue over definitions of 'weed' and 'pest' and strategies for their control in the shared, neutral or wider environments.

We are each of us sure, to varying degrees, that our knowledge is right and that therefore it should predominate, informing all our collective actions. An example of this is that we tend to imagine that the noncultivated spaces (fields two, three and four) are a type of *terra nullius,* always available for our designs and without any reference to an 'Other', human or otherwise. So far, we have lacked the skills to negotiate with other humans as different from ourselves, let alone other nonhuman species. There have been times when individuals have imposed their vision or their action without reference to any others. The only other strategy has been to withdraw completely. Neither of these strategies can be said to be an ethical engagement with the Other.

I use Marilyn Strathern's description of the encounter between a Western mining company and a group of people from Papua New Guinea because it demonstrates neatly the inability of we who are brought up within the Graeco-Western tradition to begin to approach the Other in terms other than our own. I do not imagine, on the other hand, that the Papuans have an ease of communication, or an inherently ethical engagement, with the Other. I am not saying the Papuans themselves either avoid or suffer similar pitfalls to those inherent in Graeco-European thought. I do not know.

I do not wish to fall into the traps of primitivism by imagining the Papuans have an ease, be it cultural or innate, where I do not. Instead, I wish to observe Levinas's point that it is at the very core of our Graeco-European knowledge that we have an inherent problem of imposing the self as the same and attempting an engagement with the Other as other. The point of anthropology to me is that it attempts to create an understanding of a culture in its own terms, while also understanding that this may be impossible because we can only understand a culture, an Other, through our own cultural framework. This is my understanding of an ethical engagement with the Other informed by, but also in an extrapolation of, the philosophy of Levinas. If we are to experience anything, it is that there are limitations to our understanding due to our philosophical and knowledge origins.

Levinas and 'We'

Writing 'we' throughout this chapter has contained a slippage between we, the authors, and we, the participants of *The Field*. Having written 'we' throughout this chapter, some qualification is required in an attempt to do some justice to the philosophy of Levinas. More accurately, 'I *plus* at least one other person in the group' should have been written, and even then, it should read 'I *plus* my understanding of what at least one other person in the group said at the time'. The inclusion of all implied by the word 'we' is unethical, in addition to a misrepresentation of events as they occurred. By using the term 'we', even self-consciously, the difficulties of an ethical engagement with the Other are exemplified. Moreover, this Other is not just any human other but friends, colleagues, and still we trample on the possibility of perceiving them as different to ourselves, instead imagining us in a relationship that is side-by-side and not face-to-face. Hutchens writes: 'Levinas is wary of the word "we", which is the original instrument of the ontology of power, in which individual selves stand side-by-side, not face-to-face. "We" is not a vehicle of justice, but a result of injustice, that is, there is no collective moral consciousness that is not initially a response to injustice' (2004: 105)

The Field project was started in 2008 without articulating its Levinasian aims to anyone. In the beginning, Jelinek didn't describe it as art either. We told friends, colleagues and fellow activists about those aspects of the project we imagined would be interesting to them: conservation, allotments, its proximity to Stansted airport and so forth, but we never attempted to tell participants about the project's aims. This was partly to attempt an ethical engagement on another level: to allow people to have the field experience they wanted without reference to another's aims or understanding. We believed we knew of the needs and desires of our fellow London-based ecoactivists and wanted to allow for the diversity of their needs and perceptions.

The Field is an art experiment that self-consciously explores ethics. It may or may not, in itself, be ethical. The aim of *The Field* project is to imagine difference in a nonhierarchical way, including differences across human and nonhuman species, and to engage ethically with these Others understood as other. What we have tried to describe here is how difficult is this aim, that face-to-face human relationships are fraught with difficulties in terms of responsibility. *The Field* is an attempt at understanding and appreciating those differences in a way that is nonhierarchical.

Notes

1. Institutional critique is an important strand within contemporary art practice since the 1960s. In summary, it is the artistic practice of reflecting critically on the institutional underpinnings in a site-specific artwork. The various institutional norms and practices that have been the subject of institutional critique include the funding of art institutions, art world normative structures, art world hierarchies and exclusions and the assumptions which maintain these.
2. Allotments are primarily a British phenomenon. They are areas of land set aside for growing food, which are subdivided into plots for individuals. Beginning in the late 1800s primarily as a means to supplement the diet of working-class families in urban areas, today they are also a middle-class pursuit and often understood within discourses of sustainability, food security and environmentalism.
3. To contrast hand tools with powered tools, power tools tend to have a distancing effect on the user. With the vibrations, noise and smells that are the by-product of powered tools, the latter type of technology tends to create a distance between a person and the object with which he or she is working because by-products must be actively ignored or controlled so the feeling of extending one's body through the tool becomes lost in the confusion of other sensations. In addition, the swiftness and harshness of the impact of power tools makes a mindful engagement between human, tool and tree or grassland more difficult to achieve.
4. 1 April 1960 the Letters of Administration of the estate of The Honourable Dorothy Wyndham Paget (died intestate) granted to the Honourable Lady Olive Cecilia Baillie who gifted it to Sir Gawaine George Baillie on 31 March 1965.
5. 'Bolly-woods' performed 1 July 2010, The Brady Arts Centre, 192–6 Hanbury Street, London, E1 5HU.

References

Bhatti, M., and A. Church. 2001. 'Cultivating Natures: Homes and Gardens in Late Modernity'. *Sociology* 35(2): 365–83.

Bourriaud, N. 2002 [1998]. *Relational Aesthetics,* trans. S. Pleasance and F. Woods with M. Copeland. Dijon: Les presses du reel.

Carlton, J. T. 1996. 'Biological Invasions and Cryptogenic Species'. *Ecology* 77(6): 1653–5.

Critchley, S. 1999 [1992]. *The Ethics of Deconstruction: Derrida and Levinas.* Edinburgh: Edinburgh University Press.

Dickie, G. 1974. *Art and the Aesthetic: An Institutional Analysis.* Ithaca, NY: Cornell University Press.

Dickie, G. 1984. *The Art Circle: A Theory of Art.* New York: Haven.

Dickie, G. 2001. *Art and Value.* Malden, MA: Blackwell.

Hutchens, B. C. 2004. *Levinas: A Guide for the Perplexed.* London: Continuum.

Jelinek, A. 2013. *This Is Not Art: Activism and Other 'Not-art'.* London: I. B. Tauris.

Levinas, E. 1981. *Otherwise than Being: Or Beyond Essence,* trans. A. Lingis. The Hague: Nijhoff.

Osborne, P., ed. 2002. *Conceptual Art.* London: Phaidon.

Simberloff, D. 2003. 'Confronting Introduced Species: A Form of Xenophobia?' *Biological Invasions* 5(3): 179–92.

Strathern, M. 2004. *Commons and Borderlands: Working Papers on Interdisciplinarity, Accountability and the Flow of Knowledge.* Wantage: Sean Kingston.

Wallinger, M., and M. Warnock, eds. 2000. *Art for All? Their Policies and Our Culture.* London: Peer.

Warren, C. R. 2007. 'Perspectives on the "Alien" Versus "Native" Species Debate: A Critique of Concepts, Language and Practice'. *Progress in Human Geography* 31: 427–46.

8

Hunting the Wild 'Other' to Become a Man: Wildlife Tourism and the Modern Identity Crisis in Israeli Safaris to East Africa

Rachel Ben-David

The investigation of human and animal interaction may well be one of the most fruitful endeavors of anthropology.

(Shanklin 1985: 380)

Introduction

The twenty-first century has opened up an opportunity to call into question the centrality often accorded to human beings in their dealings with nonhuman species (Escobar 1999: 1). Nonhuman species embody a unique source of knowledge, as they are often viewed as part of nature. Nature has been described as 'a window opening into a deeper, universal experience with spiritual significance' (Curtin 2009: 460). Nature and wildlife play a particular role in contemporary city life, where ecotourism serves as one of the important escape routes from the urban and the material to a realm imagined as natural and spiritual.

'Wildlife', like nature, is a controversial concept in literature. In its simplest meaning, it refers to nondomesticated animals that live in the wild. In its symbolic meaning, it refers to a fantasy and myth of savagery, wild animals roaming freely within primordial endless plains such as the Serengeti (Adams and McShane 1996). As a result of nineteenth-century historical narratives on Africa, as well as contemporary media productions and touristic representations, wildlife has become a component of the tourist gaze (Urry 1990). Modern tourists have been tempted to travel to Africa to encounter the unindustrialized, primordial landscapes and beings of their fantasies. In addition, safari tourism imaginaries such as 'The Garden of Eden' and 'Wild Africa' are subjected to glocal circulation, moving between the local and the global. As safari tourists return home after their journey, they distribute their photos of 'wildlife in Africa' on Facebook, share their romantic memories with family and friends, and ratify travel agencies' marketing discourse of Africa (Salazar 2010, 2012). In this chapter, I would like to emphasize an additional dimension of wildlife tourism—one far more experiential—which, I believe, has been neglected in safari tourism literature. I will focus on the dynamics of interactions between tourists and wild animals through the consequences of the proximate presence of the wild animals living in their natural habitat, and through the consequences of their spontaneous performance in the presence of tourists.

More specifically, I will focus on the contribution of wildlife safaris to secular Israeli tourists for whom modernity has become an obstacle to self-fulfilment, while remaining a cherished value. These tourists choose nature and wild animals as a medium for overcoming alienation and loss of an affiliation group. The notion of using wildlife to combat the decadent effects of urbanization and capitalism is not new to the literature (Almagor 1985; Haraway 1985; Curtin 2009). Through Israeli experiences of family safaris or 'Bar Mitzvah safaris' to Kenya and Tanzania, I will show how wildlife becomes an antidote to the malaise of modern alienation, which is apparently very relevant to a middle-upper-class secular Israeli lifestyle.

Starting in the late 1970s to early 1980s, affluent secular Israeli parents and grandparents have chosen to travel to East Africa with their children and grandchildren as part of a celebration of the Jewish passage to maturity called Bar Mitzvah.[1] The literal meaning of Bar Mitzvah in Aramaic, 'son of the commandments', symbolizes one who is capable of adult religious duties and subject to the law. However, in the Israeli secular context, the term Bar Mitzvah is emptied of its religious content, leaving it open to be filled with pluralistic meanings. Since the early twentieth century, Israelis have tried to bestow secularism with new meanings whilst maintaining a connection to Judaism, a notion embedded in the legitimacy of the state and Judaism as a civil religion and national culture, rather than a system of traditional belief and practice (Almog 2001: 13–33). Various forms of alternative rites of passage are chosen by parents in order to mark their children's meaningful phase in life, from a one-time fancy crowded celebrative event to a series of challenging, educational activities spread over a year-long span.[2]

Israeli rites of passage in the tourism arena have been previously discussed in literature through the phenomenon of Israeli backpackers (Noy and Cohen 2005). Young Israeli adults in their twenties leave home for long period of time (usually a few months) to go mainly to Asia and South America after completing their military service and before entering new obligations of adulthood. Noy and Cohen's study depicts backpacking journeys as a liminal time and space away from home and family, with other Israelis as a peer group, in a search for self-realization. Apparently, the study of backpackers and the present study are similar, both dealing with Israeli youths travelling around the world in a search for identities. Yet one crucial difference is that Bar Mitzvah safaris include both youths and adults, both teenagers and their parents or grandparents, who feel obliged to provide their children with an education, values and behaviour that will serve them as future adults.

Shaping the future values of Israeli youths, such as their motivation to serve in the army, has been studied in a different context: pilgrimage journeys to Polish concentration camps (Feldman 2008). Similar to those travels, Bar Mitzvah safaris provide a substitute for traditional rites of passage. The destinations obscure the way the journey supports socioeconomic hierarchies: if you pay, you go. However, Israeli youth travel to Poland is promoted and supported by national interests, as opposed to Israeli Bar Mitzvah safaris to Africa, which are promoted and supported by secular individualistic and familial interests. Both types of journey are intended to shape different aspects of Israeli identities, the difference occurring in the narratives, trends and people who are interested in shaping them.

Apparently, many parents and grandparents assume that a luxury family journey to a third-world country is an appropriate medium for preparing young people for the complexity of life within a capitalistic, postmodern society. It turns out that watching wild animals from safe jeeps provides a break from modernity as well as being an enactment of modernity. In these family safaris, almost completely unique to Israelis in the tourist industry, participants form a familial constellation in which adult figures establish a memorable, once-in-a-lifetime cultural shaping experience with their children or grandchildren. The main question encompassing this chapter is, what is the role of nature and wild animals in an enculturation of people? Or more specifically, why is a safari chosen as a medium for shaping young, affluent and secular Israelis' identity and for helping them to understand their contemporary world?

This chapter is part of a wider study, which analyses motivations of Israeli tourists for going on family safaris. Certainly, the safari serves as a social status symbol. Even if the group under study belongs to a narrow, affluent section of Israeli society, nevertheless, the social position of this group as elite reflects a dynamic cultural process. I do not make any generalizations about Israeli society as a whole.[3] Moreover, I do not intend to provide an analysis of the tourists' interactions with African locals, such as Maasai, which constitute a minor but meaningful part of the safari. These issues have been earlier addressed in tourism literature (Bruner 2005; Salazar 2010). As part of the context of this book, the examples and vignettes presented in this chapter intentionally emphasize human-animal dynamics, as a contribution to this growing field in anthropology.

Thus the focus of this study is the perception of the natural wildness of the animals (such as predation, courtship, nurturing of the young and generally their independent presence) as a cure for alienation and—ironically—a model for proper human behaviour. It is argued that wildlife performance plays a significant role in the perception that it could reconnect Israelis, preoccupied with technology and material matters, with primeval realities of human existence (so often lost in urban agglomerations) and consequently with themselves. As shown later in this chapter, the perceived mechanisms of this reconnection process include distraction from modern materialistic trends, reconnection with humanity's prehistoric past, evocation of spirituality, existential experience and, ironically, more appreciation of modern ways of life. The perceived authentic behaviour of the animals serves as model and guidance in contemporary periods of disorientation (Bauman 2000), battling anthropocentric trends and turning nature into a potential frame of meaning and belonging.

In the five following sections, the first reviews three theoretical perspectives: human-animal relationships in sociocultural studies, the perception of nature and wildlife since the rise of modernity and wildlife through the lens of tourism discourse. After a methodological section, there is a short description of the history and structure of safaris to East Africa with emphasis on the unique case of Israeli safaris. The following section discusses two pairs of modernity's important characteristics: materialism and alienation, and the search for origins and disorientation. These will be discussed as sociological motivations for Israeli families to go on Bar Mitzvah safaris. The theoretical analysis of the exploration of Bar Mitzvah safaris as an intersection of tourism, modern secularity and human-animal interactions is summarized in the conclusion.

Theoretical Perspectives

Humans and Animals in Sociocultural Studies

The analysis of individual and social identity formation through human-animal interactions is one direction of study amongst a growing number of anthropological analyses delineating human-animal relations. In a review of sociocultural studies of human-animal relationships, Mullin (1999: 201–24) indicated three central trends of anthropological research: first, the drift from relating to animals as food to relating to animals as 'good for thought', meaning the classification of animals to create boundaries between groups of people through totems (Lévi-Strauss 1963; Leach 1970); second, animals as a source of moral conflicts and contradictions, as they serve as commodities, experimental lab objects (Sperling 1988; Haraway 1989) and family members (Arluke and Sanders 1996; Caglar 1997); third, the viewing the animals as 'Others' as part of a search for individual and social identity (Geertz 1994 [1972]; Ohnuki-Tierney 1990; Guggenheim 1994). This chapter continues this last trend.

Studies such as Geertz's Balinese cockfights, Guggenheim's critical analysis of cockfighting in the Philippines, and Ohnuki-Tierney's Japanese monkeys deal with social identities and sociopolitical processes reflected in performances of captive animals, in which chickens or monkeys are contextualized in specific cultural systems. In the case of East African safaris, the animals are not kept in captivity, and their performances are allegedly free from cultural context. A closer look, however, finds that the African continent provides a geographical and symbolic context for tourists, who are exposed to myths and images of Africa produced by various social and tourist agents (Adams and McShane 1996; Bruner 2005; Salazar 2010). As this study depicts, over the course of the safari, the centrality of previously received images of the wild diminishes, giving way to an accumulation of embodied tourist experiences: hearing, smelling and viewing the wild animals from a very short distance. The proximity of the wild animals evokes in the tourists emotional reactions, as opposed to the initial static images of animals. As a result, a gradual blurring of the boundaries of the wild Other occurs. Some tourists' utilitarian and superior perception of animals changes into reflective egalitarian thoughts on the role and place of wild animals in the world. These thoughts are evoked by the similarities of living beings behaving instinctively and naturally, apparently free from cultural intervention. Eventually, some tourists seem almost to become dependent on the display of wildness of the animals, in order to preserve their own nature and well-being in the technological, materialistic world that surrounds them at home.

Modernity and Human-Animal Relationships

A definition of modernity includes varied processes such as urbanization, rational work arrangements, geographical and economical mobility and the emergence of the nation-state as the central sociopolitical unit (MacCannell 1976: 7), as well as a counterprocess characterized by dismantling collectivity and the rise of the family as a central collective unit (Bauman 2000: 8). Both early and late modernity, which are not necessarily in chronological relation, set modern societies in hierarchal opposition both to their own past and to contemporary undeveloped societies, inappropriately named 'primitive'. These modern conceptual dichotomies are the same ones that led to the colonial occupation of Africa. The structural divisions are a continuation of an old allegedly premodern common opposition separating man and animal, viewing culture as superior to nature, and maintaining a utilitarian stance towards nature (see Chapter 3). Since the rise of the Romantic period in the eighteenth century, approaches towards nature have become more appreciative and, later, changed to a more a fearful one. Nevertheless, civilization required an increasing mastery of the wild (Freud 1950), and a hierarchical view of culture over nature was preserved.

This study will problematize this perception of superiority by examining the changing human perception of people in relation to natural environments. Many preindustrialized societies believed their fate was in the hands of nature and that there should be a reciprocal relationship between humans and environment (Curtin 2009: 453). Conversely, modern nature conservationists in postindustrial society believe the environment to be fragile and in need of human protection (Curtin 2009: 453). Since the Industrial Revolution, science and urbanization have maintained an ideological hierarchy of humans over animals, reinforcing the physical separation of humans from daily contact with animals. Ironically, the consequences of science (technology, virtual mediated forms of communication) and urbanization (which is responsible for the physical separation from nature) gave rise to a contemporary process of reuniting animals and humans, as reflected in increased pet keeping, zoo visits and wildlife watching (Vining 2003: 89). This study shows a fundamental emotional difference between watching nondomesticated wildlife in natural habitats and watching mediated wild animals in National Geographic movies or captive wild animals in a zoo. Although the safari takes place within an 'environmental bubble' (Cohen 2004: 117), inside four-wheel-drive cars and expensive hotel lodges which protect (or give the impression of protecting) tourists from environmental hazards, tourists report that the open roof and the possibility to observe, hear and smell the wild animals directly afford them an intimate experience in nature. This experience involves an arousal of childlike emotions, self-reflexivity and an encounter with the 'cradle of humankind', inducing an existential experience and creating a conceptual blurring of strict human-animal categories.

Wildlife through the Lens of Tourism Discourse

Most tourism scholars agree that contemporary tourism and international movements of people are rooted in modernity. Literature often depicts wildlife watching like any other modern phenomenon of cultural display or 'sites' (MacCannell 1976; Bruner 2005). National parks are viewed as a staged attraction, often perceived simply as a museum for animals or merely as another version of a zoo, where 'habitats and species populations are managed' (Norton 1996: 369). Early studies on wildlife tourism compared its authenticity with that of the *Mona Lisa* or with the experience of watching Niagara Falls (MacCannell 1976: 81). They divided *all* touristic attractions into pairs of authentic and nonauthentic, or front-stage or backstage dichotomies (MacCannell 1976: 91). This structural approach to tourism has been thoroughly criticized (Bruner 2005; Leite and Graburn 2009; Skinner and Theodossopoulos 2011) since it is unable to catch the fine points of tourists' experiences. Accordingly, this approach misses the reasons why wildlife and nature provide an escape from modernity. The wild animals in East Africa's national parks do not display a false front for tourists, relegating their 'natural' behaviour to some invisible backstage. It is very noticeable that they act naturally and instinctively, occupied with their own activities such as sleeping, grazing, socializing, mating or preying (Figure 8.1). What you see is what you get.

In escaping alienation, safari tourists seek an 'authentic experience' in which they can feel themselves and at the same time feel part of something bigger. 'Existential authenticity', according to Wang (2000: 49), is a genuine state of being that may be activated by tourists' activity within ecotourism, such as watching wildlife in a liminal open-air environment. A successful existential experience is perceived as a potential remedy for alienation or as means of being 'true to oneself' (Wang 2000: 58). A notion of existential authenticity was reported by tourists in semi-structured interviews. Moreover, the author has felt it during her own guiding of Bar/Bat Mitzvah safaris over the last ten years.

Figure 8.1 The wild animals behave naturally in the presence of tourists. Photograph by Rachel Ben-David.

Methods

A long process of defamiliarization has enabled the author to adopt a critical perspective towards tourism, safaris and the construction of the concept of wildlife, yet maintain an intimate perception of nature. In addition to guiding, the author has been involved with human-animal relationships as an animal-assisted therapist for the past ten years. The emotional, spiritual elevation involved in watching wild animals in their natural habitats is difficult to convey to those who have not experienced East African safaris; this chapter attempts to overcome this difficulty.

This study is based on seven different periods of participant observation in Israeli organized safaris to Kenya and Tanzania, six of which the author has guided herself, and a nine-day safari that she observed in August 2010. Fieldwork included more than forty interviews held with various actors involved in safari tours, from the age of twelve to the age of eighty, including travellers and guides.[4] Additional participant observation has taken place in local settings in Tanzania, providing an opportunity to experience the so-called backstage of tourism in the Lake Eyasi district and the enactment of so-called staged authenticity by local ethnic groups.

History and Structure of Israeli Safari Tourism

Safari tourism has become East Africa's first industry, hosting about two million tourists per year. The word 'safari' is derived from the Arabic word *saa'faria* meaning 'a journey'. The first safaris (driving in vehicles for leisure hunting, as opposed to survival hunting) were held by white colonialists around the turn of the twentieth century. A few decades later, conservationists began to insist on creating protected areas where wild animals could live freely with reduced threat of being hunted. Unfortunately, the process of establishing parks supported by conservation policies around the 1950s excluded local inhabitants from all aspects of the parks.

Around that time, Israel was established as a state and, metaphorically, became a conservation park for so-called hunted Jews from all over the world. Israeli society consisted of various ethnic and national groups, all of whom brought along different traditional Jewish trends. An allegedly egalitarian ideological policy (*kur hituch*) was formulated in order to create a homogeneous Israel, giving way to secular trends, especially among elite groups. Global capitalistic trends reached Israel only around the late 1970s. The development of the Israeli market and increasing involvement with Western capitalistic trends from the 1980s to the 2000s accompanied social changes within the country. These changes were reflected in the return of Sinai (Israelis' paradisiacal playground) to Egyptian sovereignty soon after the Camp David peace agreements, which resulted in a search for new, untouched destinations. An alternative paradise was found in East Africa. From the late 1970s to the early 1980s, organized elite groups from Israel began to visit Kenya and, later on, Tanzania, with a local agency called *Hachevra Hageographit,* the Geographical Company. This travel agency began to market the first safari tours as family tours to those who could afford it, offering each Bar/Bat Mitzvah boys and girls a free ride on a hot air balloon. Over the years, the free hot air balloon ride was dropped from the itinerary (returning as a marketing gimmick only recently), the safari tours were shortened and they became more expensive (from $1,500 in 1988 to $3,800 in 2012).

The structure of an organized family safari from Israel is quite fixed, similar in structure to safari tours from other Westernized countries elsewhere. The Israeli nine-day journey is usually very intensive compared with classic vacations, both Israeli and non-Israeli. It is far from relaxing—a day begins around 6.30 a.m. and ends around 6.30 p.m.—and is intensively planned with as many as five daily visits in the whole itinerary to a game reserve or national park. Tourists' involvement with wildlife during a safari is more central than their involvement with locals. Watching, talking, listening and photographing wildlife takes up fifty per cent of the tourists' waking hours (Figure 8.2). While an encounter with local Maasai is experienced as an exciting attraction, most Israeli tourists on safari regard it as an extra experience on the itinerary, while wildlife watching is considered a central aim. This preference is related to the parents' and grandparents' appreciation of nature as educational and having disciplining value. A second explanation is rooted in the romantic, colonial,

Figure 8.2   A Bar Mitzvah boy hunting with his camera. Photograph by Rachel Ben-David.

historical engagement with wild animals as well as the reluctance to express a colonial attitude towards the locals by adopting a more convenient and politically appropriate object for the tourist gaze. Both issues will be approached in the next section.

Motivations of Safari Tourists and Modern Identity Crisis

Not all Israeli safari tourists are wildlife watchers at home. The parents' or grandparents' choice of an expensive nine-day safari tour as a milestone of their children's or grandchildren's maturity celebration is motivated by overt and hidden social factors. This chapter will focus on two semi-overt pairs of allegedly undesirable social factors rooted in contemporary modern lifestyles: materialism and alienation, the search for origins and disorientation.[5]

The most prominent motivation of safari tourists is the exoticism of Africa. Based on my findings, in accordance with other studies, tourists tend to imagine wild African animals roaming together relaxed and freely in the Serengeti plains (Adams and McShane 1996; Salazar 2010). However, the everyday experience of wild animals is far from being relaxed because animals are always alert, watching carefully for predators or scavengers. Nevertheless, in the past two centuries, as aforesaid, there has been a massive production of essentialist myths and images about wildlife in Africa, Maasai people and African tribes. These productions are responsible for the tourists' yearning for an encounter with 'primitive Others'. An example of the rooted image of Africa can be seen in a tour leader's perspective:

> Safari involves the escape to nature, the magic. It is different than Europe...The landscapes, the third world, the climate, the animals, the tribes, all are perceived very primary...very exotic. (Ari, age fifty-five)

During the seventeenth and eighteenth centuries, such so-called tribes were considered too wild, irrational and immoral to be part of the human race. Their reconsideration as humans and not animals in the nineteenth century generated anthropology as a discipline. Under the paradigm of evolutionism, which led anthropology into the twentieth century, they were regarded as occupying the lower rungs of a hierarchal scale of cultures. These conceptions, tainted with racism, facilitated colonial rule and the subsequent formation of nature parks for white colonial hunters, which led in the mid-twentieth century to the eviction of Maasai and other ethnic groups from parks and areas designated for the conservation of wild animals (Akama 2004). Although they had lived for centuries among wild animals as part of an ecological system, they have not been regarded as equal partners in the ecological and economic strategies adopted after the establishment of national parks (Adams and McShane 1996; Akama 2004). During a safari, the historical background of these locals is usually excluded from the narratives told to the tourists; thus, the Africans living in villages around the national parks become distant Others. I find the intrinsic Otherness of wild animals similar to that of local people, except that there is no political incorrectness involved. Watching wild animals does not imply any Orientalist superiority. This point, thoroughly exemplified in Haraway's analysis of taxidermy, is displayed in a memorial museum for Theodore Roosevelt, who early in the twentieth century was hunting big game in East Africa. The obsessive need to kill or hunt the animal (first with a gun and later with a camera), and then accurately reconstruct it as a display of power and control over nature, was apparently done within a context of historical crisis, when romanticism and masculinity were threatened by industrialism and urbanization (Haraway 1985). As Haraway showed, these values supported and legitimated colonialist ventures, in which animals were perceived as cleaner of moral judgment since they belong to biologically different species. Therefore, words first used to describe the so-called primitives are now shifted to describe animals. The following quote from an Israeli guide and tour company manager demonstrates such an attitude towards the primordial quality of nature:

> When a man encounters animals in nature, he reaches his roots, his essence, and the powerful forces of his life. It is really a way to connect to our primordial life, to reach the days of man's descent in Africa. (Ron, age fifty-three)

Using the same discourse relating to local people would require a more moderate rephrasing since it is gradually becoming politically incorrect. This discourse is now shifted to animals, where it is unobjectionable.

Part of this chapter's main argument is that in order to understand tourists' motivation to go on safari, one should analyse tourists' actual experiences and mental state, as well as the gaze on Africa produced by different actors within the safari industry. A few psychological benefits of human-wildlife encounters are mentioned in the literature: the experience of 'flow', stress reduction, sensual vitality, as well as a sense of privilege, well-being and spiritual experience (Curtin 2009: 460–70). When contrasting these psychological benefits of wildlife encounters with the stresses of modern life (such as a disruption of a sense of flow and an illusion of well-being through the purchase of goods), one might begin to understand tourists' attraction to animals in the wild because they do not display any of the above characteristics. The experience of flow is visible in their performance, and it is quite clear to the audience they are very tuned to their needs. Consumer society has alienated consumers from their needs and made them purchase goods as social capital. Though usually not experienced as such by the Israeli teenagers, these modern phenomena have become parents' and grandparents' main concern for their youth's development of individuality. Seeing their youth occupy most of their days buying brand-name products and striving for the most up-to-date technological goods, parents and grandparents turn to the safari as an experience that might enable children to overcome materialism and alienation.

Materialism and Alienation

Critical sociologists such as the Frankfurt School thinkers have turned our attention to the consequences of modern trends of industrialization, such as the schematization of thought and creativity (Adorno and Horkheimer 2003 [1969]). They expressed their concern for humanity in the light of the potential for mass production to prevent self-fulfilment. One of the central consequences of modern trends is an obsessive involvement with material. This study's findings show adults' concern regarding contemporary youngsters' preoccupation with material matters:

> We're living in a modern world. Thirteen-year old kids are so materialistic. (Ana, age forty)
>
> We are living in a culture of abundance; everything has to be here and now, in a pace of life disconnected from nature. Children don't know where a tomato comes from; they think it comes from the supermarket. (Galit, age forty-four)

According to these tour guides, materialism imposes a certain undesirable pace of life perceived as unnatural, which dictates an endless need for immediate objects and satisfactions. Apparently, some Israeli youth are considered materialistic. But how are wild animals expected to serve as a remedy for this ailment?

The ability of natural settings to provide spiritual experiences has been recognized long ago. While the term 'spiritual' has religious connotations, its meaning in this context is how nature and particularly seeing wildlife affects participants' 'spirit', which is 'the vital principle or animating force and fundamental emotion' (Curtin 2009: 467). Spiritual experience may be regarded by parents and grandparents as the inverse of materialistic experience. It is interesting to follow the slight change of the term materialism when it relates to animals. It is common to view animals as preoccupied with materialistic matters such as food and other survival assets. Their perceived incapacity for spirituality is one of the central human-animal distinctions. Ironically, modern culture's preoccupation with material matters brings people to look for spirituality in the wild. Safaris in Africa and the encounter with wildlife may be perceived as a distraction from modern materialistic trends and from alienation. This distraction is reflected in the following tour guide's words:

> I recommend my friends to take their children and grandchildren on safari because of its added value: the encounter with nature and with non-captive animals in their natural habitat, the encounter with Africa…This doesn't exist in their virtual world (Disney, shopping,…) and their digital world (iPhones, iPads, television)…children run around all these media products and here (in the safari) it takes them away from the story. It makes them more children. (Ari, age fifty-five)

According to Ari, when one is 'taken away from the story' or distracted from modernity's temptations, the more desired aspects of his 'self become available to him', such as 'being a child'. The reconnection between nature (especially animals) and childhood was repeated in interviews, for example:

> The safari extracts the prehistoric man in you, the child in you…something in the openness to nature, in the fact of being outside hour on hour, very close to nature, causes us to peel layers and makes people feel more comfortable with each other, to joke with each other, to return to being children. (Nava, age forty)

The notion of returning to childhood is also echoed during a safari through embodied gestures. It is most explicit when a predator is spotted. I recall grandparents tucked calmly into their seats in the jeeps, when all of sudden one of the children (searching the area through the open roof) called everyone's attention to a predator in the far or near distance; those grandparents jumped up joyfully, stood high and practised a hunt with their camera, acting exactly like their grandchildren. Wang (2000: 8) mentions that 'nature tourism is surely one of the main ways of experiencing the "real" self.' Apparently, the experience of existential authenticity contains a connection to the inner child, and reduces alienation by peeling layers to maintain a sense of flow, of discovery and creativity (Csikszentmihalyi 2000).

Paradoxically, the same infrastructure enabling tourists to travel and battle the alienation and materialism of modernity is based on modern technology. The rejected objects of technology and modernity are the same ones that enable tourists' mobility around African nature. Technology's contradictory quality within tourism has been noted in the literature (Wang 2000). Unconscious of this duality, grandparents seek the restoration of self-fulfilment and real self in their grandchildren while taking them on a luxury tour through Africa. The ambivalent view of modernity's features, respect for technology, capitalism and simplicity, along with rejection of backwardness, materialism and alienation, strengthens the children's identity as subjects of modernity. In this context, keeping in mind the dominance of modernity's features (such as technology), it is easier to understand the Bar Mitzvah as a symbolic maturation rite of passage into the modern world. So the purpose of Bar Mitzvah safaris is not to condemn modernity but to enable a critical view of it. This is reflected in the tour leader's words:

> This is a way to take the Israeli Bar/Bat Mitzvah boys and girls through a different maturation rite of passage…I expect my child to return to Israel with more appreciation for what he has, and remember that technology and materialism are important—I don't expect him to give them up—but know their appropriate weight in life, and that at the end we are all animals, and should protect the most basic values: respect and love for others, of a place and of nature. (Danny, age forty-three)

This sensibility was echoed by the teenagers themselves. In an interview a while after she returned from safari in Tanzania, Gaya said:

> I think there is a special reason this trip took place around my Bat Mitzvah. Maybe I'm maturing, and learning more things about the world. To know what's happening outside the bubble I live in…to know the Other…and the lions. Not like in the zoo, they are learning to persist and overcome difficulties. The food doesn't come directly to their hands; you can see them try, making an effort, chasing zebras and gnus. (Gaya, age twelve)

To sum up the paradox, along with humanistic values such as 'respect for others', these safaris are intended to increase teenagers' appreciation for what their parents and modern society have given them, although they express little awareness of the great privilege that enabled their parents and grandparents to pay for such safari experiences. Materialism is not condemned. It is elevated, in danger of being unappreciated. Consequently, the safari simultaneously expresses objection and confirmation of modern materialism. African safaris, I argue, provide a perfect medium for the assimilation of an essentially ambiguous secular modernity; they contain both parts of the formula, the opposite of modernity and the best of it.

The Search for Origins and Disorientation

A frequent attitude among Israeli tourists towards East African safaris is to regard them as a journey into humanity's past. Many nineteenth-century explorers and present-day travel agents subscribe to imaginaries of the past (Salazar 2010, 2012), such as a 'primordial Africa' and the biblical Garden of Eden. In one of the interviews, an Israeli tour guide voiced a common view among adult Israeli tourists:

> The more the world becomes technological, digital, materialistic and urbane, there's a turn back, an aspiration to search for the most virginal and basic, in the earth, grass, lions, zebras, horses, elephants, birds and human beings. It's a way of returning to origins. I'm not kidding when I call some gorilla tours 'a returning to roots journey'. I truly think gorillas and monkeys are our ancestors, because it's going back a long time. Not 15 years back, but 5 million! (Danny, age forty-three)

The need for a symbolic journey back to the origins of humanity is a common theme, not necessarily amongst moderns. In his book *Le mythe de l'éternel retour*, Mircea Eliade (2005 [1971]) maintained that revisiting archetypes from a mythological past provided archaic peoples with a sense of meaning in everyday life, permitting them to reconnect with creation narratives.

Jewish identity is affirmed by a similar religious enactment of historical occasions, such as the Jewish life cycle (circumcision, Bar Mitzvah and weddings) and Jewish holidays (such as Passover, Sukkoth and Hanukah). Non-Jewish aspects of secular life enter through the Jewish life-cycle window and reflect different new meanings, often related to modern alienation. An alternative frame of meaning to God's creation is natural selection, a theory which is emphasized repeatedly during the safaris. African wildlife—in its straightforward meaning of nondomesticated animals that live in the wild and not necessarily in its constructed romantic meaning—is perceived as humanity's prehistoric past. Young interviewees make a clear distinction between animals living in their natural habitat (wildlife) and animals living in a zoo, emphasizing their preference for natural habitat since it provides a context for an instinctive behaviour that the captive animals apparently do not present. Paradoxically, instinctive behaviour is usually suppressed in social situations among humans, but at the same time, it is perceived as a desirable behaviour because of its genuineness and realness. In other words, wild animals in cages are not appropriate models for natural behaviour since they are castrated from their instincts and distant from their own nature, but wild animals in their natural habitat are perceived as being themselves:

Within nature there's more realness. The animals act completely naturally. This is a capacity we have lost. (Rina, age sixty)

Looking deeply into this quote, one recognizes disorientation. According to Bauman (2000: 68), the collapse of modern political structures and the positioning of the individual instead of society as a basic unit of the political order left the individual with a need for better guidance. Living in a global world (which is accessible at home to Israeli tourists who go on safari), leaves many individuals in a search for new models of behaviour. The authority for guidance is looked for in other people's lives. This may account for the proliferating numbers of reality shows and talk shows, in which celebrities as well as common people share their successful life story with the public. Not only is there renegotiation of a mobile boundary between private and public, but there is a redefinition of the public sphere, as a scene on which 'private dramas are staged, put on public display and publicly watched' (Bauman 2000: 70). I would like to suggest broadening this definition of social sphere to include social performances by wild animals (wildlife), watched by safari tourists. As aforesaid, wildlife behaviour is perceived as more real and authentic, and therefore as a potential source of guidance. According to some of the tourists, modernity has attributed people with artificial behaviour, and wildlife can serve as models:

At the end we're all animals…We can learn from their relationships…Love, courting, intimacy, mutual fostering, when you see the monkeys clean each other, grooming…one needs to see it in order to learn how to be a human being. Personally, I'm a veteran father. I learned a lot from watching parents and their offspring in nature. It might sound like a stupid cliché, but I mean it. When I play, roll or run wild with my children on the rug or on the sofa, going under a blanket, it's like monkeys playing with their young—sorry, I will not lick them, because this is an act that humans don't do to their children, but kisses, hugs, flirting and all of that—it makes you understand how important it is. (Danny, age forty-three)

Danny did not refer to animals only for guidance. He saw them as entities with which humans may profitably measure themselves against as parents, children and partners. Tour leaders report that during safaris philosophical and existential questions are evoked among the tourists, including Israeli teenagers. An inevitable question might be, How are such significant issues aroused by watching wildlife? I believe wild animals, with their similarities and differences from humans, represent ambivalent aspects of society. 'Nature arouses ambivalent feelings, as something which is a product of society and, at the same time, a separate entity. Perhaps', Almagor writes, 'that is the reason nature remains an *enigma*' (1985: 43).

Unlike the Egyptian pyramids or the *Mona Lisa,* nature and wild animals were not created by people (though some will argue about the constructed concept of wildlife). Avoiding questions of creation by God or nature, the intrinsic difference between monuments and wildlife is seen to lie in nature's independent existence:

> Nobody told the lions to prey on the gazelles. And the gazelles, nobody told them to eat the grass. No one is directing the rains…There is some kind of an ecological order…There's no planning, managing, all these hot modern terms, and it works! (Danny, age forty-three)

When left in their natural habitat, wild animals live according to nature's cycle and adaptive survival rules. There is no human management. On the other hand, walking across the streets of Paris, looking up the Arc de Triomphe or Notre Dame, one inevitably gets the notion of human intervention and power. Looking out of the roof of a safari four-wheel drive into the plains of the Serengeti, one absorbs nature's power.

People's place in nature, their relation to nature, and culture-nature differentiation are all identity issues not receiving satisfactory attention in Israeli teenagers' busy materialistic lives. It seems that, at least in their elders' perceptions, an idealized relationship with nature may replace the relationship with God. This idea may accord for a view of safaris to Africa as pilgrimage to the holy secular space of the cradle of humankind. The contact with the sublime, wholly Other, untamed by human utilitarianism, nourishes the depleted spiritual significance of the Bar Mitzvah in this Israeli section of secularized society. This sacred contact might be hiding some unspoken aspects of modernity such as social status, postcolonial injustice towards African locals and Orientalist power within the tourist gaze of Africa. Thus, these Israeli East African safaris may be viewed as pilgrimage to the best and worst of modernity.

Conclusion

Family safaris or Bar Mitzvah safaris provide new meanings for Jewish-Israeli religious practices emptied of their traditional values. The antidote to the harmful consequences of modern everyday life is found in natural settings of wildlife in Africa. Safari in Africa is chosen as a medium for designing identity, through an evocation of connection with the past, through the encounter with wild animals that appear as models and a source of guidance and through provision of an alternative frame of meaning for life. The safari is perceived as capable of combating the ills of alienation and reaffirming 'natural' family values (Figure 8.3). The performance of the wild animals' instinctive behaviour, their educational role and connection with spirituality enables the elders and their youngsters to ignore the contradictions of the materialist infrastructure of the safari tour and the differential (postcolonial) power relations that it manifests. Among these Israeli seculars, materialism is seen as a root of decadence. Interestingly, the structure of the safari and its long physical and cultural distance from home enable tourists to attack materialism and technology as

Figure 8.3 Members of four families on safari in Tanzania. Photograph by Rachel Ben-David.

the culprit without investigating how it enables the entire safari adventure to take place. By doing it there in Africa, they do not have to change anything in their real lives back home.

This study demonstrates the uniqueness of wildlife in both human–animal interactions and in tourism arenas. The prominence of biological and survival features in wildlife makes them an ultimate Other and sought-after entities for an identity search, free of the political incorrectness often embedded in tourist-local interactions. Compared to other tourist sites or attractions, wildlife in natural habitats are in constant motion and change, acting independently according to ecological and biological laws, and apparently free of human management. Thus, instead of admiring human creations and society's productions, tourists encounter a different kind of performance, a unique kind of authenticity. They often experience a reconnection to their true self and to their own nature, similar to Wang's description of existential authenticity (2000: 49). Ironically enough, wildlife serve as models for human intuition and real behaviour, of forgotten human basic practices such as courtship and parent-child nurturing. Unintentionally, wildlife provides an alternative frame of meaning for those who seek guidance and self-knowledge in a consumer-dominated world of fluid and fractured identities (Bauman 2000).

This chapter attempted to problematize the hierarchical opposition between humans and other animals. Juxtaposing humans and animals highlights their similarities as well as differences and, at the same time, makes them both equally capable of comparison. However, despite the alleged blurring of the strict human-animal dichotomy embedded in the safaris, there is a constant objectification of wild animals through the romantic gaze on the wild, through the constant photographing of wildlife and through the use of wild animals' intrinsic naturalness in order to construct a more coherent human identity. This process is magnified through the Israeli case study of Bar Mitzvah safaris and demonstrates the potential of human-animal interactions as a fruitful field of anthropological insight.

Notes

1. For secular Jewish girls, the precise term is Bat Mitzvah, and it is celebrated at the age of twelve instead of thirteen. Because of space limits, analysis based on gender issues will not be approached in this chapter.
2. It should be noted that many Bar/Bat Mitzvah boys and girls choose to celebrate this birthday at a famous European or American city (London, Paris, New York, etc.) and go shopping with their parents. This study focuses on a special sector of society, which chooses safaris in East Africa as their destination.
3. According to Karl Mannheim (1952) in his essay *The Problem of Generations,* a generation's conception becomes consolidated through the elite nucleus of society (Mannheim [1952] in Almog 2001: 29). Therefore, this study might be able to provide interpretations relevant to a wider section of the generation, adults and teenagers, in current Israeli society.
4. In this chapter there is an emphasis on quotes related to guides, who participated in 25 per cent of the interviews in this study. Based on their close acquaintance with Israeli tourists, and given the longer period of time to contemplate issues raised in the interviews, guides frequently provided the most articulated and complex views, as can be seen throughout this chapter.
5. I refer to these factors as semi-overt since they were not revealed to me through participant observation in safari tours, but in semi-structured interviews usually held after the safaris. Some scholars might have considered them as hidden factors.

References

Adams, J. S., and T. O. McShane. 1996. *The Myth of Wild Africa: Conservation without Illusion.* 2nd ed. Berkeley: University of California Press.
Adorno, T., and M. Horkheimer. 2003 [1969]. 'The Culture Industry: Enlightenment as Mass Deception'. In M. Mey-Dan and A. Yasur, eds, *Frankfurt School* [in Hebrew]. Tel Aviv: Sifriyat Hapoalim, 158–98.

Akama, J. S. 2004. 'Neocolonialism, Dependency and External Control of Africa's Tourism Industry'. In C. Hall, ed., *Tourism and Postcolonialism: Contested Discourses, Identities, and Representations.* London: Routledge, 140–52.

Almagor, U. 1985. 'A Tourist's "Vision Quest" in an African Game Reserve'. *Annals of Tourism Research* 12: 31–47.

Almog, O. 2001. *The Sabra—a Profile* [in Hebrew]. Tel Aviv: Am Oved.

Arluke, A., and R. Sanders. 1996. *Regarding Animals.* Philadelphia: Temple University Press.

Bauman, Z. 2000. *Liquid Modernity.* Cambridge: Polity Press.

Bruner, E. 2005. *Culture on Tour: Ethnographies of Travel.* Chicago: University of Chicago Press.

Caglar, S. 1997. '"Go Go Dog!" and German Turks' Demand for Pet Dogs'. *Journal of Material Culture* 2(1): 77–94.

Cohen, E. 2004. *Contemporary Tourism: Diversity and Change.* Oxford: Elsevier.

Csikszentmihalyi, M. 2000. *Beyond Boredom and Anxiety.* San Francisco: Jossey-Bass.

Curtin, S. 2009. 'Wildlife Tourism: The Intangible, Psychological Benefits of Human-Wildlife Encounters'. *Current Issues in Tourism* 12(5–6): 451–74.

Eliade, M. 2005 [1971]. *The Myth of the Eternal Return: Cosmos and History.* Princeton, NJ: Princeton University Press.

Escobar, A. 1999. 'After Nature: Steps to an Antiessentialist Political Ecology'. *Current Anthropology* 40(1): 1–30.

Feldman, J. 2008. *Above the Death Pits, Beneath the Flag: Youth Voyages to Poland and the Performance of Israeli National Identity.* Oxford: Berghahn.

Freud, S. 1950. *Totem and Taboo: Some Points of Agreement between the Mental Lives of Savages and Neurotics.* London: Routledge and Kegan Paul.

Geertz, C. 1994 [1972]. 'Deep Play: Notes on the Balinese Cockfight'. *Daedalus* 101(1): 1–37.

Guggenheim, S. 1994. 'Cock or Bull: Cockfighting Social Structure, and Political Commentary in the Philippines'. In A. Dundes, ed., *The Cockfight: A Casebook.* Madison: University of Wisconsin Press, 133–73.

Haraway, D. 1985. 'Teddy Bear Patriarchy: Taxidermy in the Garden of Eden. New York City, 1908–1936'. *Social Text* 11: 20–64.

Haraway, D. 1989. *Primate Visions: Gender, Race, and Nature in the World of Modern Science.* London: Routledge.

Leach, E. 1970. *Claude Lévi-Strauss.* Chicago: University of Chicago Press.

Leite, N., and N. H. Graburn. 2009. 'Anthropological Interventions in Tourism Studies'. In T. Jamal and M. Robinson, eds, *The Sage Handbook of Tourism Studies.* London: Sage, 35–64.

Lévi-Strauss, C. 1963. *Totemism.* London: Merlin.

MacCannell, D. 1976. *The Tourist: A New Theory of the Leisure Class.* New York: Schocken Books.

Mannheim, K. 1952. 'The Problem of Generations'. In P. Kecskemety, ed., *Essays on the Sociology of Knowledge.* London: Routledge, 276–322.

Mullin, M. 1999. 'Mirrors and Windows: Sociocultural Studies of Human-Animal Relationships'. *Annual Review of Anthropology* 28: 201–24.

Norton, A. 1996. 'Experiencing Nature: The Reproduction of Environmental Discourse through Safari Tourism in East Africa'. *Geoforum* 27(3): 355–73.

Noy, C., and E. Cohen. 2005. *Israeli Backpackers and Their Society: A View from Afar.* Albany: State University of New York Press.

Ohnuki-Tierney, E. 1990. 'The Monkey as Self in Japanese Culture'. In E. Ohnuki-Tierney, ed., *Culture through Time: Anthropological Approaches.* Stanford, CA: Stanford University Press, 128–53.

Salazar, N. 2010. *Envisioning Eden: Mobilizing Imaginaries in Tourism and Beyond.* Oxford: Berghahn.

Salazar, N. 2012. 'Tourism Imaginaries: A Conceptual Approach'. *Annals of Tourism Research* 39(2): 863–82.

Shanklin, E. 1985. 'Sustenance and Symbol: Anthropological Studies of Domesticated Animals'. *Annual Review of Anthropology* 14: 375–403.

Skinner, J., and D. Theodossopoulos, eds. 2011. *Great Expectations: Imagination and Anticipation in Tourism.* Oxford: Berghahn.

Sperling, S. 1988. *Animal Liberators: Research and Morality.* Berkeley: University of California Press.

Urry, J. 1990. *The Tourist Gaze: Leisure and Travel in Contemporary Societies.* London: Sage.

Vining, J. 2003. 'The Connection to Other Animals and Caring for Nature'. *Human Ecology Review* 10(2): 87–99.

Wang, N. 2000. *Tourism and Modernity: A Sociological Analysis.* Oxford: Elsevier.

–9–

Becoming-animal in the Chinese Martial Arts

D. S. Farrer

[S]he who does not succeed in mastering the 'spirits' will be 'possessed' by them.

(Eliade 1974: 450)

Southern Praying Mantis is a practical fighting art from Hong Kong and Southern China. Mongkok, the Hong Kong site where I travel to learn martial arts, is the most densely populated place on Earth. Long street-markets crisscross Nathan Road, a thoroughfare of incessant screeching, hissing buses. Gold and diamond merchants jostle with massage parlours haunted by 'triad' gangsters (*hut sair wui*) serviced by the underclass of local and imported working girls (see also Boretz 2011: 176–203; Mathews 2011). In my research, Mongkok provides an ethnographic mirror to London's East End, where to borrow a phrase from Ellis Finkelstein, the East End is ever a 'tough place for hard men' (1996: 682). Although areas of Stratford received an £11 billion makeover for the 2012 Olympics, the change is cosmetic, a cover for the reality of the high rates of violent crime including rape, robbery and murder—much of it race, turf and gang-related (Dench, Gavron and Young 2006).[1] Narratives of violence, war, migration, poverty, inequality and exploitation nourished the seedling of Southern Mantis in Hong Kong. In the 1970s, this style transplanted successfully to London on the way to global expansion.

Applying Gilles Deleuze and Félix Guattari's formulation to Southern Praying Mantis is not without its difficulties. Their polysemic book, *A Thousand Plateaus: Capitalism and Schizophrenia,* resists linear, bounded, monodirectional readings to unleash the creative potentials of ambiguous rhizomic multiplicity; thankfully, theoretical deviations or offshoots are encouraged (Massumi 1992). The concept of 'becoming' is rife with permutations—becoming-intense, becoming-imperceptible, becoming-molecular, becoming-woman and becoming-transvestite, just to name a few. Becoming-animal is also illuminated in the writings of Eliade (1974), Goh (2011) and Ingold (2011a). My goal here is straightforward: to provide a framework to explore the practice of becoming-animal in Southern Mantis. This chapter examines Chow's Family Southern Praying Mantis (Chow Gar) to delineate a field of action involving animals (*dong mut*) and humans, where humans develop secret powers of the body derived from observation and self-experimentation combined with centuries of embodied—not just oral—transmission. Becoming-animal is defined here as the unleashing of hidden human potentials (affects) to inquire, 'Of what is a body capable?'[2] Might practitioners acquire the strange capabilities of becoming-telepathic, becoming-invulnerable or becoming-immovable through some bizarre animal or insect agency?

A schism between nature and culture is not necessarily assumed in non-Western languages or cultures. Chinese ontology, embodied in the physical culture of martial arts, differentiates Heaven, Earth and Hell, the realm of spirits and gods, from the lower realm of animals and demons and places humanity centrally between these polarities (Chan 2006). Although the realms are discrete, they are permeable with movement between them through reincarnation to higher- and lower-ranked forms. Through breathing exercises (*hay gong*), martial arts practitioners draw inspiration, sustenance and life force (*hay*) from clean mountain air, from the sunrise at daybreak, from celestial configurations such as The Plough (*but dou chut sing*) and from the moon, trees, oceans, waterfalls, rivers and lakes. Traditional Chinese martial arts are embodied Daoist practices, with *tangki,* Buddhist and Confucian influences, passed down from the ancestral masters and brought to life in the practice of current and future generations (Schmieg 2005; Chan 2006; Shahar 2008; Boretz 2011; Farrer and Whalen-Bridge 2011; Lorge 2012). Embodied martial legacies, such as Chow Gar, considered here, are treasure troves of esoteric skills.[3] Discussion of the development and transmission of these martial skills serves to address the theme of vital powers through the development of human potentials towards the natural capabilities of animals.

Under the glare of eagle eyes, the martial movements of Chow Gar range through mouse, plum-blossom and unicorn steps; dragon, horse, frog and crane stances; tiger, eagle and bear claws, whilst striking out with leopard, phoenix and ginger fists. The favoured weapon of Chow Gar is a seven-foot staff held at one end and twisted 'like a yellow cow's tongue'. Practitioners train to move like cats. Fluid arms slither and snake, swing like an elephant's trunk and wipe like the forelegs of a fly. Each animal and element possesses special attributes, including heaviness, stickiness, agility, ferocity, tenacity, accuracy and rapidity. Death strikes lash out with lightning speed towards acupuncture points. Considered spiritual, the Southern Praying Mantis embodiment of nature is simultaneously practical, revealing a sophisticated understanding of the human animal.

Representation and *mimicry* are prevalent terms in anthropology, performance studies, martial arts, dance and other discourses that associate martial postures, religious iconography and shamanic dance to the mimicked movements of animals—where performers, martial artists, dancers and shamans ostensibly copy or reproduce the movements of some animal, whether symbolic, mythical, imaginary or actual (Eliade 1974; Taussig 1993; Schechner 1994). In Chinese martial arts, animals operate on symbolic and mythical registers, yet mythical animals such as the dragon (a symbol of good fortune comprising aspects of horse, eagle, ox, snake, deer and fish) and the phoenix may be accorded the same or higher status than actual animals such as the tiger and crane (Hsu 1997: 197). Meaning in the martial arts is situated at the level of embodied experience, at the level of skilled practice, which lies beyond straightforward observation of the Other and beyond textual, historical, philosophical and religious inquiries that reduce animal correspondences to metaphorical, mythical or symbolic levels. Hence this chapter utilizes embodied and ethnographic experience to recount a somatic mode of attention that underscores symbolic interpretations (Turner and Bruner 1986; Csordas 1993, 1999; Welton 2011; for embodied epistemologies in dance see Ness 1992; Crosby 1997; Cruz Banks 2010).

For Deleuze and Guattari (2002 [1980]: 278–305) becoming is rhizomic; it does not depend on systems of a scientific classification or genealogy. Becoming is never imitating, nor does it proceed via representation, analogy or metaphor. Hence, according to Deleuze and Guattari's schizoanalytic perspective or nomad philosophy: 'Becomings-animal are basically of another power, since their reality resides not in an animal one imitates or to which one corresponds but in themselves, in that which suddenly sweeps us up and makes us become … "the Beast"' (2002 [1980]: 279). Although some initial imitation appears essential to learn Chinese martial arts, true skill is not reducible to the slavish reproduction of forms (that Orientalist ontology of identity) but must include skilled practices designed to induce spontaneous martial innovation (an ontology of difference) (May 2005; Schmieg 2005). The intermediate form Eighteen Swimming Dragons (*sup baat yau loong*) of Chow Gar, for example, may be combined and recombined into any number of possible configurations, where it is understood that each move refers to a type of animal-human *capacity* for movement. For dedicated martial artists practising Chow Gar, secret instruction combines with individual, experiential and creative perusal to fuse mind, body and spirit towards the attainment of skill. Must we assume, therefore, that agency, spirit or *Geist* is inherent in the acquisition of martial skill? And is *agency*—spirit—the 'becoming' in becoming-animal, becoming-intense or becoming-actual?

Because agency as active doing relates to the processes of becoming-animal in Chow Gar, we must pause to consider the objections of Tim Ingold, master of the 'dwelling perspective', to theories of agency in anthropology. Ingold accepts notions of becoming-animal while dismissing agency.[4] In *Being Alive,* Ingold (2011a: 12) regrets his earlier conceptual borrowing of 'dwelling' from Heidegger, invoking as it does a *static point,* or clearing in the forest, that with his more recent concern with *lines of movement* he now regards as better formulated via the concept of habitation (see also Ingold 2000; 2007). Thus, for Ingold, '[t]he path, and not the place, is the primary condition of being, or rather of becoming' (2011a: 12). Western philosophy aside, the path, of course, is the fundamental principle of Daoist philosophy and practice. Chow Gar is a Daoist path or Way towards individual attainment, a form of becoming-animal, as we shall see, that ultimately requires the master to awaken the animal within the acolyte. Ingold's problem with agency is scattered throughout his writings. He regards agency as 'magical mind dust' sprinkled here and there to bring dead matter to life (Ingold 2011a: 28). His main concern is that matter, things and people should not be regarded as dead and in need of ingesting some animist spirit, but as existing *in life.* From a nomadic perspective, however, failure to become animal, or become human for that matter, may lie with the withdrawal or displacement of agency, culminating in mindless ghouls inhabiting or dwelling in the environment, reenacting ritual promises in countless repetitions of habitual action with '[p]eople speaking without being fully conscious of the inhuman agency that speaks through them' (Massumi 1992: 29).

Becoming-Ethnographic

This research draws from performance ethnography conducted in Hong Kong and London and elucidates insider experience (Turner and Bruner 1986; Cox 2011).[5] Martial performance ethnography is where the researcher joins in and learns a martial art (Zarrilli 1998; Downey 2005; Farrer 2009, 2011; Boretz 2011). Contrasted to practitioner ethnography in sociology, performance ethnography derives from the anthropology of performance (Turner 1988; Schechner 1994). Recent research has combined ethnographic accounts with performance studies, literature, film, theatre and cultural studies to launch martial arts studies to 'investigate martial knowledge as it exists in the contemporary world through a discussion of embodied fantasy, of how the social body trains martial arts, and of self-construction in an era characterized by transnational diasporic identity formation' (Farrer and Whalen-Bridge 2011: 10).[6]

Chow Gar comprises a method for the development and transmission of deadly martial skills (Smith 1990 [1974]; Henning 1999). Considered as a war machine, Southern Mantis is not so much an apparatus of capture as an apparatus of murder. Chow Gar is one of four major branches of Southern Praying Mantis, including Chu Gar (Chu Gar Tong Long), Kwong Sai Bamboo Forest (Kong Sai Jook Lum) and Iron Ox (Teet Ngau)—all of which supposedly developed during the seventeenth or eighteenth century.[7] These styles are sometimes referred to as Hakka Fist or Wanderer's, Vagabond or Beggar Arts (Sect) (*lau man gao pai*), said to have originated from the martial arts with which so-called gypsy travellers equipped themselves some 800 years ago (Guldin 1997; Mark and Hayward 2012). The primogeniture of the various styles, however, does not belong to this chapter, which is concerned with becoming-animal. Becoming-animal was a theme I encountered in my research among a group practising Chow Gar in the East End of London, a practice that I followed up in subsequent research. It was the start of regular travels to Hong Kong that became a personal quest to sharpen or polish (*chup,* slang for 'to tidy up') my martial skills.

My own self-construction via Chow Gar precedes my performance ethnography by more than a decade. In 1996, after eight years of training—four years of which took five or more hours per day—I took the tenth stage exam in Chow Gar, from Sifu Paul Whitrod's school in the East End of London.[8] Turning up for the tenth stage test, I was disconcerted to see another student there to take the same examination. This student was my senior, *sihing* (elder brother), a tough, six-foot-three Jamaican man whom I had fought previously in sparring. The *sihing* was very strong, fit and skilled at boxing. A year before, during a forty-five minute round of sparring, he pummelled my face black and blue. That night I left the club sore that I had lost to him yet again. Subsequently, I said to my *sifu* (master) that if no matter how much extra I trained and learned I could not win, then what was the point?[9] Sifu's paradoxical response was to ban me from sparring for an entire year. I had to stand aside during sparring and do breathing exercises instead. For the black belt grading, my *sihing* and I performed unarmed sets, weapon sets, two-person fighting forms and other partnered exercises.[10] Next, Sifu Whitrod said: 'There is only one black sash. You have to fight each other for it. The winner takes the black sash. The loser has to leave the club for good.' My *sihing* put up an impressive fight. But trained in *hay gong,* fuelled with adrenalin, and frustrated from not being allowed to spar for a year, I overpowered him without difficulty. Sifu told me later that this was the point of the breathing exercises—a point that hitherto I had not understood.

After I won the black sash, my tearful *sihing* was quietly dismissed. Then my *sifu* said: 'I have taught you everything I can for now. Go away and learn another style, and when you are done, come back.' Sifu Whitrod and I had made fifty-five instructional films together, all on martial arts. Mostly, I was the cameraman, although I do appear briefly in fifty-three of the films. After looking around at various martial arts, and engaging in several challenge fights in London, I took up *silat Melayu,* which was billed as 'black-belt training'. But this is another story, related in *Shadows of the Prophet* (Farrer 2009).[11]

Southern Praying Mantis

Legend has it that Chow Gar emerged from the Fukien Shaolin Temple, which was destroyed when the monks became involved in the revolutionary uprisings against the Ming Dynasty (1368–1644) (Shahar 2008: 184). When their temple was destroyed, the monks went to live in the villages and taught their martial art to the villagers.[12] Some practitioner accounts of the origin of Chow Gar emphasize the founding of the style in a Daoist rather than Buddhist temple (Mark and Hayward 2012). Yet other theories claim the art is the secret family style of the displaced Ming emperors, the former rulers who lived in disguise in exile. The basis for this royal theory is that the major motifs running through the system are the Phoenix and the Dragon, the primary symbols of the Ming Dynasty emperors, subsequently disguised under the symbol of the praying mantis—the King of Insects.[13]

The Chow Gar origin myth relates how Chow Ah Naam, the system's founder (*sijo*), entered the Southern Shaolin monastery to be treated for an illness. Chow worked as a cook in the temple where a skilled fighting monk bullied the other residents. Whilst in the forest collecting firewood, Chow witnessed a praying mantis face off against a blackbird. The mantis struck out, and the bird fell. Picking up the bird, Chow saw a red line across its throat. Afterwards, Chow caught many praying mantis insects and teased them with chopsticks to learn their movements and devise his own fighting system, which he employed to defeat the bully. Abbot Chan Yin (Siem Yin Fong Jerng) witnessed the fight and decided to reveal the monastery's secret training methods to Chow Ah Naam. Leaving the temple, Chow Ah Naam, now a Buddhist monk, took Wong Fook Go as his disciple in Dong Jiang, Southern China. Wong Fook Go, who became a travelling Buddhist monk, moved to Hui Yang, a Hakka town, to escape the chaos at the end of the Manchu era and took Lau Soei, also known as Lau Sing Chor, as his disciple. Because of the Sino-Japanese war, they moved to Hong Kong where they adopted the name Tung Kong Chow Gar Tong Long Pai for the Southern Praying Mantis system. In Hong Kong, Ip Kai Shui (1913–2004) was one of the prominent disciples of Lau Soei (1866–1942), who had numerous students scattered everywhere like 'peach blossoms' (Ip Shui 1965).

Chow Gar martial skills are taught, harnessed and developed through a series of increasingly complex and sophisticated partnered training procedures. The practitioner's understanding of the human body, mind and spirit is reconfigured through the application of training methods, skills, indigenous medicines and epistemologies designed to reveal the dark or hidden powers (*um ging*) of the body. The training methods are handed down from generation to generation within the Chow Gar genealogy with each grandmaster contributing personal embellishments and wisdom over the centuries. For example, Lau Soei emphasized the praying mantis as a concept for fighting a much bigger opponent with lightning speed (*siem deen*) and the use of spring force (*tan ging*).

Chow Gar training produces powerful hand and leg techniques, using aggressive short-range strikes fired at the vital areas of the body with machine-gun-like rapidity. Chow Gar deploys the 'phoenix eye' fist, where the fore-knuckle of the index finger protrudes. Exponents are trained to strike vital points on the opponent's body using very fast, relaxed, heavy blows that rely on the generation of rib bone power (*dip gwut gong*) and shock body power (*gen tung gen*) through forces unleashed by (among other things) compressing the ribs whilst twisting the waist.[14] With its concentration on two-man patterns of exercises, from brutal conditioning such as back-hand hitting, shin bashing, hammer hand hitting (*gau choi*) and back bashing (*bic bui*) to stylized two-man fighting forms, Chow Gar is truly a social art, best trained together with a partner, rather than in solo practice, to produce a formidable fighter.

Chow Gar utilizes high rather than low stances and prefers low kicks. Southern developments contrast to Northern praying mantis (*tanglangquan*) styles, such as Seven Star Praying Mantis (Chut Sing Tong Long), which is characterized by flamboyant, flashy techniques imitative of animals and insects and utilizes high kicks and dramatically low stances. Chow Gar is not an imitative style to the same degree as *tanglangquan,* which directly mimics the movements of a mantis (combined with the footwork of an ape) (Liang and Wu 2001: 447). Instead, Chow Gar's becoming-animal embodies the spirit, essence or properties of the mantis, where the mantis is a vehicle for the development of the hidden powers of the human body. Here symbolic and embodied systems operate together and are only artificially separated.

The kung fu patrilineal kinship naming system ranks adherents within the organizational status hierarchy based on kinship terms including great-grandmaster (*tai sigong*), grandmaster (*sigong*), master (*sifu*), elder brother (*sihing*), elder sister (*sijie*), younger brother (*sidi*) and younger sister (*simui*). The fictive kinship system has considerable social and economic implications for the members where 'seniority [not age] determines a member's standing' (Amos 1997: 45). As with most families, there is some rivalry and schism. Thus many subvariants of the original, supposedly monastic Southern Praying Mantis system have splintered off, each headed by individual charismatic leaders.

Daoist *hay gong* practices include restrictions on intercourse before and directly after training and taboos on masturbation. The principle concerns controlled ejaculation so as not to waste vitality or life force. Daily, seated meditation at dawn demonstrates a principle of continuous movement and the circulation of energy through the energy cycle known as the microcosmic orbit (*siu zhou tien*) (see also Chia 1989). Partner and solo exercises are designed to achieve the capability to sense and transmit energy and to sense the opponent telepathically, an unusual sensory development outside of the Western norm.[15] The *hay gong* aspect of Chow Gar is developed only after many years of suffering the pain of ascetic physical development, and each step further into *hay gong* is accompanied by yet more brutal exercises designed to attain hidden power. Within the style, asceticism and mysticism are two sides of the same coin, the yin and the yang of a Chinese dialectical system of developing the spiritual and physical abilities concurrently. Asceticism finds its rationale in myth, and myth ascends towards reality through the pain of suffering. The acquisition of real power and skill enables practitioners to take the sheer punishment of the ascetic dimension. In a system as practical as Chow Gar, however, the mystical or spiritual dimension is not always readily developed. Eventually, some practitioners look beyond Chow Gar towards more expansive religious experiences, vis-à-vis Hinduism, Krishna Consciousness and New Age movements.

Training Methods

Chow Gar develops the hidden or dark powers (*um ging*) including sharp eyesight, strong bones, iron fingers, flexible sinews and extraordinary strength, all trained through sweat, blood and breath. Meditation heightens sensitivity to the enemy's movements, feelings and intentions. These embodied skills are taught, harnessed and developed through a series of arduous partnered training procedures, including grinding arm (*chy sau*) and dozens of specialized two-person hitting exercises such as *doi chong*. The practitioner's understanding of the human body, mind and spirit is reconfigured by the application of training methods, skills and epistemologies derived from the revelation of the human body's hidden natural potentials.

Due to adverse health issues, some great martial masters were not initially permitted to learn martial arts, so they spied upon people teaching and learning and then practised alone, fervently, in secret, until they attained skills superior to the disciples. Having demonstrated their skill in combat, a rite of passage usually involving a fight with a fierce senior student, they became disciples (*yup moon diji,* literally 'enter the door disciples') of the master, to subsequently become the next grandmaster in their turn. Hence, to teach yourself Ta'i Chi, for example, and go for occasional adjustment would seem practicable and also precedented.[16]

The teach-yourself approach, however, is ill advised in Chow Gar. Breathing exercises to develop the hidden powers of the art, if wrongly executed, may cause serious injury. Moreover, the art places great emphasis on partner work to develop sensitivity, which is well regarded as a type of 'somatic mode of attention' (Csordas 1993; Welton 2011). The practice of Chow Gar emphasizes the development of the right type of musculature, alongside correct body posture and spinal alignment, necessary to develop speed, fluidity and power. In classical kung fu, there are several requirements to attain superb martial skills including repetitive gripping and relaxing (dynamic tension), holding positions for extended periods of time (isometrics), relaxed moving meditation and the practice of forms, or sets of movements strung together in patterns.[17] Chow Gar practitioners train to develop the 'iron shirt' (*tit bo sarm*) and the 'golden bell cover' (*gum gung jow*). By repeatedly tensing and relaxing the muscles, the iron shirt works from the outside in to produce a tough layer of musculature and cartilage to protect the vulnerable parts of the body, filling out and hardening the soft cavities around the joints. Through controlled and pressurized breathing, the golden bell cover works from the inside out to a similar, though more powerful, effect.

Chow Gar practitioners train to develop the hidden powers of nine areas of the body: the neck, shoulders, chest, elbows, wrists, waist, hips, knees and ankles. These powers must be synchronized with the five small strengths (*ng sui ging*) and the five big strengths (*ng daai ging*). The big strengths include strengthening the trunk through *narn hay gung* (iron shirt power); shoulders, upper back, elbows, wrists and waist power (*yue gung*); and the mind power, or intent (*yi*). The small strengths include training the senses (such as eagle vision), gritting the teeth (to strengthen the temple, neck and jaw), attaining throat power (*how gung*), iron fingers (*teet tsee*) and toes and *dan tin gung* to strengthen the core (Whitrod 2004: 35). The following Chow Gar poem illustrates some of the powers developed:

> Explosive shock power (*geng tan ging*)—rib bone skill (*dip gwut gung*),
> Pangolin press-ups (*chune sarn gap*)—iron finger power (*teet tsee gung*),
> Seizing dragon claws (*nar loong jau*)—able to pick up a mountain (*but sarn gung*).[18]

Chow Gar emphasizes the precise and controlled application of power—power that is assisted by reflex but is not subject to reflex. The result of being struck by such power, another Chow Gar poem suggests, resembles being 'struck by lightning, felt not seen'.

Death Strikes (*Dim Mak*)

According to oral history, Wong Fook Go possessed black fingertips like steel talons. He is rumoured to have killed a man by smashing his fingertips into the man's skull. Lau Soei, before he trained Chow Gar, was master of *ma kuen* (horse fist) and was famous for killing a wolf with a kick and a stomp. An intellectual and scholar, having passed the exam to enter the Chinese court, Lau Soei killed seven men during his career as a fighter. Lau Soei struck one man in the liver with his fingertips (*chup sau*) whereupon he took three months to die. Every strike in Chow Gar is aimed at a vital point (pressure point) to disrupt the central nervous system. The principle of death touch (*dim mak* or *dim huet*) is like acupuncture (or better, acupressure) in reverse, where every acupoint has a particular way, direction and time of day to be struck to inflict serious damage. Given the sheer power developed by the mantis practitioners, the knowledge of *dim mak* may seem superfluous, granted they may snap the opponent's collar bones, rip out ribs, crush the larynx, snap and dislocate bones with a seize and twist and, in Ip Shui's words, even strip the flesh from an opponent's arm 'like removing a sock' (personal communication 1993).

The ability to sense pressure points through the fingertips is also acquired through the study of bone-setting medicine, to heal broken bones, sprains, back pain and other problems through massage, manipulation and realignment, usually involving the external application of copious amounts of bone-setting medicine (*dit dar jow*), a liniment made with Chinese herbs and alcohol.

In Hong Kong, my teacher is Li Tin Loi, a retired policeman of ferocious intensity, who teaches through continual adjustment in minute detail (Figure 9.1). Li's fingers are as hard and firm as the spikes on a heavy-duty metal rake. Invariably frowning, his eyes flick from person to person. Li's attack style is to jab sharp and quick with the hands whilst suddenly rotating his body.

A student of Sifu Li related a road-rage altercation that he had with a taxi driver, who stepped out of his taxi shouting and swinging his arms around. The student seized the taxi driver by the throat (*kum la sau*) in a move that fully executed could crush the windpipe. Such ferocity connects to one of the more disturbing aspects of the training. Intrinsic to *dim mak,* the death strike, is the ability to size up the enemy. This involves surveying the opponent to map out their weak points, vulnerable acupuncture points (*huet wai*) such as a long neck, weak shoulders, a big jutting jaw, bulging eyes and so forth. I found this training quite repulsive after six months on the London underground randomly sizing up hundreds of people every day. The plus

Figure 9.1 Sifu Li Tin Loi (left) demonstrates *yiu kui* (shake the bridge), Hong Kong, 2007. Photograph by D. S. Farrer.

side, however, is that pursued alongside the bone-setting medicine the practitioner may perceive other people's health problems, such as back, neck, shoulder and other joint problems, which prompts some Chow Gar practitioners to specialize in traditional Chinese medicine.

Grandmaster Ip Shui

Grandmaster Ip Kai Shui possessed the remarkable ability to stick to the ground as if he were a giant rock. During a demonstration in 1993, I saw five English students seize this small seventy-nine-year-old man by the arms, waist and legs, yet fail to lift him off the ground. The grandmaster was impossibly heavy for his slight frame (Figure 9.2). Ip Shui's lower back was as solid as a truck tyre, and not a millimetre of flesh could be pinched from his forearms. His throat descended at a forty-five-degree angle from his chin to his clavicles. After training, at a Chinese brunch (*dim sum*) in London, the grandmaster once invited me to press his throat. I felt an incredible mass of cartilage covering his windpipe built up through a lifetime of training the throat, temples and neck. Responding to his amused invitation, I rapped my knuckles on his

Figure 9.2   Grandmaster Ip Shui, Hong Kong, 1950s. Photograph courtesy of Sifu Paul Whitrod.

throat, which felt like knocking on hard plastic. During impromptu performances, the grandmaster would chop himself in the throat with rapid self-inflicted blows to no ill effect.

During his demonstrations, the grandmaster did not obviously tense his throat, back or body. To be relaxed in Chow Gar does not mean absolute relaxation, just as to be firm does not require permanent tension. Some practitioners did not understand the yin-yang dialectic of tension and relaxation. One advanced practitioner kept his big muscular body in a perpetual state of tension, making him look and feel tough; but this created a stiff, slow, ponderous body that waddled around like a bloated duck. Imitation is never becoming (Deleuze and Guattari 2002: 272, 305).

Grandmaster Ip Shui and his son, David Ip (the current Grandmaster Ip Chi Keung), possessed the ability to withdraw their testicles and take strikes in the groin area whilst remaining impervious to pain (*sun sook kit*). At seminars, they would invite astonished members of the audience to kick them between the legs. 'Spread 'em baldy; your ball-bag is about to head north', said one rude television presenter, who interviewed Master David Ip and kicked him between the legs to test his in-vulnerable 'skin of steel'. Despite multiple hard kicks, the blows had no effect on the master, who got revenge by kicking the presenter back. Though a groin cup shielded his vital target, the presenter collapsed to the ground. Not having learned his lesson, the presenter later playfully attempted to strike Grandmaster Ip Shui between the legs. Ip Shui was at that time sitting and enjoying a cigarette. Although 91, the grandmaster lashed out with a quick slap and a kick to the groin flooring the presenter once again.[19]

Though listed on the tenth and last stage of the syllabus, according to Sifu Whitrod, it is 'not necessary for some' to acquire the skill of 'training up the testicles' in order to complete the training. Sifu taught the relevant exercises in the seniors' class to many a ribald snicker. To train the testicles to go up, the student begins by patting his testicles from a raised horse stance, then from a high stance lifts his arms open wide and draws in the abdomen, all the while imagining the testicles being sucked back up into his body. According to the theory behind the practice, until and during the onset of puberty, the testicles may be massaged and eased up into the abdominal cavity. The practice of raising the testicles is recommended to boys who should continue the daily practice into adulthood to maintain the ability. Apparently, the testicles may be easily withdrawn or returned at any time, with no damage to virility.[20]

Beyond becoming-transvestite, raising the testicles in Southern Mantis—to render the groin impervious to strikes—invokes notions of becoming-female, which for Deleuze and Guattari (2002: 277) is the key to any becoming. Becoming-female is salient here given that the female praying mantis eats the male upon copulation:

> Lacan borrows an example from animal behavior—that of the female praying mantis, which bites off the head of her male partner during copulation—and asks us to imagine the following hypothetical situation ... You are wearing a mask that makes you look

like either a male or female praying mantis, but you do not know which; a female pray-ing mantis approaches, making you extremely anxious. The anxiety you feel may well be worse in the case in which you do *not* know whether you are disguised as a male or female, than in the case in which you know you are disguised as a male. (Indeed, in the latter case what you experience is simply *fear* of a specific fate that is soon to befall you.) Hence you may prefer to *assume* or *conclude* that your death is nigh because you are dressed as a male, even if you are not sure this is true. If we take the female praying mantis here as the Other (the real, not the symbolic Other), you may prefer to assume the Other is out to get you—to assume that you know what it is you are for the Other, what object you are in the Other's desire—than to remain anxiously uncertain. Lacan refers to the latter form of anxiety as angst (*angoisse*), which is far more upsetting and unsettling than awaiting certain death (leading to what Freud calls 'realistic anxiety'—in other words, fear). (Fink 1999: 60–1)

Donning the skin of an animal is a feature of the modernist Chin Woo Athletic As-sociation whose exponents posed as muscle men in leopard skin leotards (Kennedy and Guo 2010). This dress, however, was only the dramatic, theatrical presentation of a deeper cultural practice, neatly summed up by Eliade:

> But we must not forget that the relations between the shaman ... and animals are spiritual in nature and of a mystical intensity that a modern desacralized mentality finds hard it difficult to imagine ... donning the skin of an animal was becoming that animal, feeling himself transformed into an animal. (1974: 459)

Eliade suggests that the Chinese Daoists inherited the ancient shamanic tech-niques of ecstasy, the mastery of spirits, whereas pseudoshamans (defined as those who walk the easier path)—the exorcists, mediums and the possessed—inherited an 'aberrant tradition of shamanism' (1974: 450–6).[21] Homologous with the years of practice required to achieve genuine martial skill, the Spirit Style (*Sun Da* or Sun Gung) exponent is not a trained martial artist, but possessed by a spirit, possibly through the services of a medium or sorcerer:

> By becoming this mythical animal [Ancestor or Demiurge], man became something far greater and stronger than himself ... this projection into a mythical being ... showed the shaman his power and brought him into communion with cosmic life. (Eliade 1974: 460)

Irving Goh's (2011) notion of becoming-animal draws from fourth-century BCE Chinese philosopher Chung Tzu's parable of the butterfly: a man dreams he is a butterfly only to awaken and wonder if he is a butterfly dreaming. Goh (2011) notes that the notion of 'the pack', essential to Deleuze and Guattari's formulation, is absent from this classic example of becoming-animal. The pack, however, is ex-emplified in the case of Chinese martial arts. *Pai* means 'sect', a breakaway element, branch or separate group. Often, Chinese martial groups exhibit profound cult-like behaviour such as the swearing of oaths of lifelong solitary allegiance, ritual oaths to become a disciple (*bai si*) that share a performative tradition with the so-called triads (see Boretz 2011). Little ritual is manifested in Chow Gar as compared to other traditional systems that have become primarily ritualistic on their way to becoming-replica. Nevertheless, the pack exhibits a marked solidarity of the flesh, or corporeal sodality. Martial arts groups and triads, however, are not identical. Although there are triads among the Chow Gar practitioners, Li Tin Loi told me: 'I am a police-man, and not one of them. My master, Ip Shui was not a triad and did not like them either.' Li remembers how angry Ip Shui was when he discovered that one of his students had sworn into a triad brotherhood.

Awakening the Animal

So what has agency to do with becoming-animal, becoming-insect, becoming-mantis? And what has this to do with Ingold? Ingold (2011a) invokes Deleuze and Guattari's formula of becoming-animal to shore up his position that animal names are reduced to nouns where animals are regarded as objects or things, whereas if they were regarded as alive (in the same way as humans), they would be named individually or, better still, would be named with verbs. Hence, the fox is not a fro-zen object ossified against the snow, but a streak through the undergrowth. This is Ingold's becoming-minor, becoming-molecular, in opposition to the dominant molar positions of social theory and Western society. Yet the emergent nature of the fox, its becoming-animal, does not force us to accept the notion that animals lack conscious-ness or interiority (King 2004).

Whilst much of the information necessary to develop Chow Gar is contained within the forms and two-person practice, an expert is required to enlighten (*hoi gwong* 開光) or awaken the animal within the disciple. Awakening the animal may be easier for some practitioners than for others. Such power may make them more or less than human. Whilst awakening the animal may evoke the power of the martial deity Vajrapāṇi, in Chow Gar it awakens the intent (*yi*) of the martial artist (Shahar 2008: 37). Awakening the animal within also occurs in lion dance, in the ritual of *hoi gwong,* where prior to its first performance the lion's eyes must first be brushed with cinnabar or lustral water, so that the animal may spring into existence through the energetic performance of the pugilist dancer (who must be a kung fu practitio-ner). Minus such awakening, the lion is inert, and the martial arts and dance moves are like words on a page that have been read but never understood. The cliché that the master (*sifu*) holds onto the best fighting secrets until his or her deathbed is not just a script in *Kung Fu Panda.* The masters choose when to reveal their secrets and to whom. The practice may be scripted, but the script is subservient to the social-historical interactions of the acolytes, the disciples and the masters who are becoming-animal, becoming-insect, becoming-mantis. Even the master remains a work in progress. The key aspect of the training is the continual revelation of esoteric embodied knowledge through practice. Not everything is taught—only a quarter. The practitioner must work out the rest, a conundrum only possible through awakening the animal as outlined above.

Conclude with Open Hands

Ingold, as recounted earlier, spurns wholesale the notion of agency as a Victorian attribution of animist thought. He claims that the animist perspective, originally developed by E. B. Tylor (1913 [1871]) at the very foundation of British social anthropology, is one of spirit or 'magical mind dust', whereas Ingold locates perception (contra spirit, agency, understanding, consciousness, classificatory schema and *mentalités*) as not somehow occurring inside the actor's heads, instead emerging as human organisms dwell or navigate paths through the environment. Ingold dismisses cognitive theories such as agency in favour of a phenomenological understanding of the world as immanent and emergent, a world that folds, unfolds and refolds via the lines of individual trajectories. Aside from the influences of Heidegger, Merleau-Ponty and Gibson, Ingold's (2000) notion of perception evokes Bateson's (2000 [1972]: 135) rejection of Freud's unconscious as a problem posed the wrong way around. Therefore, Bateson formulated consciousness as an arc from the individual into the environment (other) and not merely something inside a person's head. We speak the same language that exists outside of our heads, so consciousness (agency) is not of the individual psyche but embedded in social relations (which for Ingold is the environment).

In the performance of Chinese martial arts, changing the hand changes the animal. Human hands are first of all simian and, in that sense, all kung fu begins with the monkey. For Deleuze and Guattari, the key to all becomings is becoming-female. For Chow Gar adepts who can withstand groin strikes, becoming-female is part of the journey to becoming-invulnerable. Becoming-female counters the anxiety of getting struck in the testicles—in addition to not being eaten by the female praying mantis upon copulation. Not everybody who trains in Chow Gar will attain the same dark powers in becoming-animal as Grandmaster Ip Shui. Other becomings are not precluded. Nevertheless, in Chow Gar, as in lion dance, a symbolic agency must awaken the animal for the becoming-animal to emerge.

Hence it is superfluous to dispense with agency in the problem of becoming-animal. Animals in the martial arts are not simply imitative; nor are they necessarily slippages into fantasy, mythic or theatrical registers (Holcombe 2002). In Chow Gar, becomings-animal involve *techniques du corps* inherent in our molecular animality but hidden by our molar human form (Mauss 1979: 107). Grandmaster Ip Shui became-mantis, even as others only managed to imitate. While the martial arts training counts for the most part in becoming-animal, a symbolic awakening is required on the journey to becoming.[22] Some agency beyond skilled practice is required, an agency or active doing 'in the sense in which becoming is the process of desire' (Deleuze and Guattari 2002: 272).

Chinese martial arts are rhizomic, continuously folding, unfolding and refolding into history and practice. Seemingly impenetrable boundaries between schools and systems were inevitably breached where individuals with family connections learned multiple versions of praying mantis, cognate and other styles. Such sharing is accelerated given the wide availability of materials on the Internet, especially on YouTube and other social media as people everywhere are becoming-virtual. Might we now see a new era of cooperation emerging among martial arts groups? Perhaps a whole new era of martial sophistication will emerge alongside a martial arts renaissance? The pessimistic alternative, however, is too much information, where an excess of material leads to too little practice of any one training method, resulting in the dilution of the art and the disempowerment of martial arts practitioners, where once solid powerful movements become soft and weak. Becoming-animal in Chinese martial arts requires discipline of the body, the acquisition of embodied power and the development of murderous skills. Other, implicit meanings of becoming-animal relate here, of course, to the desire of the other to 'fuck you up', as they say in the East End of London. Vicious urban street fights, and the angst, fear and grief they cause, shall no doubt fuel the acquisition of secret fighting skills for many years to come. Meanwhile, becoming-animal in the way of the old masters continues to elude the copycat.

Acknowledgement

My thanks go to the late Grandmaster Ip Shui, the current Grandmaster David Ip, Sifu Paul Whitrod and Sifu Loi Tin Loi for lessons in Chow Gar. Thanks to Ah Bun and Joe Race for partner work in Hong Kong, and to all my kung fu kindred, especially Ah Kin, Brett Thiedeke and Erten Dervish. Yong Feng and Charlie Lee participated in the fieldwork and helped with translation. This research was supported in part by research and travel grants awarded by the College of Liberal Arts and Social Sciences at the University of Guam from 2007 to 2012. This chapter springs from a conference paper, 'Becoming Animal in the Chinese Martial Arts', on the panel '"Natura Artis Magistra": Nature Is the Teacher of Artful Skill' presented at the ASA11: *Vital Powers & Politics: Human Interactions with Living Things,* September 2011. Available at: http://www.nomadit.co.uk/asa/asa2011/panels.php5?PanelID=919.

Notes

1. Regarding the estimated financial cost of the London 2012 Olympic Games, see http://www.guardian.co.uk/sport/datablog/2012/aug/13/olympics-2012-data-journalism.

2. Spinoza's question, reiterated by Deleuze and Guattari (2002 [1980]: 256; May 2005: 3).
3. See Lorge (2012: 10–1) for a summary of 'kung fu' definitional issues.
4. Theoretical discussion is truncated here in favour of ethnographic data. I have written more extensively about Alfred Gell (1998, 1999 [1992]) and agency elsewhere (Farrer 2008, 2009, 2012).
5. Cox (2011) sketches some of the processes involved in training martial arts and writing ethnography that resonate with my work.
6. This chapter examines a 'traditional' Chinese martial art, a 'primary Chinese discipline', and is not concerned with the derivative or ersatz versions prevalent in the invention of tradition of Chinese nationalist discourse (Brownell 1995; Morris 2004; Schmeig 2005: 122).
7. There is an acrimonious dispute between exponents of Chu Gar and Chow Gar regarding which is the original style and which is the offshoot, but this chapter does not concern this debate.
8. See http://www.chowgarsouthernmantis.com/instructuk.php.
9. I began training martial arts in England during the 1970s at the age of eight. From 1988 to 1996, I studied Chow Gar as an indoor student under Sifu Paul Whitrod. An 'indoor student' (disciple) trains full time and does chores instead of paying for classes: adopted by the master, they are taught beyond the regular syllabus. Throughout this period, I recorded notes after every lesson.
10. The stylized movements of Chinese martial arts contained within the sets provide a rich vein of symbolic representation and may be based on the movements of animals, outlaws, heroes, assassins, immortals and deities. Such movements proceed frame by frame and when combined form combat scenarios that rehearse a series of 'strips' of combative behaviour and premeditated responses (Goffman 1974; Farrer 2006: 30, 2011: 221–2). During instruction, the movements are frozen in space and individually named as different positions or 'stances'.
11. For visual illustration of *Shadows of the Prophet,* see my *Art of Silat:* http://www.youtube.com/watch?v=pFDAe7NR5FA.
12. Other monks took a different path to develop so-called triad organizations, which originally possessed social, religious, political and economic functions beyond the narrow British colonial definition of triads as criminal syndicates. See also Elliot (1998).
13. See http://www.chinamantis.com/.
14. Relax (*sung* 鬆, literally 'loose') is a difficult term to translate, learn or teach. In Chinese martial arts, 'relax' does not mean soft, listless, floppy movements but refers to a nonrigid fluid power full of energy and intent.
15. Howes and Ingold have engaged in several rounds of intellectual sparring concerning perception and the senses that indicates the strengths and weaknesses of their respective positions; see, for example, Howes (2011) and Ingold (2011b).

16. Huo Yunjia, legendary founder of the Chi Woo Athletic Association allegedly learnt his art this way.
17. 'Routine', 'form and 'set' are interchangeable concepts that refer to specific choreographed sets of movements passed down within various styles of kung fu. A 'style' of kung fu refers to a type of kung fu, such as Praying Mantis, that is constituted of sets of movements alongside other specific exercises. A 'school' of kung fu is a social organization of one or more styles. See Farrer (2011: 228n3).
18. See http://www.southernmantis-litinloi.hk/fist.sturture.html.
19. See http://www.youtube.com/watch?v=hyNmV2Y43ko.
20. Martial art novitiates could well consider the following advice for cross-dressers, transvestites and pre-op transsexuals: 'The easiest way to learn to tuck [the testicles away] is to lie flat on your back with your feet flat on the floor, and find the place to push them into your abdomen. This will generally be straight up, relative to your body... With a bit of practice, you can do the tuck in less than a second while standing up and pulling your panties on...' (source: http://www.transgenderzone.com/library/pr/fulltext/50.htm).
21. On Chinese exorcists (*tang-ki*'s), see Chan (2006) and Sutton (2003).
22. Abram (2011: 132), a philosopher who independently develops a dwelling perspective from his own experiences, says, 'our actions have resonance only to the extent that they are awake to the other agencies around us, attuned and responsive to the upwelling creativity in the land itself.' This presents further dimensions to the problem of dwelling and agency and opens vistas for further research.

References

Abram, D. 2011. *Becoming Animal: An Earthly Cosmology.* New York: Vintage.
Amos, D. 1997. 'A Hong Kong Southern Praying Mantis Cult'. *Journal of Asian Martial Arts* 6(4): 31–61.
Bateson, G. 2000 [1972]. *Steps to an Ecology of Mind.* Chicago: University of Chicago Press.
Boretz, A. 2011. *Gods, Ghosts and Gangsters: Ritual Violence, Martial Arts, and Masculinity on the Margins of Chinese Society.* Honolulu: University of Hawai'i Press.
Brownell, S. 1995. *Training the Body for China: Sports in the Moral Order of the People's Republic.* Chicago: University of Chicago Press.
Chan, M. 2006. *Theatre Is Ritual, Ritual Is Theatre: Tang-ki: Chinese Spirit Medium Worship.* Singapore: Singapore Management University and SNP.
Chia, M. 1989. *Iron Shirt Chi Kung.* Vol. 1. New York: Tuttle.

Cox, R. 2011. 'Thinking through Movement: Practicing Martial Arts and Writing Ethnography'. In T. Ingold, ed., *Redrawing Anthropology: Materials, Movements and Lines.* Farnham: Ashgate, 65–76.

Crosby, J. 1997. 'The Dancer's Way of Knowing: Merging Practice and Theory in the Doing and Writing of Ethnography'. *Etnofoor* 10(1/2): 65–81.

Cruz Banks, O. 2010. 'Of Water and Spirit: Locating Dance Epistemologies in Aotearoa/New Zealand and Senegal'. *Anthropological Notebooks* 16(3): 9–22.

Csordas, T. 1993. 'Somatic Modes of Attention'. *Cultural Anthropology* 8(2): 135–56.

Csordas, T. 1999. 'Embodiment and Cultural Phenomenology'. In G. Weiss and H. F. Haber, eds, *Perspectives on Embodiment: The Intersections of Nature and Culture.* New York: Routledge, 143–64.

Deleuze, G., and F. Guattari. 2002 [1980]. *A Thousand Plateaus: Capitalism and Schizophrenia,* trans. Brian Massumi. London: Continuum. (Original edition *Capitalisme et schizophrénie 2: Mille plateaux.* Paris: Les Éditions de Minuit.)

Dench, G., K. Gavron and M. Young. 2006. *The New East End: Kinship, Race and Conflict.* London: Profile Books.

Downey, G. 2005. *Learning Capoeira: Lessons in Cunning from an Afro-Brazilian Art.* Oxford: Oxford University Press.

Eliade, M. 1974. *Shamanism: Archaic Techniques of Ecstasy,* trans. Willard R. Trask. Princeton, NJ: Princeton University Press/Bollingen.

Elliot, P. 1998. 'The Boxers: The Fists of Righteous Harmony'. In *Warrior Cults: A History of Magical, Mystical and Murderous Organizations.* London: Blandford.

Farrer, D. S. 2006. 'Deathscapes of the Malay Martial Artist'. Special edition on Noble Death, *Social Analysis: The International Journal of Cultural and Social Practice* 50(1): 25–50.

Farrer, D. S. 2008. 'The Healing Arts of the Malay Mystic'. *Visual Anthropology Review* 24(1): 29–46.

Farrer, D. S. 2009. *Shadows of the Prophet: Martial Arts & Sufi Mysticism.* Dordrecht: Springer.

Farrer, D. S. 2011. 'Coffee-Shop Gods: Chinese Martial Arts in the Singapore Diaspora'. In D. S. Farrer and J. Whalen-Bridge, eds, *Martial Arts as Embodied Knowledge: Asian Traditions in a Transnational World.* New York: State University of New York Press, 203–38.

Farrer, D. S. 2012. 'The Performance of Enchantment and the Enchantment of Performance in Malay Singapore'. *Moussons* 20(2): 11–32.

Farrer, D. S., and J. Whalen-Bridge. 2011. 'Martial Arts, Transnational Affiliations and the Paradoxes of Embodied Knowledge'. In D. S. Farrer and J. Whalen-Bridge, eds, *Martial Arts as Embodied Knowledge: Asian Traditions in a Transnational World.* New York: State University of New York Press, 1–28.

Fink, B. 1999. *A Clinical Introduction to Lacanian Psychoanalysis: Theory and Technique.* Cambridge, MA: Harvard University Press.

Finkelstein, E. 1996. 'Status Degradation and Organizational Succession in Prison'. *British Journal of Sociology* 47(4): 671–83.

Gell, A. 1998. *Art and Agency: An Anthropological Theory.* Oxford: Oxford University Press.

Gell, A. 1999 [1992]. *The Art of Anthropology, Essays and Diagrams.* London: Athlone Press.

Goffman, E. 1974. *Frame Analysis: An Essay on the Organization of Experience.* Boston: Northeastern University Press.

Goh, I. 2011. 'Chuang Tzu's Becoming-Animal'. *Philosophy East and West* 61(1): 110–33.

Guldin, G. 1997. 'Hong Kong Ethnicity: Of Folk Models and Change'. In G. Evans and S. M. Tam, eds, *Hong Kong: The Anthropology of a Chinese Metropolis.* Honolulu: University of Hawai'i Press, 25–50.

Henning, S. 1999. 'Academia Encounters the Chinese Martial Arts'. *China Review International* 6(2): 319–32.

Holcombe, C. 2002. 'Theater of Combat: A Critical Look at Chinese Martial Arts'. In D. Jones, ed., *Combat, Ritual and Performance: An Anthropology of Martial Arts.* London: Praeger.

Howes, D. 2011. 'Reply to Tim Ingold'. *Social Anthropology/Anthropologie Sociale* 19(3): 318–22.

Hsu, A. 1997. *The Sword Polisher's Record: The Way of Kung Fu.* Boston: Tuttle.

Ingold, T. 2000. *The Perception of the Environment: Essays in Livelihood, Dwelling, and Skill.* London: Routledge.

Ingold, T. 2007. *Lines: A Brief History.* London: Routledge.

Ingold, T. 2011a. *Being Alive: Essays on Movement, Knowledge and Description.* London: Routledge.

Ingold, T. 2011b. 'Reply to David Howes'. *Social Anthropology/Anthropologie Sociale* 19(3): 323–7.

Ip Shui 葉 瑞. 1965. *Mantis Kung Fu San Sao* 螳螂拳散手. 香港:錦華出版社. Hong Kong: Jinhua.

Kennedy, B., and E. Guo. 2010. *Jingwu: The School That Transformed Kung Fu.* Berkeley, CA: Blue Snake Books.

King, B. 2004. 'Social Communication as Dance'. In *The Dynamic Dance: Nonvocal Communication in African Great Apes.* Cambridge, MA: Harvard University Press, 1–41.

Liang, S., and W. Wu. 2001. *Kung Fu Elements: Wushu Training and Martial Arts Application Manual.* East Providence, RI: Way of the Dragon.

Lorge, P. 2012. *Chinese Martial Arts: From Antiquity to the Twenty-First Century.* Cambridge: Cambridge University Press.

Mark, G. F., and R. Hayward. 2012. *Kwong Sai Jook Lum Gee Southern Praying Mantis Kung Fu: History, Principle, Technique.* St Paul, MN: Shu Kuang Press.

Massumi, B. 1992. *A User's Guide to Capitalism and Schizophrenia: Deviations from Deleuze and Guattari.* Cambridge, MA: Swerve/MIT.

Mathews, G. 2011. *Ghetto at the Center of the World: Chungking Mansions, Hong Kong.* Chicago: University of Chicago Press.

Mauss, M. 1979. *Sociology and Psychology: Essays,* trans. Ben Brewster. London: Routledge and Kegan Paul.

May, T. 2005. *Giles Deleuze: An Introduction.* Cambridge: Cambridge University Press.

Morris, A. 2004. 'From Martial Arts to National Skills: The Construction of a Modern Indigenous Physical Culture'. In *Marrow of the Nation: A History of Sport and Physical Culture in Republican China.* Berkeley: University of California Press, 185–229.

Ness, S. 1992. *Body, Movement and Culture: Kinesthetic and Visual Symbolism in a Philippine Community.* Philadelphia: University of Pennsylvania Press.

Schechner, R. 1994. 'Ritual and Performance'. In T. Ingold, ed., *The Companion Encyclopedia of Anthropology: Humanity, Culture and Social Life.* London: Routledge, 613–47.

Schmieg, A. L. 2005. *Watching Your Back: Chinese Martial Arts and Traditional Medicine.* Honolulu: University of Hawai'i Press.

Shahar, M. 2008. *The Shaolin Monastery: History, Religion and the Chinese Martial Arts.* Honolulu: University of Hawai'i Press.

Smith, R. 1990 [1974]. *Chinese Boxing: Methods and Masters.* Berkeley, CA: North Atlantic Books.

Sutton, D. 2003. *Steps of Perfection: Exorcistic Performers and Chinese Religion in Twentieth-Century Taiwan.* Cambridge, MA: Harvard University Press.

Taussig, M. 1993. *Mimesis and Alterity: A Particular History of the Senses.* New York: Routledge.

Turner, V. 1988. *The Anthropology of Performance.* New York: PAJ.

Turner, V. W., and E. M. Bruner, eds. 1986. *The Anthropology of Experience.* Urbana: University of Illinois Press.

Tylor, E. B. 1913 [1871]. *Primitive Culture: Researches into the Development of Mythology, Philosophy, Religion, Language, Art and Custom.* London: Murray.

Welton, M. 2011. 'From Floor to Stage: Kalarippayattu Travels'. In D. S. Farrer and J. Whalen-Bridge, eds, *Martial Arts as Embodied Knowledge: Asian Traditions in a Transnational World.* New York: State University of New York Press, 161–84.

Whitrod, P. 2004. *Close-in Fighting Skills of Chow Gar Hakka Southern Praying Mantis Gung Fu.* Stratford: n.p.

Zarrilli, P. 1998. *When the Body Becomes All Eyes: Paradigms, Discourses and Practices of Power in Kalarippayattu, a South Indian Martial Art.* New Delhi: Oxford University Press.

–10–

Anthropomorphism, Anthropocentrism and the Study of Language in Primates

David Cockburn

Kanzi

This chapter will focus on a presentation—in the book *Kanzi's Primal Language* (Segerdahl, Fields and Savage-Rumbaugh 2005)—of a famous study of the language abilities of the bonobo.[1] I will be concerned, in particular, with questions about the *aims* of such research and with charges of anthropomorphism or anthropocentrism that may be levelled at this and other forms of ape language research.

First, however, I must say something about what is distinctive of this study. I will try to give a flavour of the kinds of behaviour displayed that grounds the claim that the bonobo under study have language. Here are two examples:

> The film illustrates how Kanzi's language emerged in activities that are normal to apes, such as travelling in the woods and finding food, but these activities were enriched with linguistic interaction...Sue asks Kanzi to break some sticks for the fire they are making and he immediately does so. In another scene Kanzi suggests, on the keyboard, that he wants to go to a particular place in the forest but Sue is not sure what he means, so she makes guesses in English to which Kanzi listens attentively. When she finally guesses correctly, Kanzi nods and begins to walk. (Segerdahl et al. 2005: 14)
>
> Caregivers continually ask Kanzi what he wants to eat or do, they inform him what is about to happen, they ask him for help to collect and return bowls and toothbrushes, and if occasionally a caregiver tries to organize these matters without coordinating linguistically with Kanzi or Panbanisha, she soon has to deal with a group of very obstinate bonobos. (Segerdahl et al. 2005: 39)

I found such descriptions striking. What I want to highlight here is the *form* of the behaviour that is considered relevant to the claim that Kanzi might have language. What I have in mind comes out most clearly by contrast with examples from the more scientific approach adopted in earlier work with Kanzi. Typical tests here were of this form:

Kanzi wears headphones and responds to word recognition tasks formulated by a researcher in an adjacent room. In other tests, Kanzi responds to novel sentences formulated by Savage-Rumbaugh, who hides her face behind a welder's mask. The purpose of the test design was to eliminate the gestures, glances and other contextual features that also characterize normal communication between humans, but that are seen by many linguists and ape language critics as 'extra-linguistic assists'. (Segerdahl et al. 2005: 14)

The crucial contrasts highlighted by Segerdahl and colleagues might be summarized in terms of two features of the later research. First, the research involves giving a central place to the idea of a culture: 'First-language acquisition focuses on *doing* things together, on *living* together while communicating' (Segerdahl et al. 2005: 22). It is the way in which the gestures and sounds that the apes make are woven into such joint activities—into a 'culture', or shared ways of living—that, it is suggested, demands that we mark them out as *speaking.* Second, and closely linked with that, the authors stress the importance to identifying another as speaking, and to our grasping what the other says, of the *expressive* behaviour that surrounds what we might think of as the specifically linguistic gestures:

Kanzi's gestures are scarcely extra-linguistic, but function as criteria for the linguistic nature of his keyboard utterances. If we doubt whether Kanzi really means something by pointing to various symbols, our doubts vanish when we see his utterances together with gestures such as those just described...When Kanzi emphasizes his meaning he seeks eye contact and uses gestures that indicate the cultural matrix of his signs. (Segerdahl et al. 2005: 59)

While I think it is very easy to imagine how Kanzi's seeking eye contact might give an inescapable impression that he is at least trying to speak to you, some will insist that in so far as we are moved by this kind of thing, our judgement of what we are confronted with is clouded: the emotional impact of such behaviour is getting in the way of a cool-headed assessment of whether this creature really does have the skill we are trying to identify. By contrast, in the eyes of the Kanzi researchers, that insistence flows from a highly intellectualized picture of language use, one that construes it as a *skill,* as a manipulation of symbols in accordance with a system of rules. Part of the background to the Kanzi project is an idea that this picture is open to serious question, and, with that, part of the aim of the project is to dislodge such pictures. In brief, if the starting point of our thought about language is *talking,* in a familiar sense in which talking—conversation, chat—is a pervasive and fundamental feature of everyday human life, there is little ground for taking rules, grammar and so on to be what is definitive of language.[2] In so far as we give central place in our thinking about language to the idea that it is a particular form of interaction between living creatures, we should be open to the suggestion that 'Kanzi's organ of speech is his entire body as it functions in a broad variety of cultural activities'

(Segerdahl et al. 2005: 59) and, with that, open to the suggestion that, for example, Kanzi's attempts to seek eye contact, far from clouding our judgement, are a legitimate, perhaps inescapable, part of the basis for a consideration of whether he has language.

The above remarks connect closely with a central feature of the form of the research. The authors write:

> Language is not an inanimate object. It is unclear what it would mean to sit undisturbed outside an enclosure and decide objectively whether that object is inside. According to the apes, the observer is a person they can talk with...The language Par thought it was his duty to detect by careful observation was thrown straight into his face by an ape who used language simply the way language is used: to communicate with someone when you have something to say to that person. [In Par's first encounter with the apes he is rebuked by one of them for talking at an inappropriate time.]...Morally, then, there is no such thing as a neutral observer of the apes' language. The observer is a living being, and language is a form of communication between fellow-creatures. (Segerdahl et al. 2005: 89–90)

This is, I take it, in part a *moral* judgement on other ways of approaching the study of language in apes: where the ape is treated as an object of study to be put through a series of tests in order to see if he makes the mark. But it is also an observation of a kind of absurdity into which the researcher may find herself falling when she struggles to adopt a pure 'objectivity' of approach in relation to a particular bonobo. As the authors remark, Par 'cannot both feel ashamed because he was just recently rebuked in dramatic language and treat the ape's language as an interesting hypothetical possibility' (Segerdahl et al. 2005: 90), and 'trying to prove that an ape has language, when you constantly talk with her in order to organize the proof, is not much less comical' (Segerdahl et al. 2005: 42). This, in turn, is linked with something else:

> The moral relation to the apes must be the overriding factor of the work, its first principle, which means that the apes are allowed to affect us, just as we affect them: the emerging Pan/Homo culture is an intermediary form of life. Otherwise, there would be no talking with each other. By acting respectfully (and occasionally disrespectfully) towards the apes, as humans do towards each other, we bring into our interactions precisely the linguistically relevant aspects of our human ways of life. Kanzi demonstrates that nature responds to this respectfulness. With regard to many animals, and certainly with regard to the great apes, moral bonds function as links to the reality we observe in studying language. (Segerdahl et al. 2005: 99)

I think we might usefully distinguish two points here. A first is that it takes a context of such respect for talk to be drawn from a creature (whether human or other): it is only in living with others who display appropriate attitudes towards it that a creature will develop a capacity for speech, or be predisposed, on particular occasions, to *say* anything. But further, the central quality that is called for if we are seriously concerned with determining whether a particular creature (again, human or other) might be speaking is not an ability to weigh evidence in the precise and disinterested ways that we may think of as the hallmark of proper science, but an openness to being personally affected by—moved by—the other. As the authors provocatively express the point: what is needed is not *evidence,* not a proof that Kanzi speaks, but rather an overcoming of a form of autism from which many of us suffer in relation to nonhuman creatures (Segerdahl et al. 2005: 134).

In a remark that captures a central theme of the book, the authors write: 'If one cannot talk freely with the ape before, during and after the test, the ape cannot be said to have language, no matter how impressive the test results are' (Segerdahl et al. 2005: 40). This articulates well something that many will find particularly attractive in this whole approach: an insistence that it is no more appropriate to treat a bonobo *purely* as an object of disinterested scientific investigation—as we might conduct tests to determine the properties of a chemical substance—than it would be so to treat a human being.[3] At the same time, the remark may highlight what some will find seriously problematic in this research, for it may seem unambiguously to embody the deeply anthropocentric assumption that the decisive test of whether a creature has language is whether we—*human beings*—can talk with her. We may be usefully reminded at this point that a desire to overcome any taint of human centredness is one of the motivations of the distancing/objectivizing/scientific approach—an approach that gives central place to recording and measuring in a way that is maximally independent of the potentially idiosyncratic responses of those engaged in the research[4]—that some of us may take much pleasure in scorning. Now while I believe that there is a confusion in that felt pressure to objectivize and, with that, that the emphasis the authors put on our being able to talk with Kanzi does not reveal a problematic human centredness in their approach, I do not think that the issues here are completely plain sailing. Much of the rest of this chapter will be an attempt to make some progress in sorting out the difficulties here.

Anthropomorphism and Anthropocentrism

Segerdahl and colleagues address the concern about 'human centredness' in the following passage:

> For what is anthropocentrism in connection with the human-animal divide? Is it not the natural tendency to take our best-known human standards for granted and to impose them on the animals, simply because they are *our* standards, the ones *we* use? For instance, we naturally assume we know what language is, at least in our own species, and ask if apes can learn language in this sense. What could be more natural? The ape language advocate

believes that apes can learn language, but the sceptic thinks that this is over-interpreting the data and seeing language where there is none: that it is a case of the error called anthropomorphism (projecting human terms on nonhuman realities). But if the very posing of the question presupposes the imposed human standard, does it not follow that the ape language advocate and the sceptic are equally anthropocentric? They both take it for granted that we already know what language is in our own species and ask if apes can acquire language in this sense. Is it not this unique human standard that de Waal himself uses, as if it were unassailable, when he expresses his suspicion that ape language research is anthropocentric? Is his notion that 'there is something inherently unfair about judging them on our terms' itself based on an almost irresistible form of anthropocentrism? What if his notion of 'our terms' can be questioned? What if a closer study of the animals could overturn our taken-for-granted standards, even in their application to us? (Segerdahl et al. 2005: 109–10)

The authors speak here of anthropomorphism as 'projecting human terms on non-human realities' (though suggesting later that this understanding may itself reflect a distorted view of the situation), and anthropocentrism as 'the tendency to take our best-known human standards for granted and to impose them on the animals, simply because they are *our* standards, the ones *we* use'. Some may have difficulty keeping this distinction clearly in focus. The fundamental distinction here is, I believe, between two different forces carried by the qualification 'human'. The phrase '*human* terms (or standards)' is ambiguous between 'terms (or standards) that humans use' and 'terms (or standards) that have application to humans'. We might then say, very roughly, that anthropomorphism is to be construed as applying terms (standards) that *have application to humans* to nonhuman realities, while anthropocentrism is applying terms (standards) that *we humans employ* to nonhuman realities.

If we still have trouble keeping a firm hold on this distinction, this may, at least in part, reflect a tendency to doubt whether it is really as marked as my formulation is designed to make it appear. Thus, we may take it to be clear that any terminology *employed* by human beings is more or less bound to be a terminology that is human-*centred,* in the sense of being primarily fitted to the description of (having its primary application to) human beings, and so that a description of nonhuman creatures in terms of thoughts, desires, personality, speech and so on manifestly involves an extension—legitimate or illegitimate—of this terminology from its original home. But while there *may* be some kind of truth in the suggestion that human beings are generally more interested in human beings than they are in other things, and so can be expected to have a language that reflects this fact, we should not, in the absence of some formidable argument, take it to be an inescapable or universal feature of human life that human interests are necessarily human-centred. Perhaps the inclination to assume this may be weakened by reflecting on the suggestion that it is an inescapable truth that men are more interested in men than they are in other things—such as women.

'The angle from which we look at things' is not at all the same thing as the natural focus of our attention. Now, if there is an important distinction between the idea of a terminology *employed by* human beings and that of a terminology that has its central *application to* human beings, we might hope that the distinction between anthropocentrism and anthropomorphism could provide a useful tool for disentangling potential confusions in this area. My own suspicion, however, is that the condition of this terminology is one of terminal decline to an extent that renders it somewhat worse than useless.

Consider, first, anthropomorphism. Amongst definitions of the term to be found in the literature are 'the act of attributing human traits to other animals', 'the misattribution of human qualities, in particular mental states, to animals', 'the error of projecting uniquely human qualities onto something that isn't human' and a number of variations on these.[5] With this, judgements on anthropomorphism range from its being, by definition, something to be avoided (see above), through the suggestion that it is 'a logical starting point when it comes to animals as close to us as apes' (de Waal 2001; quoted in Segerdahl et al. 2005: 112), to the claim that the notion itself is a symptom of a confused anthropocentrism (Sharpe 2005: 167). A good bit of sorting out of the terminology is clearly going to be needed before useful disagreement can even begin.

A first stab at some sorting out might be along the following lines. If we think of the term anthropomorphism roughly as I suggested above—'applying terms (standards) that have application to humans to nonhuman realities'—we will have to bear in mind that the expressions 'is five feet tall' and 'weighs 130 lbs' are ones that have application to humans; since nobody is going to suggest that there is a confusion in attributing features of *these* kinds to nonhuman animals, we might wonder whether this is a useful basis for discussion. At another extreme, definitions of the form 'the misattribution of human qualities, in particular mental states, to animals' manifestly beg all the questions before the discussion has even begun. Perhaps something along the following lines captures better what is characteristically at issue in disputes about anthropomorphism: 'projecting terms that have their primary application to human beings on nonhuman realities'. Now if *this* is how the expression is to be read, we should note that there appear to be no grounds for any suggestion that the ascription of, say, pains, emotions or thoughts to nonhuman creatures involves anthropomorphism, for there appear to be no grounds for the assumption that ascription of such states to certain nonhuman creatures is not as primary (in any relevant sense of that rather fluid term) as is their ascription to human beings. But perhaps it can be agreed that the ascription of language to certain nonhuman creatures is, in this sense, an instance of anthropomorphism.

I say 'perhaps' to mark a sense that the term 'projection' may still be slanting the discussion in a way, and the expression 'primary application' may be slippery in ways, of which we should be wary. My concern is that we need to be absolutely clear that if we do characterize what is involved here as 'anthropomorphism', then this is not, so far, to suggest that there is anything suspect in what we are doing. It may be helpful to bear in mind here that there is probably a straightforward sense in which the term 'language' has its primary application to *English,* as the word 'speaking' has its primary application to what passes between speakers of English (and as the word *hablando* has its primary application to what passes between speakers of Spanish). I will return to considerations that relate closely to these concerns.

What of the term 'anthropocentrism'?[6] Segerdahl and colleagues suggest that traditional forms of ape language research are guilty of anthropocentrism in that the question of whether a particular ape has language is taken to be the question of whether there is something in his life that meets certain standards that *we humans* have laid down, these standards generally involving reference to some form of complex grammatical structure. But if *this* is what anthropocentrism is, then one might wonder whether there is not something slightly odd in suggesting—as Segerdahl and colleagues, along with many others, do—that it involves some kind of mistake. For if someone wants to know whether a particular creature has language, what he wants to know is whether it has *language.* To appreciate the force of this platitude, compare someone who asks whether a particular creature can run at twenty miles per hour (mph) and is given an answer of the form: 'Given our standards for judging that something can run at 20 mph, this creature no doubt can't; but with what right do we impose *our* standards on *them.*' The truth is that nobody is here imposing anything on this creature. (So far, at least. If they go on to judge these leaden-footed mice to be a collection of couch potatoes, then matters are rather different.) We are answering the question, 'How fast can they run?' and we will only be doing that if, in doing so, we employ the standards embodied in our—in particular, the questioner's—use of that phrase. Similarly, isn't it clear that there cannot possibly be anything objectionable in answering our question about the bonobo by appealing to the standards embodied in our use of the word language? How *else* are we to answer it? There may be room for legitimate protests about our *asking* that question and about our attaching to that question the significance that is sometimes attached to it. ('If they don't have language, they don't have an immortal soul, don't have rights') But if we ask this question, then the answer, it might seem, *must* appeal to our standards.

For a number of reasons, however, the situation may be less straightforward than is suggested by those remarks. We can ask first, *whose* standards are at issue when Segerdahl and colleagues object to 'the tendency to take our best-known human standards for granted and to impose them on the animals'? In fact, it is clear that the standards they are speaking of are those that operate within the professional culture of the ape language researcher. There may be a sense in which those are the best *known* human standards, but that is not to say that those standards have a significant place in the thought of the rest of us, in particular, in our use of the term 'language'. The core of the charge may, then, be this: 'A familiar form of scientific research into the linguistic capacities of nonhuman creatures takes as its touchstone for "language" the standards that operate within a particular professional culture; the fact (in so far as it is a fact) that a particular species is incapable of meeting those standards—lacks the capacity for "language" in *that* sense—does not entail that it lacks the capacity for language in the everyday (one is tempted to say "human") sense of that term.' One might wonder whether 'anthropocentrism' is an appropriate label for such a procedure. That aside, if there is such a failure of match between our everyday use of the term 'language' and its employment in the professional culture of ape language research, there is ground for concern. It is, perhaps, imaginable that there should be good professional reasons for giving a familiar term a particular technical sense within the context of certain forms of research. But if we fail to keep clearly in mind that this *is* a technical sense, there will be a risk of serious confusion in the specialists' reporting of results to a lay audience, and perhaps also in the significance that they themselves attach to them.

But there is a further point here. I asked, isn't it clear that there cannot possibly be anything objectionable in answering our question about the bonobo by appeal to the standards embodied in our use of the word 'language'? But the question of whether something has a certain feature is not always, perhaps is not generally, the question of whether it meets a certain standard. A standard is something one may place beside, and with which one may compare, an object or activity that is the focus of our interest (as one places a measuring rod beside the child): something to which the object or activity does, or fails to, measure up. But not all judgements of a thing's features take this form. Consider, for example, the recognition of emotions in others. When I identify fear, anger or affection in another's face, I do not, characteristically, judge what is there through comparison with a standard. I see the anger straight off, not, for example, by way of identifying features that the distorted face shares with other faces that provide a standard of an angry face. And suppose that someone, perhaps an anthropologist or psychologist who is interested in cross-cultural expressions of emotion, proposes a standard of some form: a paradigmatically angry face that is to serve as an object of comparison or a set of criteria involving dilation of the pupils, flaring of the nostrils and so on. Whatever the possible merits of such a proposal, we would, I suppose, judge the proposed standard by how well it picks out faces that we judge straight off—judge, that is, without the use of standards—to be angry. And if it is objected that such a procedure would be flagrantly unscientific, we might note that it is a necessary truth that there is more to life than science (in the sense presupposed in the objection). For there would be no judgements that involved an appeal to standards were there not judgements that did not do so. One way to make this point is to note that if the judgement that some object (for example, the boy) meets some standard (reaches this mark on the measuring rod) itself involved comparison with some standard, we would be embarked on a regress that could only be brought to a halt with a judgement that involved no such comparison.

Anthropocentrism, as explained by Segerdahl and colleagues, is 'the tendency to take our best-known human standards for granted and to impose them on the animals, simply because they are *our* standards, the ones *we* use'. Despite a superficial case for the judgement that there cannot possibly be anything objectionable in that tendency, I have argued that, in two respects, anthropocentrism, so understood, may be less innocent than it can appear. There is, I believe, a third respect in which this is so. One of the most striking features of the Kanzi language project is the way in which it involves a challenge to a conception of the 'we' that may be at work when we speak of 'the language *we* use'. In developing this point, it will be helpful first to stand back a bit and ask, what is the *point* of research into the linguistic capacities of the bonobo?

The Point of the Research

It might seem clear that the point of this research is to learn whether the creatures studied have a capacity for language. The general emphasis in the *Kanzi* book is, however, different. First, the authors' emphasis is, rather, on what we may learn about *ourselves* as human beings. And second, and closely linked with that, they argue that we should not picture the situation in terms of the researchers bringing to their study of bonobo a fully adequate notion of language, their question being whether these creatures do, or can, satisfy the criteria for having *this.* The situation is, rather, that in finding that we can speak with bonobo—in finding that we can interact with bonobo in ways that we cannot help but characterize as *speaking* with them—we learn something important about what language is, what speech is, *in us.* And this change in our self-understanding is not readily separated from a change in us (the self that is to be understood) that may come about through the research. I will take this in a number of steps.

Someone might ask, 'If the most important thing about this research is what it may teach us about *ourselves* would we not do better simply to study ourselves explicitly and directly, not by way of a study of other creatures with whom we may interact?' They might add, 'Would this approach be, not only a more direct one, but also a more moral one? Even if the work with bonobo does not involve any cruelty to them, it certainly involves removing them from their natural habitat and the form of life that is proper to them in a way that is, at best, going to call for some serious justification.' The authors have some interesting (and no doubt controversial) things to say about such appeals to the notion of the 'natural' (Segerdahl et al. 2005: 202). Rather than pursue that, however, I want to consider their grounds for believing that studying the bonobo is a way to come to understand *ourselves*—we human beings—better. A central thought here is this: 'Precisely because we are confronted with language where we do not expect to find it—in forms of everyday life shared with bonobo—ape language research opens our eyes to dimensions of language neglected by our Western intellectual tradition' (Segerdahl et al. 2005: 4). We, or at least some of us, are inclined towards an overintellectualized view of language, one that identifies *the* essential thing about language as being vocabulary and, above all, complex grammatical structure. This tendency may have a number of connected roots. Some relate to features of the professional culture of scientific research—in particular, a need to bypass any dependence on subjective human reactions of the researcher—in ways on which I touched earlier. Rather different pressure may come from the idea that the most important feature of some phenomenon—what, in that sense, is essential to it—must be something that marks it off from other phenomena. This idea may lead us to suppose that we see what is most important about language in features, such as complex grammar, that are manifestly absent in other phenomena that are in some way related (such as the babbling of a baby) yet are clearly not language. Moving up a level, we may suppose that the most important thing about *us*—we human beings—must be something that marks us off from all other creatures: the idea that it is language that is the decisive difference having, of course, a long history. But the idea that the most important feature of some phenomenon must be something that marks it off from others is not one that we have to accept.[7] At any rate, there is no reason to rule out in advance the possibility that much that is most important in human life is to be found in some form in the lives of nonhuman creatures.

The Kanzi researchers suggest, first, that language is one such feature and, second, that by means of seeing it in the life of a creature that is in many ways significantly different from ourselves—seeing it in a form in which some of what normally, in our own experience, surrounds it is absent—what is fundamental to language stands out more clearly. In seeing that what is going on between Kanzi and us is unmistakably *talk,* we may come to see what is going on in linguistic interactions between human beings in a different light: in a light in which, for example, the complex grammatical structures that are (sometimes) involved are less prominent, and the gestures, facial expression and so on in which the talk is embedded are more so.[8] Our sense of what it is for something to be language and, perhaps with that our use of the word 'language', may change.[9] More generally, our encounter with creatures such as the bonobo may prompt a rethinking of contrasts—nature and culture, body and mind, gesture and speech—that may structure our thought over a wide area. (It is simply the other side of this that where the contrasts, in their familiar philosophical form, are deeply entrenched in our thought, they may inhibit our appreciation of what is to be found in such encounters [see King 2002: 87].)

It might be replied: 'Having a grammar in a rich sense may not be crucial to what is most important in the place that this phenomenon—language—has in our lives. What is most important to that place may be, as we might express this, features of its physical embodiment. But this is quite consistent with an acknowledgement that it is having a grammar that makes this thing *language*—with the claim that if something does not have this, it is not language. And if that is how things are, if we want to determine whether bonobo can develop language, it is *this* that we must look for.'

But what kind of basis could such a claim about what is essential to something's being language have? The things that we encounter in everyday life and that we unhesitatingly take to be language have a number of features: they have grammatical structure, they have dictionaries that may be consulted, they play a central role of a huge variety of kinds in interactions between creatures ranging from greetings to papers at scientific conferences, they also have a written form and so on. So long as we lead relatively sheltered lives, there may be no need for, indeed no place for, a question: which of those are essential to its being *language?* It is only when we are confronted by creatures (human or nonhuman) whose lives display some but not other of these features that the question arises. Now it might not be *totally* groundless to say that something that lacks a written form is not language—writing is, after all, a central feature of what language is in our (whose?) lives. Similarly, though perhaps with rather better grounds, it might not be totally groundless to say that something that lacks a complex grammatical structure is not language. Indeed, there may be particular theoretical contexts in which this terminology has much to be said for it. If we resist such a move—resist the insistence that this is a necessary condition for something's being language—it will be on the grounds that the absence of rich grammatical structure (or of a written form) does not detract from the central importance of something in the character of interactions between members of the group that is *common* to their lives and ours. And while there are no doubt other ways in which what is common might be marked—while we could, in principle, simply hand the words 'language', 'speech' and so on over to the specialist whose focus is on grammatical structure and adopt some other terminology for our purposes here—there may be good reasons for refusing to do so. We might struggle to find other ways of speaking of what is going on in our interactions with the bonobo that are adequate to the phenomenon. With this, this range of words has rich connotations—connotations that may be central to their meaning and cannot simply be discarded at will. We may, then, do well to use them in a way that honours those connotations so far as possible. For example, the question of whether a creature has language, or the capacity for language, is (rightly or wrongly) linked in the minds of many with questions about the forms of treatment or respect that it may deserve. It is vital that we are clear whether the scientist who reports the results of her research might be using key terms in ways that are not in complete harmony with how we are inclined to take them: absolutely clear, that is, about *what* we are being told when we are informed that a certain species does, or does not, have the capacity for language.[10]

Finally, I want to return to my suggestion that one of the striking features of the Kanzi language project is the way it involves a challenge to our conception of the 'we' when we make reference to how *we* speak. I remarked earlier that the word 'language' is *our* word. Therefore, if our question is whether the bonobo in this study have *language,* there cannot possibly be anything objectionable in answering it by appeal to the standards embodied in our use of the word 'language'. Indeed, if we did anything else, we would not be answering *that* question. It might be added that it is an inescapable platitude that any terminology employed by human beings is bound to be a terminology that expresses our human interests. While it may well be that our interests stand in need of some developing, and that the encounter with the bonobo may make a profound contribution to that, however they develop they will still be the interests of we human beings, and the language that we speak will still be an expression of those, perhaps radically modified, interests. And the fact that the ways in which we speak reflect those, human, interests rather than the interests of a dog or a whale is no more something to be regretted or embarrassed about than is the fact that my expression of joy on receiving some good news is *my* expression of joy (rather than that of the man who lives next door).

If one takes it to be obvious that any language we speak is bound to be one that reflects the interests of human beings, one should, I think, also find it obvious that the language that a Scotsman speaks is bound to be one that reflects the interests of a Scot, the language that an athlete speaks one that reflects the interests of an athlete and the language that I speak one that reflects *my* interests. And while there is, no doubt, some kind of truth in all of those, the examples should remind us that speech is a communal activity and that there is no necessity in the relevant community being specified, in all cases, by the term 'we human beings'. In practice, there is a sense in which it is, in fact, never *all* human beings that make up that community. (Though some of the ways in which we fall short of that ideal may be manifestly something that merits reproach.) And one aspect of the significance of the work with Kanzi, and of the lives of others who in some more or less rich sense live *with* creatures of some nonhuman species, is the possibility that they may challenge the 'we' of 'we human beings' in the other direction. Thus, Segerdahl et al. stress that in the researchers' interactions with the bonobo, a new, intermediary, Pan/Homo culture developed. Now a community of human beings and bonobo will share a life that is, inevitably, different in important respects from any life shared solely by human beings or solely by bonobo.[11] The differences between that shared life and the shared life of any English-speaking human beings will be expressed (will be embodied), in part, in differences in the language spoken. The point here is not simply that *our* language may be transformed in certain respects by our interactions with the bonobo. The point is, further, that in speaking of 'our' language we (that is, those closely involved in Pan/Homo culture) will no longer be speaking of the language of a particular group of *human beings*. 'Our' vocabulary, including our specifically linguistic vocabulary—'tell', 'ask', 'reply', 'promise' and the term 'language' itself—will no longer be simply that of a human community; the standards embodied in it (in so far as standards are embodied) will no longer be specifically human ones: or better, those to whom we must answer in our use of that language is not restricted to other human beings.[12]

Notes

1. For other useful discussions, with which I am in broad sympathy, of this and related studies, see the papers by Barbara King (2002) and Stuart Shanker (2002) in *Anthropology beyond Culture* (Fox and King 2002). One *difference* between these papers and the *Kanzi* book—a difference that is relevant to my concerns

in this chapter—is the strong emphasis in the latter on interactions between the bonobo and the human beings studying them.

2. See the discussion of the contrast between 'generative' and 'interactionist' approaches to the study of language in Shanker (2002: 130–1, 137–8). The significance of my italicization of *talking* can best be appreciated through a contrast with the following remark made by Gopnik and quoted by Shanker: '[U]ttered surface forms provide evidence about the properties of the abstract rules, but do not in themselves constitute language. It is the grammar, the set of abstract rules producing the utterances, that constitutes language' (Gopnik, Dalalakis, Fukuda and Fukuda 1997: 114). A consideration of the deep philosophical pressures towards such startling, though extremely common, assumptions, while very relevant to the concerns of this chapter, is beyond its scope.

3. The 'purely' is important. We do, of course, sometimes treat a human being as an object of disinterested scientific investigation. But we (hopefully) generally ask her permission, welcome her when she arrives, perhaps chat with her as we attach the wires and so on. (Or at least, pay someone else to do that bit.)

4. King's dismissal of these concerns seems to me entirely appropriate (King 2002: 88), though I suspect some will find it a little too rapid.

5. For references to these, and other, uses of the term, see Lynne Sharpe (2005: 159–67). See also *The Stanford Encyclopedia of Philosophy* (http://plato.stanford.edu/contents.html) entry on 'Animal Cognition', and *The Internet Encyclopedia of Philosophy* (http://www.iep.utm.edu/) entry on 'Fallacies'.

6. The variation in usage of this term is every bit as marked as is that of the term 'anthropomorphism'. To give a very limited indication of this variation, we can note the following examples: 'An anthropocentric value theory (or axiology), by common consensus, confers intrinsic value on human beings and regards all other things, including other forms of life, as being only instrumentally valuable, i.e., valuable only to the extent that they are means or instruments which may serve human beings' (Callicott 1984: 299). A very different approach is seen in the suggestion that to call certain properties anthropocentric is to imply that they 'depend upon aspects of our make-up (our sense-modalities, or our sensibilities) that might be lacking to creatures with an equally discriminating grasp of how the world works' (Price 1986: 215–28). On a related, but different, understanding, a view is anthropocentric if it insists that 'the value of non-personal natural (and artifactual) objects remains dependent upon human subjects' (Nelson 2005: 426).

7. The importance of this point was forcefully brought home to me by discussions with Anniken Greve.

8. Thus, I fully endorse Lynne Sharpe's more general suggestion that 'rather than learning about others by analogy from our own case, we learn about ourselves as we learn about others, and that "others" here does not refer only to human beings' (Sharpe 2005: 165).

9. As, I would suggest, in coming to appreciate that what is going on between human beings whom she does not understand (French or Chinese speakers, for example) is talk, the child's understanding of what language is changes.

10. For a closely related response to the suggestion that we would do best simply to drop the term 'language' from discussion of these issues, see Shanker (2002: 126, 141–4). Shanker presents a forceful case for the claim that it is important that those with 'interactionist' sympathies do *not* simply abandon the terminology of 'language' and 'culture', despite its often problematic character. For a related discussion, focusing specifically on the word 'culture', see King (2002: 103).

11. There may be room for questions here about the richness with which we can speak of a 'shared life' in a context, such as this inevitably is, in which, presumably, both parties to it, human beings and bonobo, have a more or less rich life outside the area that is shared and from which the other is, for fundamental reasons, excluded; and where, further, the area that is 'shared' is brought into being and sustained, for reasons of their own, by one set of the participants in it. I will only remark here that the force of such reservations depends as much, almost certainly more, on details of the functioning of the communities in question as on the fact that the 'shared life' in question involves more than one species.

12. In an observation that is very relevant at this point, Par Segerdahl has, in private correspondence, stressed the place that talk *about* language has in the Pan/Homo culture of which he has had experience, suggesting, in a way I take to be enormously plausible, that speaking about our speaking (for example, asking someone whom he meant when he said 'she' was late) is partly constitutive of what it is to speak. See also on this point Shanker (2002: 133). I am grateful to Par Segerdahl for his very helpful remarks on this point. I would like to thank Lynne Sharpe for ongoing discussions that have had a very significant impact on my thinking about these issues. I would also like to thank Patrick Cockburn and Maureen Meehan for detailed and extremely helpful comments on earlier drafts of this chapter.

References

Callicott, J. B. 1984. 'Non-anthropocentric Value Theory and Environmental Ethics'. *American Philosophical Quarterly* 21(4): 299–309.

de Waal, F.B.M. 2001. *The Ape and the Sushi Master: Cultural Reflections by a Primatologist.* London: Allen Lane.

Fox, R. G., and B. J. King, eds. 2002. *Anthropology beyond Culture.* Oxford: Berg.

Gopnik, M., J. Dalalakis, S. Fukuda and S. Fukuda. 1997. 'Familial Language Impairment'. In M. Gopnik, ed., *The Inheritance and Innateness of Grammars.* New York: Oxford University Press, 111–40.

King, B. J. 2002. 'On Patterned Interactions and Culture in Great Apes'. In R. G. Fox and B. J. King, eds, *Anthropology beyond Culture*. Oxford: Berg, 83–104.

Nelson, M. T. 2005. 'Loving Attention: A Realist, Projectivist Theory of Value'. *Religious Studies* 41(4): 415–33.

Price, A. W. 1986. 'Doubts about Projectivism'. *Philosophy* 61(236): 215–28.

Segerdahl, P., W. Fields and S. Savage-Rumbaugh. 2005. *Kanzi's Primal Language: The Cultural Initiation of Primates into Language*. Houndmills: Palgrave.

Shanker, S. 2002. 'The Broader Implications of Borderline Areas of Language Research'. In R. G. Fox and B. J. King, eds, *Anthropology beyond Culture*. Oxford: Berg, 125–44.

Sharpe, L. 2005. *Creatures Like Us?* Exeter: Imprint Academic.

Dressed in Furs: Clothing and Yaghan Multispecies Engagements in Tierra del Fuego

Penelope Dransart

The term 'extinction' carries a potent emotional charge. During the twentieth century, it was associated with a growing awareness of human responsibility for the loss of species, habitats and human ways of life. This term acquires great resonance in that the subjects of this chapter, the peoples of Tierra del Fuego, provoked the naturalist Charles Darwin to consider the human condition of people he met in relation to the nonhuman species he studied. His characterization of both Yaghan as a people and of individual Yaghan persons he met has exerted an enormous influence on subsequent writers. Such is his status as an observer of living species, that some social anthropologists have been known to rely on his writings, causing them to overlook the published fieldwork of ethnographers of the southernmost inhabitants of the Southern Hemisphere.

At the time of Darwin's travels in South America in the 1830s, local people were being displaced by the hunting of marine mammals on an industrial scale. Their subsistence economy, based on fishing, gathering and hunting, relied largely on the marine species of the cold Humboldt Current, which takes a northerly course from the Antarctic to the shores of Chile. This chapter is concerned with a way of dressing oneself that was no longer being observed at the turn of the nineteenth and twentieth centuries. Using fragments garnered from the sources consulted, I seek to reconnect them in a historically contingent milieu and to locate them, as advocated by John Comaroff and Jean Comaroff (1992: 16), in 'a world of meaningful interconnections'. These interconnections were enmeshed in different sorts of multispecies engagements making it possible to interpret the historical interdependency between humans and sea mammals, both as prey (for example, fur seals, whales and otters) and in the form of fellow predators (for example, orcas).

Fuegian ethnography is appealing to think with precisely because Darwin's powerful voice concerned the divide between animality and humanity (using Western terms to characterize relationships between human and other animal species). The author of *On the Origin of Species* wrote for a readership schooled in a peculiarly Western tradition that divided humanity from animality and gave a special status to the former.

In the context of this chapter, both local Yaghan and nonlocal sealers valued fur seals for their pelts. Yaghan dress standards, however, stood for a way of life that many outsiders struggled to respect because it did not fully accord with their expectations concerning human behaviour. When Fuegians led a fishing-gathering-hunting way of life, they seemed to demonstrate what Ted Benton (1991: 22) characterized as the possession of 'morally and socially significant powers and dispositions which are in-tuitively non-adaptive' (particularly in their reluctance to clothe themselves fully by European standards). At the same time, however, people in the Northern Hemisphere prized seal fur, which was destined to clothe the rich in a luxury market.

It is appropriate to review historical Yaghan ethnographic evidence in the light of recent arguments concerning changing perceptions of the relationship between hu-mans and other animal species. The conceptual gulf between the two, apparently in existence in European thought during the nineteenth and twentieth centuries, seems to be narrowing. In declaring certain nonhuman species to be 'uniquely special', environmental activists discussed by Niels Einarsson (1993: 78) provide examples of an intellectual tendency in which whales occupy 'a Pan-like role' because they straddle the gulf between being human and being animal.[1]

Since the 1970s and 1980s, philosophers and sociologists have taken issue with the notion of there being a human-animal divide, and they have engaged in debates concerning a human–animal continuism in relation to animal rights (Benton 1993: 17). At first sight, it might seem that authors who argue for a continuity rather than a divide between humanity and animality share a common perspective. Donna Haraway (1990: 151–2) thought that a 'boundary breakdown' was occurring between humans and animals, but Benton (1993: 224n15) did not accept her argument, and he emphasized the importance of recognizing the uniqueness of each species. His argument drew attention to the significance of a 'moral tradition' among Western activists concerning the extinction of species that are vulnerable and relatively rare (Benton 1993: 69–70).

Benton's emphasis on the character of the difference between species led Law-rence Wilde (2000) to reject his discussion of Marx's allegedly contradictory views on animals in what Benton (1993: 42) termed a 'species imperialism', in which ani-mals were seen to be inferior compared to the superior 'species being' of humans. Marx defined humanity in essentialized terms through productive activity, but Wilde (2000: 43–4) objected to Benton's approach of diminishing the differences between human and animal uses of tools (that is, by overlooking diversity in the capacity to produce) while at the same time admitting that there is strong variation between the productive activities of different human groups.[2] The point I wish to make here is that authors who share similar aims of treating animals with compassion fall out with each other over the double bind in having to conduct their debates in languages using terms for humanity and animality that have acquired oppositional status. Tim Ingold (1994: 23) pointed out 'a paradox at the heart of Western thought, which insists with equal assurance both that humans are animals and that animality is the very obverse of humanity'.

This aporia does not provide a secure basis for considering how Fuegians themselves conceived of their relationships with the nonhuman species on which they relied. Ethnographic evidence suggests that Fuegian recognition of the individual characteristics of different animal species was based on a different ontological view of what it is to be human to that broadly represented by a Judeo-Christian tradition or by a Darwinian notion of survival of the fittest. Fuegian hunting of marine mammals did not take place in a context of human-animal opposition but one in which competing human interests vied against each other, especially when outsiders from the Northern Hemisphere competed for the very same animals with which the Fuegians fed and clothed themselves.

It is likely that Fuegians did not give special status to human beings as persons against the other species of their environment. They wore the skins of the prey species, and they anointed their own skins with oil extracted from those animals. Their shamans were able to forge relationships with spirits of the dead through the medium of orcas. My discussion of Fuegian relationships with orcas in the hunting of other animal species for clothing and food (see below) should be seen comparatively in the light of Alfred Irving Hallowell's (1960) interpretation of Ojibwa views concerning mutual interdependence between species (Ingold 1994: 24–5) and Nurit Bird-David's (1993, 1999) comparative analysis of concepts among gatherer-hunter societies. Such analyses demonstrate that interspecies relatedness was conceived of in terms of personal relations. They provide evidence for a 'relational ontology including other-than-human persons' (Halbmayer 2012: 12).

Social anthropologists have been able to discuss different ontologies regarding relationships between entities including people, nonhuman animals and plants in terms of animism and perspectivism. There has been, however, some discussion over the character and extent of such relational ontologies (Turner 2009; Halbmayer 2012). Perspectivists claim that animals, normally thought to be natural beings, identify themselves as cultural (that is, human) beings while animists endow human and non-human beings, including plants and other phenomena such as astral bodies, with the possession of a spiritual essence. Terry Turner (2009: 9) argued that anthropologists' explorations of 'the common subjectivity of cultural and natural beings' in their discussion of lowland South American ethnographic materials are intended to reformulate the Lévi-Straussian categories of nature and culture, while still being predicated on the 'categorical opposition' of those terms. Turner (2009: 38) also thought that such interpretations make it possible to conceive of the body as subject to transformational processes, in which both a 'subjective perspective and objectified bodily form' are produced. In assigning importance to the formal treatment of people's bodily surfaces, he acknowledged that the notion of a 'social skin' draws on the 'natural bodily content of senses and powers' as it emerges 'through a series of stages' culminating in 'the physical dissolution of death and the separate disintegration of spirit and body' (Turner 2009: 38).

For Yaghan, the development of this social skin served to embody subjective identities formed through activities such as wearing the skins of marine mammals and through participation in the ceremonies during which youths were initiated into adult ways of being. To be successful in catching prey, hunters had to acquire the knowledge to be like marine mammals. It should also be noted, however, that in her contribution to this volume, Veena Das recognizes that human beings 'are capable of internalizing animal modes of being within their own worlds but yet they cannot assimilate these forms completely'. This observation should be taken into account when considering Yaghan wearing of animal skins to clothe their nakedness.

The peoples of Tierra del Fuego are known in the ethnographic literature as Alakaluf (or Kawéskar), Yaghan (or Yamana), Ona (or Selk'nam) and Haush (Furlong 1917; Chapman 1977, 1997).[3] Seals supplied vital ingredients such as fur hides, meat, oil and other substances that could be converted into products, providing people with vital substances for food, warmth and light. By the nineteenth century, trade in fur seal pelts formed a major contribution to the economies of southern Chile and Argentina.[4] The control over who had access to the hides of fur seals, however, signalled inequitable relationships that resulted in the displacement of local people by northern whalers and sealers and the establishment of encampments run by missionaries for the few surviving Yaghan people.

Extraction of resources (for consumers who were not part of the local milieu from which those resources had been taken) meant that the inhabitants of the Northern Hemisphere came to rely heavily on the finite resources of oil obtained from the spermaceti in the heads of sperm whales and the fur pelts from seals. In more recent times, coal, gas and oil have supplied consumers, especially in industrialized nations, with energy. Populations of seals have begun to recover,[5] but the ways of life of the local peoples, which were characterized by their interdependence with animal and plant species, have not.

The history of Tierra del Fuego provides an important demonstration that the needs of species, both human and nonhuman, must be considered in an interconnected manner, taking into account the relational ontologies of the people. My next section outlines the historical evidence for the documentation of Fuegian ways of life. It is followed by an examination of Yaghan notions of dress and how the act of dressing oneself in Fuegian terms necessarily entangled people in a series of multispecies interrelationships.

Contact Histories

The peoples of Tierra del Fuego became known to northerners through the reports of mariners. A history of their contact with such outsiders has been chronicled comprehensively by Chapman (2010). In addition to the observations made by Charles Darwin (1839; Keynes 2001), Anglican and Salesian missionaries produced reports. A series of volumes followed a French scientific mission to Cape Horn in 1882–3 (Milne-Edwards 1891). Most detailed, however, are the publications of anthropologists, including those by Martin Gusinde and Anne Chapman. Father Gusinde was a priest of the Order of the Divine Word, who made four study visits to Tierra del Fuego in 1918, 1920, 1921 and 1922–3. In the 1980s, Anne Chapman conducted fieldwork with Yaghan women, especially with two sisters, Úrsula and Cristina Calderón, as well as with Rosa Clemente. Another important source of information is contained in the life history of Lakutaia le kipa, or Rosa Yagán as she was known in Spanish, and recorded by the Chilean journalist Patricia Stambuk (1986).

There is an overwhelming sense in many of the accounts that Yamana have not survived as a people. In his employment for the Museo de Etnología y Antropología, Chile, Gusinde wrote a series of reports based on his field visits to Tierra del Fuego. In the first, originally published in 1920, he argued that, given the reduced Yamana population, it was not necessary for the Chilean government to reopen the Anglican Mission while the Lawrence family retained their concession on Navarino Island, where some Yamana families had a refuge, but it would be

a highly humanitarian and patriotic act to concede some land to these last remnants of a people who are becoming extinct, where they can live the few years of existence remaining to them in peace, where they would not be molested or exploited, since they can accommodate themselves to an island, or whatever location, moderately adequate to their few primordial needs of subsistence. (Gusinde 2003: 46)[6]

The message concerning Yamana extinction is more stark in the subtitle that Patricia Stambuk (1986) used for Rosa Yagan's oral narratives; she was 'the last link'. Rosa opened her account by saying that, of five Yamana lineages, she was 'the last of the Wollaston clan'. This statement is rather more measured than the utter solitude implied by naming her as the 'last link'. Nevertheless, the theme of extinction in the literature is pervasive. Gusinde's request on behalf of Yamana for a reservation of land was couched in terms intended to persuade the Chilean government of the feasibility of his proposal. Given his authority as a sympathetic and perceptive field researcher, his views were influential. He must surely have been disappointed in the lack of progress on such an important matter during his lifetime.

Since then, environmental and ecological concerns have led to the establishment by Chile of protected zones administered by CONAF, the National Forestry Corporation (Sielfeld 1997: 88). In 2005, UNESCO recognized the Cabo de Hornos Biosphere Reserve, which is listed in the MAB Biosphere Reserves Directory. The description in MAB's programme listing presented the zone somewhat contradictorily as 'one of the unique areas where non-fragmented or altered temperate forests are conserved'. It recognized the diversity of the invertebrate and mammal populations and that the resident human community includes 'the indigenous community of Yagán descending from the first colonists…the most threatened of the Chilean indigenous cultures' (MAB Biosphere Reserves Directory 2011). UNESCO recognition was the result of increased attention given to the environmental and cultural aspects of the ecoregion. This activity included Chilean research conducted with Úrsula and Cristina Calderón to extend the register of bird names that have been recorded in the literature on the Yaghan language (Massardo and Rozzi 2004).

To collect the animal materials with which to clothe themselves, Yaghan relied on predation and, on occasions, interspecies cooperation to obtain the necessary materials. At the time Gusinde did his fieldwork, people were virtually all wearing Western-style garments. His informants provided him with a detailed record of what people used to wear, which he compared to the published literature. Imported garments were proving to be remarkably unsuitable for their needs. They provided a home for fleas, which were introduced by Europeans along with the clothing; older people reported that fleas of the body (rather than those of the head, which seemingly were not an innovation) were unknown in previous times (Gusinde 1982: 405). Perhaps, however, the serious inconvenience of having constantly to scratch oneself was in itself less of a consequence than the wetness people had to endure in European-style garments. Gusinde (1982: 402) observed that Yamana people dried themselves by sitting close to a fire because they did not have appropriate materials for such a task. In his opinion, garments soaked by the rain and sea water made a deleterious impact on the health of Yamana because they had to dry on the body of the wearer, who kept them on day and night (Gusinde 1982: 335). He considered clothing to be one of a number of major factors that contributed to the sudden decline in people's health after they came into regular contact with missionaries.

Being Properly Dressed

An early description of how Fuegians clothed themselves came in 1578 from the sailors on the *Golden Hind,* whose captain was Drake. On one of the islands of the Pacific, perhaps at Desolate Bay, the chaplain Fletcher reported seeing 'men, women, and young infants wrapt in skins, and hanging at their mothers' backs' (as described in Chapman 2010: 18). In 1711, the Jesuit Père Labbé and a group of French sailors observed about thirty Haush men and women dressed in skins of 'sea wolf' (or fur seal) and bracelets and necklaces made from sea shells (Brosses 1756 2: 434–5, cited by Chapman 2010: 36). A 1766 account provided by the Nodal brothers presented details in respect of the dress worn by about fifteen Haush men they and their crew met at Good Success Bay, named after one of their caravels, *Nuestra Señora de Buen Suceso.* The men had painted their bodies with red pigment, and their faces were 'covered with whitish clay'. Their cloaks were of guanaco hide (which the Europeans called 'sheep' skin). They also wore leather girdles, 'pretty' bracelets of shell and headdresses made from white down bird feathers (Chapman 2010: 23). Captain Cook also met Haush in 1769 and in 1774. Both these encounters took place in Good Success Bay. He thought they were 'a little, ugly, half-starved beardless Race' and that they were 'almost naked', with sealskins over the shoulders. Some of the men wore cloaks consisting of two or three skins sewn together and reaching to knee length. The women had aprons of sealskin, but the children were 'as naked as they were born; thus they are inured from their infancy to Cold and hardships' (cited in Chapman 2010: 41). These descriptions, often brief, are separated in time, but they appear to present a consistent picture which, in the course of time, enabled outsiders to develop stereotypes concerning the identification of different ethnic groups in Tierra del Fuego.

The picture that emerged, and that was elaborated in engravings (Figure 11.1), is one of a scantily clad people with a cape-like skin wrapping.[7] This characterization of Fuegians entered the imaginations of people living in the Northern Hemisphere. In a chapter focusing on the anthropology of dress in a recent text book, Carol Delaney mentioned that people 'borrowed' fur garments from nonhuman animals for protection from the extremes of climate.[8] She went on to argue, however, that not all human groups have the same need for such protection. Appealing to the work of Darwin, in reference to the Fuegians, and to the work of Spencer and Gillen, in the case of the inhabitants of the Torres Straits Islands, Delaney (2011: 297) maintained that these people had the ability to endure severe temperatures while being relatively undressed. In her view, they

> were able to withstand inclement weather and tolerate significant changes in the temperature without being significantly discomfited. Some practitioners of meditation and yoga claim that they, too, are able to ignore changes in temperature. Whether they actually ignore these changes or are able to make their bodies feel warm when they are cold and cool when they are hot, I am not sure, but in either case it is an issue of mind over matter. (Delaney 2011: 297)

In this view, some groups of people have been able to develop their mental capacities in order to counteract certain basic physiological needs when they experience inclement climatic conditions. It contradicts the observation made from close quarters by Martin Gusinde (1982: 1423), who observed that Yamana '[c]ertainly feel the cold and heat, the frost and the solar rays, the sharp stones on the ground and the hardness of their bed, the wounds and injuries, but they put up with whatever inconvenience with indifference and suffer in silence'.

In her textbook account, Delaney did not quote Darwin's words directly when she cited the assertion that the 'all naked' Fuegians 'were some distance from the fire and yet perspiration streamed down their bodies'. Rather than accept what Darwin wrote at second or third hand, it is worth consulting his words directly. I have found two sources relating to January 1833:

> At night we arrived at the junction with Ponsonby Sound; we took up our quarters with a family belonging to Jemmys or the Tekenika people.—They were quiet & inoffensive & soon joined the seamen round a blazing fire; although naked they streamed with perspiration at sitting so near to a fire which we found only comfortable.—They attempted to join chorus with the songs; but the way in which they were always behind hand was quite laughable. (Darwin in Keynes 2001: 135)

Figure 11.1 Illustration of a Fuegian family published in John Hawkesworth's account of voyages to the South Pacific (1764–71). By courtesy of the Roderic Bowen Library, University of Wales Trinity Saint David.

The second is similar:

> At night we slept close to the junction of Ponsonby Sound with the Beagle channel. A small family of Fuegians, who were living in the cove, were very quiet and inoffensive, and soon joined our party round the blazing fire. We were well clothed, and though sitting close to the fire, were far from too warm; yet these naked savages, though further off, were observed to our great surprise, to be streaming with perspiration at undergoing such a roasting. They seemed, however, very well pleased, and all joined in the chorus of the seamen's songs: but the manner in which they were invariably a little behindhand was quite ludicrous. (Darwin 1839: 240)

While Cook thought that Fuegians were 'wretched' and lacked 'sagacity...to provide themselves with such necessaries as may render life convenient' (cited in Chapman 2010: 43), Darwin, regardless of his opinions on the effectiveness of their dress, nevertheless thought that their lives were worth living:

> There can be no reason for supposing the race of Fuegians are decreasing, we may therefore be sure that he enjoys a sufficient share of happiness (whatever its kind may be) to

render life worth having. Nature, by making habit omnipotent, has fitted the Fuegian to the climate & productions of his country. (Darwin 1839: 237)

The writings of Darwin have exerted much influence on subsequent authors. An 1891 report of the 1882 French scientific expedition to Cape Horn included an account of experiments conducted on Yaghan subjects by Paul Hyades to explore their tactile sensibility by using a device known as Weber's compass. The subject was instructed to close his or her eyes while the researcher applied both points of the compass to the skin and asked whether he or she could feel one point or two. Certain areas of the body are more sensitive than others—including the tip of the tongue, the lips and the ends of the fingers. According to Nélia Dias (2007: 55–6), the natural scientists who collected data from places such as Tierra del Fuego wished to establish whether or not there were differences in tactile sensitivity between European and non-European peoples. Hyades thought that this experiment provided a measurable indication that Fuegians had a greater threshold of sensibility than Europeans. She indicated the 'supposed paradox' noted by Hyades of how it was possible that Yaghan were more sensitive to the tips of the compass than Europeans when their skin was exposed to such a rigorous climate. This problem was related to Darwin's reaction, when he had been surprised by the apparent resistance of Fuegians to the cold (Dias 2007: 57).

There was of course more to dress than some of these eighteenth- and nineteenth-century accounts might lead one to suppose. By the mid-twentieth century, detailed accounts of Yaghan dress had been reported in different European languages (see, for example, Cooper 1946: 86–7; Gusinde 1982 I: 387–92). Robert Lowie (1952: 3) said of Yaghan that a man 'does not expect to be kept warm by his skin cape; for that end he relies upon his fire, which is truly indispensable, and on the grease he applies to his body in exceptionally cold weather'. The oil supplied by seals and whales was an equally important element of dress as the capes and pubic coverings with which Fuegians protected their modesty. Úrsula Calderón, in discussion with Anne Chapman, remembered that people living round about Cape Horn did not feel the cold precisely because they used seal oil to protect themselves against rain and from illness. She recalled that there 'were thousands of Indians everywhere, like them—naked' (cited by Chapman 2010: 53). In addition to dressing their bodies with seal oil, they carried whale and seal oils in bladder containers to drink.

The perceived nakedness of Fuegians derived from preconceptions borrowed from the dominance of Spanish speakers in Chile. In a dictionary based on the Yaghan dialect spoken by the people of Ushuaia, the Revd Thomas Bridges (1933: 287–8, 496, 534) listed adjectives related to being naked, undressed or exposed, as well as verbal forms such as to undress oneself, to take one's clothes off or to 'throw or wear over one's shoulders a skin or piece of cloth or blanket' (Figure 11.2). His son, Lucas Bridges (1948: 63), born in Ushuaia in 1874, wrote that a poor person was referred to as *api tupan* (body only). Despite the constant references made by outsiders to nakedness, late nineteenth-century Yaghan concepts of being dressed fell within the definition of what constitutes dress offered by Joanne Eicher and Mary Ellen Roach-Higgins (1992: 15): 'an assemblage of body modifications and/or supplements displayed by a person in communicating with other human beings'.

One of the two main garments Yaghan wore before the introduction of European clothing was a cape made from fur seal or otter skins (Figure 11.3). Gusinde (1982 I: 390) reported that women preferred to use two to four otter skins, in some cases stitching together up to eight or ten hides. They prepared the skins by pulling out the long coarse hairs, leaving an undercoat as soft as velvet. In the north, a cape made from two or three fox pelts was sometimes worn, and, in the south, the skins of cormorants or penguins might be used. According to Gusinde (1982 I: 390), cormorant capes were considered the most beautiful. Both men and women wore their capes with the fur or feathers on the outside—apparently Yaghan people found the contact with the fur to be disagreeable (Gusinde 1982 I: 388). The skin of the cape became lubricated with the seal oil with which the wearer had anointed his or her own skin, but Yaghans did not treat their capes with any care. Within a few weeks, they became rigid and torn at the edges, although the cape's owner continued to wear the garment for half a year.

Another essential skin garment was a pubic covering, made from smooth leather from which the fur had been removed. It was triangular or trapezoidal in shape and men's were larger than women's. According to Gusinde (1982 I: 388), older men who did not wear this covering caused other people in the community to suffer embarrassment, but no one dared to reprimand their elders for exposing their genitals. Male commentators found that women were fearful of being seen without a pubic covering, especially in male company. Gusinde (1982 I: 392) described the garment as being made from a piece of soft leather, preferably guanaco, which was scraped on both sides and then anointed with fish oil. Girls and young women used a piece of otter or guanaco hide without removing the fur, and they wore the garment with the fur in contact with the body. The pubic covering was attached by means of a strip of leather or a plaited tendon cord passed round the hips from one upper corner of the triangle or trapezoid to the other.

In contrast to the cape and the pubic covering, footgear seems to have been optional. While women went barefoot, men sometimes wore leather sandals like those of Selk'nam (Gusinde 1982 I: 388). Necklaces and bracelets were often worn. Rosa Yagán (in Stambuk 1986: 89) recalled how, in former times, people made necklaces from bird bones and bracelets for wrists or ankles from leather. She, too, made necklaces from shell, washing the shells in river water before grinding a hole in each one. Next, she threaded them on a reed until she was happy that they were even, after which she strung them on a cord plaited from whale sinew.

Figure 11.2 Karougoyopak kipa holding a duck. She wears a pubic covering, but note the mission clothing behind her. Mission scientifique du Cap Horn 1882–3. Photograph ©Photo SCALA, Florence and by courtesy of Musée du quai Branly.

Figure 11.3 Biloush Lachaiakana with his wife and their child, L'île Hermite. Mission scientifique du Cap Horn 1882–3. Photograph ©Photo SCALA, Florence and by courtesy of Musée du quai Branly.

These accounts of Yamana dress from the past convey a sense of completeness, not only in the garments made from the skins of animals and birds that the people hunted, but also with the seal, whale or fish oil with which they anointed their own skin. In addition they had complementary accessories, in the form of necklaces and in the bladder containers of seal or whale oil, which they took with them wherever they went. The missionaries were in error when they thought that by making Fuegians don European garments they were clothing their nakedness.

There is a sense, however, that the local and foreign ways of dressing could not be mixed. Rosa Yagán (in Stambuk 1986: 89–90) remembered only one woman in the Río Douglas mission who possessed necklaces and bracelets, and Rosa bartered a shell necklace she made to an outsider, 'a dude' (*un futre*) on his way to Santa Rosa, for foodstuffs (in Stambuk 1986: 96). After her husband died, Rosa met up with a Chilean from Chiloe who discouraged her from collecting shells for making necklaces, which evidently were not appropriate for use with Western-style garments. Equally, when Martin Gusinde (1982 II: 813) became a participant observer in *chexaus* puberty rituals in 1920 and in 1922, he found that formerly the initiates crossed their limbs and torso with long strips of down-covered hide, but it was now no longer possible to use this item on top of European clothing because 'it would not have the least effect'. Úrsula Calderón recounted to Chapman (2010: 590) that Emilia (Kapumucus-kipa) was one of the last to wear sealskins until finally her Christian Yaghan husband burnt the skins to prevent her constant lapses from wearing mission garments. The wearing of imported clothing broke the intimate connection between Yaghan and the hunting and fishing activities, which supplied the pelts and oils that they applied to their skin.

Interspecies Cooperation

Because oil was both a foodstuff and an item of dress, the hunting of whales took place both before and after Western-style clothing was imported by outsiders. Yamana, however, rarely hunted healthy whales and, unlike sealers from the Northern Hemisphere, they did not always club seals to death. From the writings of Martin Gusinde, Lucas Bridges and Anne Chapman, it appears that orcas were more successful in killing marine mammals than human predators. Lucas Bridges commented that his father knew of one instance alone in which a group of Yaghan people hunted a whale to death. Apparently a 'whole fleet of canoes was used, and the attack lasted over twenty-four hours' (Bridges 1948: 77). In the deep waters south of the Strait of Magellan, whales swam and sometimes became stranded on the shore. Anne Chapman (2010: 56) reported that Yaghan shamans learned of the location of a beached whale in their dreams.

Much as people relished eating whale meat and drinking its oil, she discovered that Rosa Clemente, Úrsula and Cristina Calderón and Hermelinda Acuña enjoyed talking to her about orcas. They referred to them using the Spanish term *pez espada,* or swordfish, probably on account of the large fin which emerges in a sword-like manner from the water when the orcas approach the surface.[9] Chapman (2010: 53–4) described how three or more orcas would surround a whale, biting 'into its lips and tongue, which they eat, and leave the whale to die—a miserable death'. On seeing a whale stranded in such a condition, Yaghan would harpoon it to finish the killing. Therefore, they held the orcas in great esteem, claiming the orcas worked for them. Rosa Clemente told Chapman (2010: 54) 'that the orcas wounded seals and whales for her people to eat and that it was forbidden to even attempt to kill them'. Citing a comment made by Thomas Bridges, Chapman (2010: 53) added that orcas nearly always killed the whales the Yaghan obtained and that they 'consequently esteem them as sacred' and that they were 'very happy' on such occasions.

Yaghan shamans spoke with orcas, which were believed to bring back the spirits of dead shamans. Because these spirits threatened to take the spirits of living children, parents ordered their children to hide themselves from the presence of orcas. Rosa Clemente explained:

> We [the children] had to stay hidden, inside [the hut]. They didn't allow us to look at them. I heard her [old Mary] because she shouted so loud. On the beach there were a lot of old people. My grandfather was there and my papa was there. There were not many orcas, only two or three. The orcas stayed above, nearly on top of the water, listening to old Mary. She talked to them for quite a while and the orcas stayed there listening to her. Afterward they said good-bye to her, by moving their fins and went nearby to the Island of the Seals…They [the old people] went right away to the coast of that little island and found a lot of dead seals…[the orcas had killed for them]. (cited in Chapman 2010: 55)

In conversation with Chapman (2010: 55), Rosa Clemente described the loneliness of the *kashpi*—the soul or spirit—of deceased shamans who would return to the living, travelling in the body of an orca, hoping to ensnare one of their family members to join them. Cristina Calderón compared an orca to a boat bearing the spirit of a deceased *yekamush* (shaman). She repeated the warning given by adults to children; if they saw an orca in such a condition, their own *kashpi* would be endangered (Chapman 2010: 55–6). One of the last Yaghan shamans to survive was Julia who, despite holding the orcas in awe, conversed with and sang to them. Nine or ten years after the death of her shaman husband, Alfredo, she recognized his *kashpi* in a pod of orcas in a bay off Navarino Island. Fearing that he had come to take her to the abode of the *kashpis,* she shouted at him, accusing him of leaving her and refusing to go with him. Hermelinda recalled that Julia forbade her and other children from leaving the hut for three days, during which Julia fasted and chanted day and night while resisting the force of his *kashpi* (Chapman 2010: 56).

These women's memories illustrate the depth of character in the engagement between human beings and orcas as copredators of marine mammals and fish. Biologists have observed orcas snatching seal pups from surf zones or from the shoreline of Patagonia. Two or more orcas cordon off the seals, preventing them from escaping, while one of them swims towards the beach, temporarily grounding itself at the moment before the seal can escape into the water. With subsequent waves, the orca lifts its head and tail, arches its body and rocks itself free back into deeper water, with the prey in its mouth, if it has been successful (Lopez and Lopez 1985: 182).

It seems that Yaghan were well aware of the tactics used by orcas to hunt. Orcas committed the ferocious attacks on pinnipeds, but human beings were also beneficiaries. Yaghan respect and awe for them meant that they regarded them as powerful nonhuman mediators in a moral universe. Young people also learned to experience the world from a seal's perspective during the *chexaus* ceremony, during which male and female adolescents were initiated into adult life. The events took place in a communally constructed building, referred to in the literature as a large hut. This structure became the equivalent of a rock shelter at sea level (*alain*) during the ceremony; it symbolized the abode of seals (Gusinde 1982 II: 803).

Not Only Did They Shiver

Yaghan felt the cold on many occasions despite using seal, whale and fish oil to keep warm. In addition to covering themselves with these oils, they always maintained a fire in their canoes—the men tended it, and the women dived into the icy water to fish and take the canoe into land (Bridges 1948: 63–4). Rosa Yagán remembered being wrapped up in clothes, rather than being under seal and otter skins, at the end of her parents' dugout canoe, as would have been the case in former times: the 'fire was always lit... on top of sand and turves, and the warmth was felt from prow to stern, but I felt very cold' (in Stambuk 1986: 18).

Despite the alleged physiological adaptation which Delaney's textbook account attributed to the peoples of Tierra del Fuego, Chapman (2010: 93–4) pointed out that Fuegians were exposed to the keen wind and shivered when visiting European ships to barter with the sailors. People put aside their skin capes when climbing up and down the rope ladders to gain access to the ships. She observed, however, that they did so not only to have their hands free. Just as the seals learned to hide from human predators, Yaghan learned to hide the sealskins from European eyes, such was the acquisitiveness for them.

Although outsiders took the animal skin and fur garments as worn by Yaghan to be a sign of a primitive condition, when worked on by European furriers, the same materials carried connotations of sophistication. From the end of the eighteenth to the beginning of the nineteenth century, fur seal populations were decimated by sealers from northern countries (including British, French, Spanish and Yankee sailors). Seals are largely defenceless when attacked in their rockeries by human beings armed with clubs. After the 1780s, the depredation by Europeans grew worse, and seals learned to hide in more inaccessible rock ledges, making it difficult for Yaghan to reach them. Lucas Bridges (1948: 62, 67) observed that the Yaghan 'lived almost entirely on fish and limpets; they had very few skins with which to clothe themselves'.

By 1879, it was estimated that 200,000 seal fur pelts were being taken annually from the waters of the Southern Hemisphere and preserved by salting, after which they were packed into hogsheads (Backus 1879: 837). The best skins were thought to be from the Antarctic Ocean; the fur was considered to be 'fine beyond comparison; pelt very pliable, light, and thin and firm. Value salted, from £2 to £10' (Backus 1879: 839). Seasoned sealskins were treated to remove the coarse hairs, leaving the fine underfur, and dyed to ensure an even colouring. Furriers in London gained a reputation to have outdistanced all competition in this process.

A particular instance demonstrates the relative economic values of seal fur in an international market. The explorer Julius Popper prepared an album of photographs taken during the expedition he had been granted in 1881 to prospect for gold in southern Patagonia and Tierra del Fuego (Scarzanella 1995: 629). He delivered an account of this expedition at a lecture in the Instituto Geográfico Argentino in 1887 when he took the opportunity to donate the album to Miguel Juárez Celman, the president who had granted him permission to explore Argentinean territory. The visual record for this search for gold was bound in the skin of a fur seal.[10]

Enclosed within the fur cover, the album presented an outsider's perspective on the coexistence of human and nonhuman species in the Patagonian and Fuegian 'borderlands' (in the sense of the term as used by Kirksey and Helmreich 2010: 548). The photographs included a sequence of views of dead animals—a guanaco, birds, the head of a sea lion—followed by a posed picture of some of the men from Popper's expedition, guns raised to the shoulder as if they were poised to shoot, and in the foreground the body of a naked dead Selk'nam with a bow in his outstretched hand. Observing the graphic juxtaposition of dead animals and dead humans as though a hunter were displaying his prey, María Paz Bajas Irizar (2005: 5) argued that one should view these photographs in the light of the text of the 1887 lecture. In it, Popper claimed to have been hunting guanaco with his men, when they were confronted by 'some 80 Indians' and they opened fire with their Winchesters, leaving two men dead. Bajas Irizar (2005: 5) commented on the justification that Popper provided for the graphic images of dead Selk'nam, highlighting his choice of the phrase '[t]wo Indians *this time* remained dead on the ground' (emphasis added). Were there, she asked, other occasions when hunting expeditions had similar results? The images and text do not supply an answer. Her discussion of the question, however, demonstrates an extreme example of the lack of concern for the interests of local human and nonhuman species that occurred as outsiders engaged in the quest to extract economic value out of the resources of Tierra del Fuego.

Conclusion

This chapter has explored how dressing oneself in Fuegian terms necessarily enmeshed people in a series of multispecies engagements. It has explored the recorded memories of Yaghan people and ethnographic representations of them, seeking to place them in a historically meaningful world, one in which Yaghan relational ontologies might achieve a little more salience. The richness of this material is striking, but it is surprisingly unfamiliar to many English speaking readers. Yaghan cultural histories have struggled to compete with views based on the notion that Fuegians had undergone a different physiological adaptation than Europeans, based on Darwin having seen seal or fish oil on human skin, which he seems to have thought was perspiration.

My exploration of dress in relation to the vitality of humans led to a consideration of orcas as human collaborators, whether as hunters of fur seals or as psychopomps whose personae were recognized by Yaghan shamans. Interaction between sea mammals and human fishers as copredators is a phenomenon that marine biologists have reported from other parts of South America (Simões-Lopes, Fabián and Menegheti 1998; Zappes et al. 2011). The ethnographic information considered here indicates, however, that such a relationship is more than just an economic activity on the part of the human collaborators. Yaghan explanations of interspecies collaboration relate human existence to that of nonhuman and supernatural beings, with orcas mediating different levels of worldly and spiritual existence.

Cristina Calderón's comment that an orca was like a boat bearing the spirit of a deceased *yekamush* (shaman) is a significant one given that Yaghan believed that animals, birds and trees were once human. Yaghan spoke of a time before a great flood when animals and birds were humans (as recorded by Rosa Yagán in Stambuk [1986: 76, 103]). They also believed that trees were formerly human beings. During the *chexaus* rituals, Gusinde discovered that trees acted as witnesses to the actions of the young people who underwent the puberty rituals. Gusinde was instructed: 'You mustn't believe that these trunks are nothing more than wood! No way, they are other people who during the great revolution a long time ago turned into trees' (Gusinde 1982: 840). The animal skins with which people wrapped themselves and the bark 'skin' provided by trees to make canoes served as a potent bodily metaphor which constituted Yaghan society in Turner's terms because these outer surfaces constituted 'subjective perspective and objectified bodily form' (Turner 2009: 36).

Orcas, like human counterparts, have long lives and a long period of maturation, and they benefit from the presence of older family members to train them as successful hunters. Yaghan *chexaus* ceremonies formed part of the process for training young adults in the essential activities of gathering and hunting. During the ceremonies, the adults took great delight in acting the roles of prey species, including whales and seals, for the benefit of the initiates. To be a successful fisher, hunter or gatherer, adults developed an acute awareness of the habits of other living species.

The children learned to be a fur seal, precariously resting on the shoreline within the reach of a powerful orca. From that position of vulnerability, they acquired the skills to dress and feed themselves as Yaghan people. Those skills were irrevocably lost when northern sealers extracted in excess the pelts of fur seals to supply the demands of international trade in an unequal quest for what outsiders perceived to be a luxury good.

Notes

I wish to thank for their perceptive comments an anonymous peer reviewer, Felicia Hughes-Freeland, Lynne Sharpe and Jonathan R. Trigg for reading previous versions of this chapter. Pamela Wace directed me to the Backus (1879) reference. Any inaccuracies or infelicities remain my responsibility.

1. In this volume, David Cockburn (Chapter 10) discusses a cultural trajectory in which human researchers and bonobo developed a shared language.
2. Wilde (2000: 52n1) wrote that Benton's objection to Marx's discussion of differences between species 'is jejune'.
3. In this chapter, the terms Yamana and Yaghan (or, in the older literature, Yahgan) are used synonymously. For a discussion on how they have been used, see Chapman (2010). Following a literary device adopted by Evans-Pritchard (1940) who, excepting the title of his book, tended to speak of Nuer in preference to the Nuer, I avoid 'the Yamana' because it tends to treat people in an overgeneralized manner.
4. The economic contribution of fur trapping to the building of the Canadian nation has inspired studies focusing on fur as cultural capital, as witnessed in the life histories collected in Southern Yukon Territory by Cruikshank (1990: 339). She suggested that these narratives had an enduring quality because they addressed wider concerns in response to social upheaval at a time of governmental consolidation and industrial growth. Different scholarly approaches to the fur trade have examined the sexual politics of fur and its incorporation into libidinal economies generated by international fashion industries (Emberley 1998; Nadeau 2001). These approaches indicate the extremes of cultural meaning with which fur may be endowed in the appropriation of the skins of fur-bearing animals for both local consumption and an outside market.
5. According to Sielfeld (1997: 94), the status of *Arctocephalus australis* in the Región de Magallanes is categorized as being 'out of danger'.
6. My translation of: [*U*]*na obra altamente humanitaria y patriótica conceder a esos últimos restos de una raza que extingue, algún terreno, en donde puedan pasar con tranquilidad los pocos años que les quedan de existencia, donde no se les persiga y no se les explote, ya que ellos se conforman con una isla o un sitio culaquiera, medianamente adecuado a sus pocas necesidades primordiales de existencia.*

7. Figure 11.1 is reproduced from John Hawkesworth's (1773) account of the voyages made in 1764–71 to the South Pacific. Commissioned by Lord Sandwich in his capacity as First Lord of the Admiralty, on publication it attracted considerable criticism. According to Katrina Williamson (2006), the attacks were threefold: the first came from 'the captains for tampering with the texts of their journals', the second from 'prudish readers for reprinting descriptions of the sexual freedoms of the South Sea islanders' and the third from 'devout churchmen for impiety in the general introduction to the work, in which Hawkesworth had rashly challenged the doctrine of providential intervention'.

8. One should note the euphemism in Delaney's account in the light of Veena Das's comments in Chapter 2. The 'borrowing' of a fur skin conceals the violence of the killing while assuming that the prey animal has given its consent. It also, she argues, is a ruse enabling the sacrificer to evade confronting his or her own death.

9. The story of Asoulaxipa, a female member of Delphinidae, featured in one of the myths collected by Gusinde (1982 I: 1235). In it, Asoulaxipa outwitted sea monsters called *lakuma,* which were thought to drag women to the bottom of the ocean, by saying, 'Very well. Here goes another little grandfather' every time she saw one when paddling her canoe. Gusinde (1982 II: 1235n220) referred to her as a 'small orca, *Pseudorca crassidens,* also known as "killer whale"'. The myth has been published in English in Wilbert (1977, myth no. 42), who identified the creature as either *Pseudorca crassidens* or *Orca magellanica.* Elsewhere in his ethnography of the Yamana, Gusinde (1982 I: 502) described human hunters joining in as orcas started to chase a young whale. The Yaghan name for the orca with the powerful dorsal fin was *ëpaiači,* which he identified as *Orca magellanica,* the 'lord', who might be accompanied by other species (Gusinde 1982 I: 503). The name *Orca magellanica* is not listed in the third edition of Wilson and Reeder (2005), and the Linnaean name of *Orcinus orca* has been used in this chapter. Both it and *Pseudorca crassidens* visit the waters of the Región de Magallanes, but according to Sielfeld (1997: 94), the current status of these species is 'insufficiently known'.

10. Whereas Columbus failed to find sufficient gold in the Caribbean at the end of the fifteenth century and ended up trading slaves to finance his expeditions, at the end of the nineteenth century, Popper seems to have drawn attention to the trading of pelts stripped from fur seals as a high value alternative to gold.

References

Backus, M. M. 1879. 'Fur'. In *The Encyclopaedia Britannica: A Dictionary of Arts, Sciences, and General Literature.* 9th ed. Vol. 9. Edinburgh: Adam and Charles Black, 836–9.

Bajas Irizar, M. P. 2005. 'Montaje del álbum fotográfico de Tierra del Fuego'. *Revista Chilena de Anthropología Visual* 6: 34–54.

Benton, T. 1991. 'Biology and Science: Why the Return of the Repressed Should Be Given a (Cautious) Welcome'. *Sociology* 25(1): 1–29.

Benton, T. 1993. *Natural Relations: Ecology, Animal Rights and Social Justice.* London: Verso.

Bird-David, N. 1993. 'Tribal Metaphorization of Human-Natural Relatedness: A Comparative Analysis'. In K. Milton, ed., *Environmentalism: The View from Anthropology.* London: Routledge, 112–25.

Bird-David, N. 1999. '"Animism" Revisited: Personhood, Environment, and Relational Epistemology'. *Current Anthropology* 40 (Supplement): 67–91.

Bridges, L. 1948. *Uttermost Part of the Earth.* London: Hodder and Stoughton.

Bridges, T. 1933. *Yamana-English: A Dictionary of the Speech of Tierra del Fuego.* Mödling, Austria: Missiondruckerei St Gabriel.

Chapman, A. 1977. 'Economía de los Selk'nam de Tierra del Fuego'. *Journal de la Société des Américanistes* 64: 135–48.

Chapman, A. 1997. 'The Great Ceremonies of the Selk'nam and the Yámana: A Comparative Analysis'. In C. McEwan, L. A. Borrero and A. Prieto, eds, *Patagonia: Natural History, Prehistory and Ethnography at the Uttermost End of the Earth.* London: British Museum Press, 82–109.

Chapman, A. 2010. *European Encounters with the Yamana People of Cape Horn, before and after Darwin.* Cambridge: Cambridge University Press.

Comaroff, J., and J. Comaroff. 1992. *Ethnography and the Historical Imagination.* Boulder, CO: Westview Press.

Cooper, J. M. 1946. 'The Yaghan'. In J. Steward, ed., *Handbook of South American Indians.* Vol. 1. Washington, DC: Smithsonian Institution, Bureau of American Ethnology, Bulletin 143, 81–106.

Cruikshank, J. 1990. *Life Lived Like a Story: Life Stories of Three Yukon Native Elders.* Lincoln: University of Nebraska Press.

Darwin, C. R. 1839. *Narrative of the Surveying Voyages of His Majesty's Ships Adventure and Beagle between the years 1826 and 1836, Describing Their Examination of the Southern Shores of South America, and the Beagle's Circumnavigation of the Globe. Journal and Remarks 1832–1836.* London: Henry Colburn.

Delaney, C. 2011. *Investigating Culture: An Experiential Introduction to Anthropology.* Malden, MA: Wiley-Blackwell.

Dias, N. 2007. 'Une pointe ou deux? Le destin anthropologique du compass de Weber'. *Terrain* 49: 51–62.

Eicher, J. B., and M. E. Roach-Higgins. 1992. 'Definition and Classification of Dress: Implications for Analysis of Gender Roles'. In R. Barnes and J. B. Eicher, eds, *Dress and Gender: Making and Meaning in Cultural Contexts.* New York: Berg, 8–28.

Einarsson, N. 1993. 'All Animals Are Equal but Some Are Cetaceans'. In K. Milton, ed., *Environmentalism: The View from Anthropology.* London: Routledge, 73–84.

Emberley, J. V. 1998. *The Cultural Politics of Fur.* Ithaca, NY: Cornell University Press.

Evans-Pritchard, E. E. 1940. *The Nuer.* Oxford: Clarendon Press.

Furlong, C. W. 1917. 'Tribal Distribution and Settlements of the Fuegians Comprising Nomenclature, Etymology, Philology, and Populations'. *The Geographical Review* 3(3): 169–87.

Gusinde, M. 1982. *Los indios de Tierra del Fuego*. Tomo Segundo: Los Yámana. Buenos Aires: Centro Argentino de Etnología Americana.

Gusinde, M. 2003. *Expedición a la Tierra del Fuego*. Santiago de Chile: Editorial Universitaria.

Halbmayer, E. 2012. 'Debating Animism, Perspectivism and the Construction of Ontologies'. *Indiana* 29: 9–23.

Hallowell, A. I. 1960. 'Ojibwa Ontology, Behaviour, and World View'. In S. Diamond, ed., *Culture in History: Essays in Honour of Paul Radin*. New York: Columbia University Press, 19–52.

Haraway, D. 1990. *Simians, Cyborgs and Women: The Reinvention of Nature*. London: Routledge.

Hawkesworth, J. 1773. *An Account of the Voyages Undertaken by the Order of His Present Majesty for Making Discoveries in the Southern Hemisphere, and Successively Performed by Commodore Byron, Captain Wallis, Captain Carteret, and Captain Cook, in the Dolphin, the Swallow, and the Endeavour*. London: Printed for W. Strahan and T. Cadell in the Strand.

Ingold, T. 1994. 'Humanity and Animality'. In T. Ingold, ed., *Companion Encyclopedia of Anthropology: Humanity, Culture and Social Life*. London: Routledge, 14–32.

Keynes, R. D., ed. 2001. *Charles Darwin's Beagle Diary*. Cambridge: Cambridge University Press.

Kirksey, S. E., and S. Helmreich. 2010. 'The Emergence of Multispecies Ethnography'. *Cultural Anthropology* 25(4): 545–76.

Lopez, J. C., and D. Lopez. 1985. 'Killer Whales (*Orcinus orca*) of Patagonia, and Their Behavior of Intentional Stranding While Hunting Nearshore'. *Journal of Mammology* 66(1): 181–3.

Lowie, R. H. 1952. 'The Heterogeneity of Marginal Cultures'. *Selected Papers of the XXIX International Congress of Americanists* 3: 1–7.

MAB Biosphere Reserves Directory. 2011. Cabo de Hornos, UNESCO: The MAB Programme. Available at: http://www.unesco.org/mabdb/br/brdir/directory/biores.asp?mode=all&code=chi+08. Accessed on 11 April 2013.

Massardo, F., and R. Rozzi. 2004. 'Etno-ornitología yagán y lafkenche en los bosques templados de Sudamérica austral'. *Ornitología Neotropical* 15 (Supplement): 395–407.

Milne-Edwards, A. 1891. 'Mammifères'. In Ministères de la Marine et de L'Instruction Publique, *Mission Scientifique du Cap Horn. 1882–1883. Tome VI. Zoologie*, Première partie. Paris: Gauthier-Villars et Fils.

Nadeau, C. 2001. *Fur Nation: From the Beaver to Brigitte Bardot*. London: Routledge.

Scarzanella, E. 1995. 'Indiani e "cacciatori d'ombre" in Tierra del Fuego: note su fotografia, etnografia e storia'. *Storia Contemporanea* 26(4): 619–35.

Sielfeld, W. 1997. 'Las áreas protegidas de la XII Región de Chile en la perspectiva de los mamíferos marinos'. *Estudios Oceanológicos* 16: 87–107.

Simões-Lopes, P. C., M. E. Fabián and J. O. Menegheti. 1998. 'Dolphin Interactions with the Mullet Artisanal Fishing on Southern Brazil: A Qualitative and Quantitative Approach'. *Revista Brasileira de Zoologia* 15(3): 709–26.

Stambuk, M. P. 1986. *Rosa Yagán. El último eslabón.* Santiago: Editorial Andrés Bello.

Turner, T. S. 2009. 'The Crisis of Late Structuralism. Perspectivism and Animism: Rethinking Culture, Nature, Spirit, and Bodiliness'. *Tipití: Journal of the Society for the Anthropology of Lowland South America* 7(1): 1–40.

Wilbert, J., ed. 1977. *Folk Literature of the Yamana Indians: Martin Gusinde's Collection of Yamana Narratives.* Berkeley: University of California Press.

Wilde, L. 2000. '"The Creatures, Too, Must Become Free": Marx and the Animal/Human Distinction'. *Capital and Class* 24: 37–53.

Williamson, K. 2006. 'Hawkesworth, John (*bap.* 1720, *d.* 1773)'. *Oxford Dictionary of National Biography.* Oxford University Press. Available at: http://www.oxforddnb.com/view/article/12658. Accessed 7 September 2012.

Wilson, D. E., and D. M. Reeder, eds. 2005. *Mammal Species of the World: A Taxonomic and Geographic Reference.* 3rd ed. Baltimore: Johns Hopkins University Press. Available at: http://www.bucknell.edu/msw3/. Accessed 4 August 2012.

Zappes, C. A., A. Andriolo, P. C. Simões-Lopes and A. P. Madeira Di Beneditto. 2011. 'Human-Dolphin (*Tursiops truncatus* Montagu, 1821) Cooperative Fishery and Its Influence on Cast Net Fishing Activities in Barra de Imbé/Tramandaí, Southern Brazil'. *Ocean & Coastal Management* 54: 427–32.

Appendix: Modes of Being and Destinies of Living Beings in a Mexican Book of Fate

Penelope Dransart

Why was a suite of images taken from a nineteenth-century facsimile of a Mexican book of fate chosen for the cover of this book? These images present two pages taken from a pre-Hispanic Mixtec-style screenfold manuscript known as the Codex Fejérváry-Mayer, which is in the collections of the National Museums Liverpool, as published in 1831 in a series of hand-coloured lithographic plates commissioned by Edward King, Viscount Kingsborough. The layout of the manuscript is based on a divinatory cycle consisting of 260 days, divided into 20 periods or *trecenas* of 13 days. On the first page (not illustrated here) there is a cosmogram representing the continuous flow of time, threading its way from one cardinal direction to the next in four periods of 65 days (Boone 2007: 114). The cardinal directions are associated with deities, colours, trees and birds. Intercardinal loops between these directions are associated with colours, plants, animals, year birds and the body parts of the deity Tezcatlipoca. According to Elizabeth Hill Boone (2007: 116), time passes, moving from 'one part of the cosmos to another, absorbing the mantic meaning of each direction', enabling the diviner to assess the position of each *trecena* and the forces which govern its lapse of days, depending on its position in this spatial and temporal map.

The two pages reproduced from the Kingsborough facsimile on this book's cover are from the verso of the manuscript. Each page, one placed above the other, consists of two registers. The upper register on both pages forms part of a sequence known as a birth almanac. Each section of this sequence represents four days. The sequence flows through the lower of the two pages, where three of the four-day periods are associated with a different deity manipulating the umbilical cord of the foetus. In the uppermost sequence, Mictlancihuatl, Lady of the Land of the Dead, gives birth to the baby by expelling the infant upwards into the land of the living. The next divinity cuts the umbilical cord and, in the top right hand corner, the divinity Mayahuel presides over her four-day period by suckling the newborn child (Boone 2007: 140–1). Mayahuel was the deity of *pulque,* a sweet liquor fermented from the sap of the maguey cactus. It is rich in vitamins and resembles milk. Boone (2007: 141) explains that the fate of the infant was controlled by the particular divinity who presided on the day of the birth; if it took place on one of the first four day signs, the birth process would be associated with 'vegetation and abundance', but those born on day signs whose patrons were the deities of 'death and blood sacrifice' would be fortunate to survive.

Adult life is represented in another sequence appearing in the lower register on each of the two pages. Humans and nonhumans participate in the productive activities of work. There are two morally different sequences, one auspicious and the other inauspicious. The lower register on the left side of the uppermost page depicts a wood cutter legitimately attempting to clear a field to grow crops, but a jaguar attempts to defend the forest as he does so. As the jaguar and the man come face-to-face, the wounded limb of the tree exudes blood-like sap. The image on the lower right of this uppermost page presents two intertwined snakes, one of which, in Gordon Brotherston's (1995: 141) interpretation of the scene, 'tamely licks the carrier's hand, as he sweats blood under his load'.

The lowermost scenes on the lower of the two pages depicted on this book's cover include a woman, identified by Brotherston as an adulteress, because she follows a 'bent waterway', carrying a water jar from which a phallic snake emerges (Brotherston 1995: 141). She comes face-to-face with a crayfish (or a water scorpion). The scene in the lower register of this page depicts a man offering fire to a two-headed coral snake which, according to Brotherston (1995: 141), represents 'hissing, two-tongued gossip' as the temple bursts into flames. These two scenes belong to the inauspicious cycle.

Trees bleed and cactuses lactate in this parallel view of the cycles of life and death experienced by human, nonhuman and plant beings. The Mexican books of fate dramatize human and nonhuman roles in the productive activities that are represented, but vitality for human beings in this moral economy is hypostatized and is accessible to an individual in a positive manner if that person was born on auspicious day. In contrast to the fecund fate of the fortunate individual, a child born on an inauspicious day was likely to encounter scarcity rather than plenitude.

Destinies, however, were never simple and it seems that pre-Hispanic Nahuatl speakers did not accept fate unquestioningly. In a study of a form of speech known as 'ancient words', Miguel León-Portilla (1992: 190) argued that Nahuas were trained to wear a wise countenance and to make the 'heart firm'. Attributed to a father, the following 'ancient words' were recited to a noble daughter when she reached six or seven years of age, to prepare her to confront with fortitude the challenges of a life of sorrows:

> Hear well, O my daughter, O my child, the earth is not a good place. It is not a place of joy, it is not a place of contentment. It is merely said it is a place of joy with fatigue, of joy with pain on earth; so the old men went saying. In order that we may not go weeping forever, may not die of sorrow, it is our merit that our lord gave us laughter, sleep, and

our sustenance, our strength, our force, and also carnal knowledge in order that there be peopling…

And now, O my daughter, hear it well, look at it deliberately; for behold, here is thy mother, thy noble one. From her womb, from her breast thou wert chipped, thou wert flaked. It is as if thou wert an herb, a plant which hath propagated, sprouted, blossomed. It is also as if thou hadst been asleep and awakened.

See, hear, and know how it is on earth…They say the earth is a dangerous place, a fearsomely dangerous place, o my daughter, O dove, O little one. Know that thou comest from someone, thou art descended from someone; that thou wert born by someone's grace; that thou art the spine, the thorn, of our lords who went leaving us, the lords, the rulers who already have gone to reside beyond. (Sahagún 1969: 93–4)

The reference to the chipping of stone relates to Nahua beliefs in the sparks created by the divine couple in the heights of heaven when they chipped flint or used a fire drill; these sparks were believed to animate the foetus in the womb of mortal women (Sahagún 1969: 202; Graulich 2000: 358). In juxtaposing metaphors based on stone, plants and birds, this speech alludes to Nahua metaphysical concepts concerning the animation of living beings.

In León-Portilla's (1992: 189) analysis, Nahuas were 'possessors of a face, possessors of a heart'. It is clear that for them face-to-face ethical relationships were not just established between organisms with a physical reality (as, on the cover of this book, between the woman and the crayfish and the man and the jaguar). Nahuas also conceived of relationships between themselves and spatiotemporally conceived time itself. The chapters in this book have examined human modes of being and destinies in relation to other living beings, including nonhuman mammals, insects and plants. The authors have addressed concerns regarding regeneration, spiritual renewal and violent action as well as the extent to which communication is possible between human and other living beings. Native Mexican texts and books of fate also provide particular insights into such matters.

References

Boone, E. H. 2007. *Cycles of Time and Meaning in the Mexican Books of Fate.* Austin: University of Texas Press.

Brotherston, G. 1995. *Painted Books from Mexico: Codices in UK Collections and the World they Represent.* London: British Museum Press.

Graulich, M. 2000. 'Aztec Human Sacrifice as Expiation'. *History of Religions* 39(4): 352–71.

Kingsborough, Lord [Edward King]. 1831. *Antiquities of Mexico, Comprising Facsimiles of Ancient Mexican Paintings and Hieroglyphs,* vol. 3. London: Robert Havell and Colnaghi.

León-Portilla, M. 1992. *The Aztec Image of Self and Society: An Introduction to Nahua Culture.* Salt Lake City: University of Utah Press.

Sahagún, B. de. 1969. *Florentine Codex: General History of the Things of New Spain,* no. 14, part VII, trans and eds C. E. Dibble and A. J. Anderson. Santa Fe, NM: School of American Research and the University of Utah.

Index

212 · *Index*